COMPETITION AND CHOICE
IN ELECTRICITY

COMPETITION AND CHOICE IN ELECTRICITY

Sally Hunt *and* Graham Shuttleworth
National Economic Research Associates

JOHN WILEY & SONS
Chichester · New York · Brisbane · Toronto · Singapore

Copyright © 1996 by S. Hunt and G. Shuttleworth
Published by John Wiley & Sons Ltd,
Baffins Lane, Chichester,
West Sussex PO19 1UD, England

National 01243 779777
International (+44) 1243 779777

Reprinted July 1996

Other Wiley Editorial Offices

John Wiley & Sons, Inc., 605 Third Avenue,
New York, NY 10158-0012, USA

Jacaranda Wiley Ltd, 33 Park Road, Milton,
Queensland 4064, Australia

John Wiley & Sons (Canada) Ltd, 22 Worcester Road,
Rexdale, Ontario M9W 1L1, Canada

John Wiley & Sons (ASIA) Pte Ltd, 2 Clementi Loop 02-01,
JinXing Distripark, Singapore 0512

Library of Congress Cataloging-in-Publication Data

Hunt, Sally.
  Competition and choice in electricity / Sally Hunt and
Graham Shuttleworth.
      p.   cm.
  Includes bibliographical references and index.
  ISBN 0-471-95782-8
    1. Electric utilities—Great Britain.   I. Shuttleworth, Graham.
  II. Title.
  HD9685.G7H86   1996   95–41280
                                                                           CIP

British Library Cataloguing in Publication Data

A catalogue record for this book is available from the British Library

ISBN 0-471-95782-8

Typeset in 10/12pt Times by Keyword
Printed and bound in Great Britain by Bookcraft (Bath) Ltd, Avon
This book is printed on acid-free paper responsibly manufactured from sustainable forestation,
for which at least two trees are planted for each one used for paper production.

CONTENTS

ACKNOWLEDGEMENTS

It is customary to thank those who have contributed to the development of the ideas in the book. In this case, the primary thanks must be to the people who made us work out how to set up an electricity market in the first place—our clients at National Power with whom we worked constantly for two years, and especially Tim Russell, David Tolley, Keith Miller, David Hadfield, Peter Clubb and to John Baker who decided to run with the Pool, even though it was totally untried; to Larry Ruff, Steve Roberts, Peter Bird and Oliver Letwin, Charles Davies and Geoff Horton, who were working for other parties in the UK privatisation; to our colleagues Paul Joskow, David Robinson, Rod Frame, Paul Dawson, Laura Brien, Penelope Rowlatt and Paul Plummer; to our clients in other systems with other problems—Jan Moen, Roger Kearsley, Ramón Pérez Simarro, Yvan Capouet, Noureddine Berrah, Juan Altimari, John Ballance, Ann Cohn, Jim Kritikson; and to our gurus and teachers Fred Kahn and Ralph Turvey who have with great generosity made comments on various parts of this text in various contexts. Any of them would have written it differently; but we thank them all the same.

PREFACE

This is a book of applied economic theory. It is the direct result of a remark by a utility regulator to one of the authors. He said, approximately:

> *I grew up in the world of planning and marginal cost pricing. I know how to make tariffs and calculate rates of return . . . I know how to choose the next supply source and how to estimate demand . . . I can do cost allocations . . . But in this new world of competition, I seem to need to know about markets and contracts and risk allocation, and how to structure an open transmission system. Most of all, I need to know whether I want the industry that I regulate to be in this new world.*

This book is for him, and all the utility planners, executives and regulators throughout the world who find the developments of the late 1980s and the early 1990s have left them with gaps in the useful bag of conceptual tools they are accustomed to bringing to matters of policy. The tools they need apply to the newly emerging world of competition in production and choice for consumers. Most of our work has been for the electric industry, but many ideas are applicable also to other regulated industries, particularly gas.

The underlying micro-economic theory comes from transport economics, industrial organisation, the theory of markets and the economics of risk, property rights, contracting and transactions costs. Graduate students who can live with the absence of double integrals and economic jargon may find it useful. They, like us, will eventually be translating abstract ideas for use by busy people who naturally think of "welfare" as a government handout, and have never wanted to know what a second-order condition was.

We originally developed most of the sections of the book for clients (companies, governments and regulators) who needed theoretically sound alternative answers to practical questions. We have been immensely fortunate in having clients who commissioned us to think out answers to new problems. They have worked with us continuously as we tried out ideas on them. They have made us write in plain English and keep our eyes on the actual situation in their countries and industries. We have also benefited enormously from the comments of colleagues who were ruthless with their criticism, and generous in their contributions. This then is really the work of National Economic Research Associates (NERA) and its clients on all six continents over the past six years.

This is not a work of advocacy for any particular model of industry organisation. The aim is to present the conceptual tools needed to think through the alternatives. Although our initial work in this area was in developing the market system for electricity currently in operation in the UK, we are very well aware of the problems of the UK system, and the difficulties in applying it elsewhere. We have worked closely with clients who favour alternative models, which has enlarged our view of both the possibilities and the pitfalls.

ABBREVIATIONS

CCGT	combined cycle gas turbine
CEGB	Central Electricity Generating Board (UK)
CfD	contract for differences
DGES	Director General of Electricity Supply
DSM	demand side management
EC	European Community
EDF	Electricité de France
EPAct	Energy Policy Act (USA, 1992)
EU	European Union
FERC	Federal Energy Regulatory Commission (US)
IPP	independent power producers
kW	kilowatt
kWh	kilowatt hour
LOLP	Loss of Load Probability
LRMC	long-run marginal cost
MO	Market Operator
MVC	marginal value to consumers
NGC	National Grid Company (UK)
NPV	net present value
OFFER	Office of Electricity Regulation (UK)
PPA	power purchase agreement
PPP	Pool Purchase Price (UK)
PSA	Pooling and Settlement Agreement (UK)
PSP	Pool Selling Price (UK)
PURPA	Public Utilities Regulatory Policy Act (USA, 1978)
REC	regional electricity company
RPI	retail price index
SvK	Svenska Kraftnät (Swedish Grid Company)
SM	Statnett Marked (Norwegian State Electricity Market)
SMC	system marginal cost
SMP	System Marginal Price

SRMC	short-run marginal cost
TSO	transmission system operator
TP	transmission provider
TUOS	transmission use of system
VOLL	Value of Lost Load

1   INTRODUCTION

The big idea which underlies the new world of competition and choice in electricity is that it is possible and desirable to separate the transportation from the thing transported. That is, electric energy *as a product* can be separated commercially from transmission *as a service*.[1] In more mundane terms, we have been used to thinking of electricity as a product that we only use at the point of delivery, and pay for in a single delivered tariff. The question now is, could the bill be "unbundled" into an electricity and a delivery charge? Even if the delivery service remained a monopoly,[2] could the customer choose who would supply the electricity over the wires? Could the wires be "common carriers" even though the physics of the system dictate that the product is fully intermingled and indistinguishable?

This seemingly simple question is central to understanding what is going on in the electric industry today. For a hundred years, it has been assumed that electricity and the delivery of it were inevitably intertwined: like an egg baked into a cake, you could not go back and reconstitute the egg once the cake is mixed. But if it is possible to define and separate the transport service, so that it can be provided separately from the electricity itself, electricity becomes a product that can be bought and sold and transported from place to place, much as any other product. Electricity markets are opened to alternative producers and alternative purchasers. The economic analysis required for this type of world is the analysis of *transactions*—what is the product being bought and sold, at what time, in what place; who is the buyer, who is the seller, what is

---

[1] There are of course precedents for separating transportation from the thing transported. The US *Hepburn Act* 1906 introduced the "commodities clause" into the *Interstate Commerce Act*, prohibiting railroads from carrying their own freight. But on the railroads it is clear which specific goods are associated with a supplier. In electricity, such specific attribution is physically impossible.

[2] It is usually thought that the delivery system remains a monopoly because there is only one set of wires going into a building and only room for one set of wires on the street. However, while there may physically be room for more than one set of wires, economies of scale in covering the territory with the wires have traditionally led to the conclusion that transport of electricity is a natural monopoly. This assumption is maintained throughout the book, although in industries such as telephone, technology is making delivery service much more competitive.

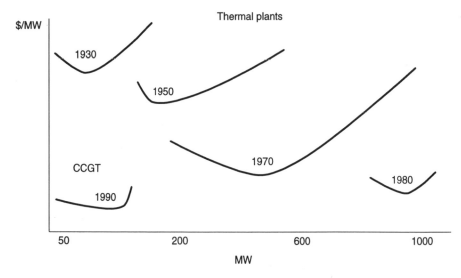

Figure 1.1   Optimal plant size per-MW cost curves (1930–1990). (From Casten, T. R. (1995) "Whither electric generation? A different view", *The Energy Daily*, September 7.)

the price, how is it determined; what are the conditions of the sale? This is the world of markets and contracts.

Perhaps the need to separate the transport from the product would not have arisen but for the realisation that generation was no longer a natural monopoly. This in turn was due to the changes in generating costs that characterised the 1980s. The generating portion of the industry had been thought of as a natural monopoly because of the economies of scale that could be obtained by purchasing large and more efficient plant. These plants were large with respect to the size of the market. Even as markets got larger, and the use of electricity increased, so did the optimal size of plant. As Figure 1.1 shows, the optimal size of generating unit rose through the period 1970 to 1980, as it had for the previous 50 years. Then things began to turn around. Technology imported from materials science and the space programme made turbines much more efficient than they had ever been. At the same time, the price of gas declined, and the prohibitions on gas burning which the western countries had imposed[3] were repealed. The way was then clear for smaller and cheaper generating units to be built economically; they were the cheapest form of new construction but, more important, in many cases the all-in cost of a new plant was lower than the customers were paying for the sunk costs of old plant. Customers began to

---

[3] The US and Europe had similar prohibitions on burning gas for electricity production during the 1980s.

think about building their own plant, and wanted to know why they could not change suppliers to get cheaper products.

There were two sorts of answers: one that it was physically or institutionally impossible to separate transmission and generation; and two that as a matter of equity, the customers had in some way committed themselves to pay for the sunk costs of the old technology. The latter question is one to which we will allude later in the book when we consider how the structural alternatives create and can be used to deal with stranded costs of this type. The assumption of physical or institutional impossibility kept the question off the front burner for some time.

It is certainly true that transporting electricity is physically more complicated than transporting most other goods. Transmission requires split-second timing of electricity flows from producers, or the system will go out of control with disastrous consequences. In physical terms, transport and production are inevitably closely related. As we show in Chapter 5, a transmission company must have access to electric energy (beyond that transported) to be able to run a transmission system. In the past, the need for central control of production and transportation resulted automatically in "*vertical integration*": generation and transmission and local distribution were integrated within the same firm. Distribution might be provided by a separate company, but with each distribution company tied to only one generating company by contract. Some have argued that this is necessary because of the physical relationships, as the eggs and cake analogy suggests. However, the more subtle (and to our mind more defensible) argument is an analysis of the costs and benefits of separating them.

TRANSACTIONS COSTS

As Joskow and Schmalensee pointed out in *Markets for Power*,[4] it is theoretically possible to replace command-and-control relationships (within a firm) with "contractual" relationships (between firms). "Contractual" relationships in this context may mean any agreement about the terms on which transactions take place between the separate firms. However, as they also point out, the difficulty of fully specifying all the necessary terms of the contract so that all possible situations are covered may be so great, and so expensive to negotiate, execute and litigate, that it is not worth attempting; it is more efficient to keep the activities with a single firm where one manager manages both activities. The technical term for the costs of negotiating, executing and litigating the required contracting mechanisms are *transactions costs*.

[4] Joskow, P. L. & Schmalensee, R. (1983) *Markets for Power, an Analysis of Electric Utility Deregulation*, MIT Press, Cambridge, MA.

Transactions costs are the costs associated with making contracts to replace command and control. Joskow and Schmalensee spelled out these difficulties in the institutional and technical context of the electric industry; they noted that free entry would require, among other things:[5]

- a regional transmission-coordination system with interconnected generating plants;
- a mechanism for dispatching generating plant that recognises the need for physical control second by second, but permits and encourages economic (least cost) dispatch;
- some method for coordinating unit commitment and maintenance;
- some method for ensuring that adequate generating capacity is built;
- some method for ensuring minimum cost investment, system wide;
- some method for dealing with emergencies.

Then it was widely agreed that these requirements were correct, but that the difficulties were insuperable because the transactions costs of separating transmission from generation and distribution were simply too great (some would argue, physically inconceivable). Vertical integration from production to consumption was the natural condition of the industry, because of the transactions costs of separating them.

MOVEMENT TO COMPETITION

However, this did not necessarily rule out competition entirely. Although the utility needed to maintain control over plant construction decisions and the operation of the transmission system, there could be some competition to build and operate plant. In the US, the *Public Utilities Regulatory Policy Act* (1978), known as PURPA, introduced the idea of competition in generation. Established utilities were required to purchase power from independent generators at prices that equalled their "avoided costs". After initial skirmishes in the courts, the independent generators (called Independent Power Producers or IPPs) flourished. However, they were not allowed to sell to end consumers but had to sell all their output to the local monopoly utility.

Somes states overestimated avoided costs so badly that they induced excessive amounts of new independent capacity; as a corrective measure, during the 1980s, competitive bidding to build and operate capacity, and contracts for

---

[5] As for footnote 4. See page 113. This list does not address all Joskow and Schmalensee's concerns, which are found throughout the book.

the output of the plants, became standard procedure for new plants in many states. The growth of the IPPs demonstrated forcefully that economies of scale in generation were no longer a sufficient consideration to dictate that generation was a natural monopoly. By 1993, some 50% of new capacity in the US was being constructed by IPPs. Competition in generation was now possible. Even if the utility had become a sort of purchasing agency for generation, there was still no question of giving the US electricity customers a choice of who would supply them.

By the mid-1980s there was near-universal agreement that the industry was naturally vertically integrated (although some competition at the generation level was possible if a purchasing agency coordinated everything). Into this conventional wisdom stumbled the British government in early 1988. They published a White Paper proposing that the electricity privatisation[6] should include breaking up the Central Electricity Generating Board (CEGB), the nationalised industry that owned all the generating plants and the transmission system. (The distribution system was also government-owned as twelve separate companies, each with a local monopoly over customers, and each able to purchase electricity from only the CEGB.) Existing plant would be divided between two generating companies; new entry of competing independent generators would be encouraged; a separate transmission company would be established; the distribution companies would provide local transport, and customers would choose their suppliers, to encourage competition. The previous privatisations of the telephone and gas industries as private sector monopolies had apparently not convinced the government that they were reaping all the benefits that private sector disciplines were supposed to provide. So electricity (electricity!) would be made competitive.

It would be nice to be able to say that there was a clear understanding then of the conceptual problems of transactions costs. It would be even nicer to be able to claim that the problems of replacing a command structure with a system of contracts had been solved. However, this was not the case. None of the drafters of that White Paper now claims to have had any idea how the commercial separation of generation and transmission would be accomplished. Indeed, most people thought it impossible at the time.

After two years of negotiations, false starts, massive computer programs

---

[6] The privatisation of the England and Wales system. We will refer to this as "the UK privatisation" throughout this book, for convenience, although it is inaccurate. There are in fact three UK systems, and there were three UK privatisations of three different government-owned companies, done by three different ministries with three separate teams of advisers. England and Wales, with 48 000 MW maximum demand, was privatised by the Department of Energy under what we will later refer to as a Model 3 system. Scotland, with 5500 MW was privatised by the Scottish Office under a Model 1 system. Northern Ireland, with 1400 MW, was privatised under a Model 2 system by the Northern Ireland Office. A NERA team advised the Northern Ireland Office, and we have relied heavily on their insights on contracting. The authors of this book were advisers to National Power in the England and Wales privatisation.

commissioned and abandoned, the current market structure took form, and was implemented in March 1990. The new structure, which separates the product from the transportation at all levels, consists of competing generators, regulated transport companies at two levels (transmission and distribution) and competing retailers.[7] The UK system is a highly organised market with more rules than a normal market, to ensure system stability. This central commercial structure has worked remarkably well. The complaints about the UK system, of which there have been many, relate to the winners and losers during the changes, and to the small number of competitors. None of the complaints relate to the feasibility of setting up a disaggregated commercial system.

The effect of the success of this operation is hard to overestimate: "it" could be done. It was shown to be feasible to arrange contracts that allowed open access to transmission and distribution wires, at least in a single island with a single transmission company. The restructuring met the Joskow and Schmalensee list of requirements in principle, and as far as could yet be ascertained, in practice. The effect has rippled through the electricity industries of the whole world. Everywhere, there is interest in the implications of introducing more competition.

However, the fact that something is technically feasible does not make it necessarily desirable: the transactions costs may still be too high. The side-effects of opening the market for electricity after years of providing service as a monopoly utility are legion—we will return to them later. Many countries are strongly opposing a move to open access: the European Community Council turned down such a proposal, although it is considering opening generation to competitive bidding, believing competition in generation to capture most of the benefits and few of the costs of open access. The European Union may also offer some access to large customers. The US has been moving gradually towards choice for at least some customers; particularly for independent distribution companies, known as wholesale customers, who have previously been tied to a single supplier. The US *Energy Policy Act* of 1992 (EPAct) permitted wholesale customers a choice of supplier, and obligated utilities to transmit ("wheel") power across their territory to accomplish this (this is known as "wholesale wheeling"). However, the same Act prohibited the federal authorities from mandating choice for retail customers ("retail wheeling"), although individual states may permit it, and some are now considering doing

---

[7] In the UK, the retail function is, confusingly, called "supply" (confusing because production or generation is often referred to as "supply"). "Suppliers" (i.e. retailers) in the UK need a "supply licence". A supplier who also owns the local monopoly distribution company has a "first-tier supply licence". Anyone may get a "second-tier supply licence" for the same territory, and retail in competition with the first-tier supplier. Second-tier suppliers are generating companies, or brokers, or the local distribution company, or distribution companies who own wires in another location. We have always found it more useful to use the term the "retailer" of electricity, and in this book we refer to the new function as the retail function.

so. California announced that it intended to go to "direct access" or competitive markets for all consumers, in April 1994, a move that has been compared to an earthquake.

Restructuring the electric industry is conceptually different from privatising it, which is a change from public to private ownership. In the UK, the restructuring of the commercial relationships was done with the privatisation. Elsewhere (and in other industries in the UK) privatisation has taken place without restructuring. In other countries, notably the US, where the sector has been largely private for many years, restructuring is taking place without changes of ownership. China is considering restructuring without relinquishing government ownership.

It is not therefore surprising that confusion reigns in this area. The number of options seems limitless. The tools for addressing them are being developed in a fairly unsystematic way, in response to particular concerns in particular countries. We developed the analysis in this book in answer to questions posed by our clients in the UK, the US, the EC, the World Bank, China, Norway, Sweden, Venezuela and Spain. Our NERA colleagues have worked on electricity industry problems in Northern Ireland, Greece, Jordan, Chile, Russia, Bulgaria, Latvia, Czechoslovakia and its offspring, Egypt, Morocco, India, New Zealand and Australia.

THE SCOPE OF THIS BOOK

We have limited ourselves in this book to the four problems about which we are most often asked. There is no doubt an entire textbook to be written on important areas we have relegated to footnotes or have not mentioned at all. Our excuse for not being exhaustive is that there appeared to be an immediate need for some coverage of these topics, however abbreviated. Limiting the scope has, however, allowed us to expand the depth, by giving concrete examples and cases that we hope will illuminate the concepts.

The four areas we have chosen to concentrate on are the central analytical problems on the new competitive world:

● alternatives for restructuring;
● the structuring of contracts;
● the development of spot markets;
● transmission pricing.

These issues relate to each other as follows: there are four broad options for structuring an electric industry, which we characterise as Models 1, 2, 3 and 4, corresponding to the levels of choice. In Part 1 we review these alternatives, the positive and negative points of each, and the main variations on these themes.

In Part 1 we also review what it takes to move from one model to another. Institutionally, such a move can be complex and depend on the initial situation: it requires legal changes, arrangements to compensate losers, and many other features that we are not attempting to cover in detail in this book.

In Part 2, we concentrate on analysing the three main changes required in commercial arrangements for transactions. These are: contracts for the sale of power; spot market and pooling arrangements; and transmission pricing.

We have called them "agency problems"—the economist's term for setting up arrangements where the agents (the traders or the regulated entities) are induced to behave efficiently when they behave in their own interests. Part 2 of the book investigates what is needed to ensure economic efficiency in these new mechanisms.

Part 1

ELECTRICITY
SECTOR
STRUCTURES

2 RESTRUCTURING AND PRIVATISATION

All over the world, governments and regulators are considering whether to restructure and/or privatise their electric industries. Mostly their aim is to increase efficiency through better investment decisions, better use of existing plant, better management and better choices for customers. Sometimes they are driven to it by customers who feel they can purchase more cheaply elsewhere; sometimes shortages force a search for new sources of capital; sometimes the incumbent utility has become inefficient and the problem is to introduce incentives; sometimes the utilities themselves want to be freed from inhibiting intervention. Whatever the reason, they need to know their alternatives, and the implications of a change.

Restructuring and privatisation are different dimensions of change.

- *Restructuring* is about commercial arrangements for selling energy: separating or "unbundling" integrated industry structures and introducing competition and choice.
- *Privatisation* is a change from government to private ownership, and is the end-point of a continuum of changes in ownership/management.

In the UK, when the electric industry was privatised, it was also restructured. The two need not go together. They are two almost separate dimensions of change. However, there is a practical logic linking the two decisions.

If a government decides it wants to privatise its electric industry (or any industry) it needs to place a value on the assets. The value of the assets will depend upon the revenues the assets can earn. To provide investors with sufficient information to decide what the assets are worth, the government must itself decide what system will be adopted to determine the flow of revenues. If the industry being privatised is the rubber industry, estimates of the world price of rubber are needed. If the industry is the electric industry the sources and certainty of revenues will be crucial. Regulatory systems are put in place to control costs and prices and to make investment decisions in the absence of competition—regulation is a surrogate for competition, to be used when competition is unworkable. However, once it has been shown that competition is feasible, the question must arise as to whether it would make sense to introduce it and how much to introduce. Hence, the question of restructuring inevitably arises in conjunction with considerations of privatisation.

In this chapter, we look at the broad range of issues that interest governments contemplating changes in a nationalised monopoly industry: changes in management and ownership on the one hand, and changes in structure (competition and choice) on the other. Privatisation is the end-point of changes in the management/ownership dimension. Competition is the end-point of changes in the structural dimension.

THE MATRIX OF STRUCTURE AND OWNERSHIP/MANAGEMENT

We start by asserting that there are really only four ways to *structure* an electric industry. We say this knowing that the reader will already be saying "there must be at least a hundred". But the alternatives divide into four groupings, and it is convenient for the purposes of exposition to consider these four as the basic models, and other variations as extensions of them. We introduce the four models in more detail in subsequent chapters. At this point it is sufficient to say the models are defined by the degree of competition.[1]

- Model 1 has no competition at all.
- Model 2 allows or requires a single buyer or purchasing agency to choose from a number of different producers, to encourage competition in generation.
- Model 3 allows Distcos[2] to choose their supplier, which brings competition into generation and wholesale supply.
- Model 4 allows all customers to choose their supplier, which implies full retail competition.

---

[1] These models are considered in much more detail in Chapter 3 and the remainder of Part 1. We are aware that other commentators choose different "models" for exposition purposes, often based on the structure of companies within the industry. For example, models might be defined by the question of whether transmission is separated, or whether distribution is separated. To our mind, these are not the most fundamental questions of structure: company structure questions follow from the high-level decision of how much competition is desired. Parts of existing companies may need to be separated to avoid conflicts and self-dealing. Some parts of separate companies might need to be consolidated to take advantage of economies of scale or scope. These issues are dealt with later in the text.

[2] We have used the following terminology. A "Distco" is a company which both owns the distribution wires and retails electricity. A retailer is a merchant who sells electricity to final customers, but does not necessarily own the wires over which the electricity is transported. All Distcos are retailers—not all retailers are Distcos.

The ownership dimension can conveniently be divided into three levels:

● in some countries, the electric industry is a government department, with no separate accounts, and often with responsibilities that are only remotely connected to electricity production (such as providing housing and schools for employees);
● the next level is a distinct government-owned company, or nationalised industry;
● the third level is a privately owned industry.

A useful way to look at these two dimensions is as a matrix in which a country might be anywhere on the matrix: the horizontal axis is competition and choice; the vertical axis is the degree of government control.

Figure 2.1 shows in broad outline how the two dimensions fit together, and where countries fitted on the matrix in 1994. Different levels of competition and choice, represented by the four models, are shown on the horizontal axis; on the left is full monopoly, on the right is full competition. On the vertical axis the dimension is the degree of government control. It starts at the top with a government department with full control, passing through a government-owned, but separate company, and ending with a privately owned company. The countries of the world have electric industries all over this matrix. Many are moving from one place to another, but all the movement is from top to bottom, and from left to right—a reduction in government control, and an increase in competition and choice.

New Zealand has moved across the matrix: it has restructured without change from government ownership. By contrast, in the US most companies have long been privately held and regulated monopolies. In 1978, competing generators were introduced. Since the *Energy Policy Act* of 1992, the industry is also in the painful process of moving to wholesale and perhaps retail competition. These moves do not entail changes in ownership—they are horizontal moves across the chart. In the UK, the restructuring for full competition was concomitant with privatisation—a move both horizontally and vertically. France has elected to stay in exactly the same place as a government-owned company with a full monopoly.

Most countries with government-controlled power sectors are moving to corporatisation and commercialisation: examples are India, Australia, New Zealand, Korea, Jordan and Malaysia. In China, commercialisation is the major government policy for all industries. Some of these countries are also experimenting in the other dimension, with competition in generation, and introducing independent generators to sell to public-sector industries.

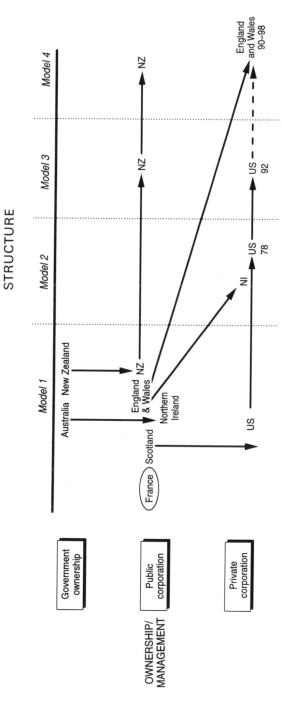

Figure 2.1 Country matrix: structure and ownership

THE FORMS OF OWNERSHIP AND MANAGEMENT

Many of the global changes in the electric industry are changes in ownership and management. These changes are concerned with putting pressures on enterprises to behave more commercially, but without necessarily changing the structure of the industry. Since this book is only tangentially concerned with the economic issues arising in these types of change, we devote this section to considering what the issues are, mainly so that we can draw a boundary around them and exclude them from further discussions. We begin by defining the key terms.

Owners are defined as those "who are entitled to the profits of the industry"; owners appoint *managers* to ensure that the enterprise is run efficiently, give them authority to do so, and hold them accountable for the results. The three most common forms of ownership/management are:

1. *Direct government ownership*: the government both owns and has direct managerial control over the industry, as in China at present (and as was formerly the case in many countries). The same people are owners, regulators and managers, although sometimes they have different "nameplates" in their different roles. Investment is done with government appropriations, prices are set by, and revenues are remitted to, the government. The government focuses on central planning, perhaps in conjunction with other industries; it should be concerned with investment appraisal and efficiency, but that is not its primary focus. The industry is viewed as "infrastructure". The government may impose other tasks on the electric industry, such as responsibility for schools and hospitals in a region.

2. *A government-owned corporation*: the government owns a corporation which manages the industry so that government is one step removed from day to day control. The board of the corporation sets the goals, and appoints different people, the management, to achieve those goals. The corporation may still be required to carry out other government policies such as support of supplying industries, but it is under some obligation to show a profit in its activities. There may be an independent regulatory agency, or the government department may approve prices and investment policy. This is the case with Electricité de France (EDF) in France, and used to be the case in the UK under the Central Electricity Generating Board (CEGB).

3. *A privately owned corporation*: a third form of ownership is private ownership of the corporation and its assets, as in the US and now the UK. These companies (joint stock companies[3]) may be listed on the stock exchanges,

---

[3] A joint stock company (a limited liability company whose shares may be quoted on a stock exchange) may be a completely private company, or the government may own enough shares to control the company. One way of gradually privatising an enterprise is to form a joint stock company with only a minority of shares held privately, then gradually sell the government shares.

and are expected to make profits for their shareholders (who may be the employees of the company). The managers are accountable to the Board, which represents the shareholders. These companies are generally regulated by an independent regulator.

These distinctions are never rigid in practice: the government may in effect have total control even over private companies. The level of government control may depend more on the intentions and behaviour of the government than on the organisation of the sector.

1. *Commercialisation* happens when the government relinquishes detailed control, in favour of autonomy for the enterprise and a focus on profitability. This is a change in behaviour rather than organization. It normally involves adoption of commercial accounting practices, economic tariffs, and an effort to separate the core business from other activities.
2. *Corporatisation* is the formal and legal move from direct government control to a legal corporation with separate management. This may be a government-owned corporation. The ownership of assets and the capital structure need to be determined before this step is taken. The government also needs to set out the objectives for the corporation, and the process by which public policy objectives are taken into account. Economic regulation may be introduced at this stage to oversee pricing and investment policies.
3. *Privatisation* is the move from a government corporation to a privately held corporation. Incentives for efficiency are considered even greater if management is subject to the disciplines of stock market valuation of the company, which happens when the enterprise is privatised. Privatisation may also be undertaken to increase the company's access to capital markets. Privatisation is accomplished by a flotation on the stock market or a trade sale. This requires a valuation, a prospectus and registration on a stock exchange. It is accompanied by an increase in external regulation of the monopoly elements of the industry.
   This progression is shown in Figure 2.2.

Many important economic issues arise when a system is commercialising, corporatising and privatising: we and our colleagues have worked on problems of tariff policy, investment appraisal, regulatory regimes and valuation in many places. But because this book is focused on the requirements of the more competitive structures, and because there is already a substantial literature available on more traditional regulatory economics, we simply summarise, in Table 2.1, the economic issues which will arise at each stage as changes in the ownership/management dimension, which we have described above, are implemented.

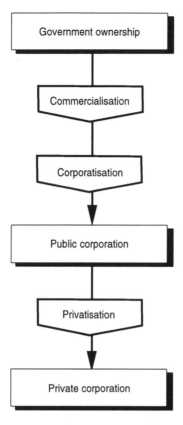

Figure 2.2 Changes in ownership/management dimension

Table 2.1 Economic issues in reform of ownership and management

Ownership/Management	Issues
Government Department	Planning, efficiency incentives, investment appraisal
Commercialisation	+Accounting policy, +Tariffs policy
Corporatisation	+Capital structure, +Dividend policy
Government-owned Company	+(Regulation)
Privatisation	+Valuation
Privately owned Company	+Regulation

EXPERIENCE WITH DIFFERENT FORMS OF OWNERSHIP AND MANAGEMENT

Commercialisation and Corporatisation

Government-owned monopolies have often been regarded as the preferred model, in spite of the more recent swing of the political pendulum to favour private ownership. Nationalisation of small local companies often produced large and previously unexploited opportunities for coordination and scale economies. Electricité de France was a pioneer in rational pricing, and was also able to develop a large nuclear programme through standardisation. At one time, the CEGB in the UK was regarded as a model of efficiency.[4] There is some evidence that government ownership itself is not a bar to efficiency: in the UK, Nuclear Electric, which remains a government-owned corporation, has also shown large efficiency gains, suggesting that competition rather than private ownership was the determining factor in the UK.

Government ownership permits investment in public goods such as rural electrification. Markets will not support these investments because the benefits flow too widely to be captured by the investors. The benefits can only be recaptured from the beneficiaries through taxation. In this sense, covering the country with an electric grid can be seen as the equivalent of building roads, and a natural role for the government. It is possible to force the private sector to make these investments, but it is easier for the government to do it directly through ownership.

The ability of the government to raise "low cost" capital is both a plus and a minus for government ownership. It enables infrastructure investment, but it can result in overbuilding of risky and capital-intensive projects, which only look good at low costs of capital, and which the market would never support. But public ownership can work the other way, especially if the ability to set rational prices is constrained by the political necessity to keep inflation under control. This can result in the starvation of the government-owned industry of investment funds.

In some countries, where the electric industry is seen as a government department, revenues and costs are completely separate, the revenues being treated as a tax, and the costs as a budget item. Commercialisation into a real business unit, with profit and loss statements, is a prerequisite to private investment. Tariffs have to be raised to remunerative levels and a proper accounts system installed.

---

[4] See Kahn, A. E. (1946) *Great Britain in the World Economy*, Columbia University Press.

Privatisation

The gathering momentum of privatisation around the world rests partly on governments' desires for cash for the treasury, but also on a growing belief that private ownership and the pressures of organised stock markets will increase the efficiency of formerly nationalised industries.

However, when a monopoly utility is to be privatised, the form of the regulation will dictate the valuation of the industry. The sale value is the net present value of the revenues minus the costs: the revenues depend on the regulatory framework. Therefore, developing the new regulatory framework is crucial to the privatisation of a monopoly.

The US, Spain and Germany have long had private power companies, as well as government-owned companies. They also have long-established and complex regulatory systems for economic control of the private industry. Regulatory regimes always have an intrinsic conflict between financial security for the industry and incentives for efficiency. Establishing the regulatory regime is a major consideration in privatisation. Indeed, until a decade ago it was the only method available for constraining private monopolies.

Regulation is generally viewed as a surrogate for competition and, if competition is feasible, it is often considered during privatisation. The restructuring question therefore often arises during the privatisation process. Arguments of feasibility, and economies of scale and scope are considerations that must be carefully examined. If it is feasible and efficient to restructure the industry and introduce competition, then it must be considered as an alternative to economic regulation.

Many countries are following the privatisation route as a general policy for many public-sector industries, but electricity is seldom at the top of the list. We have observed that once it becomes obvious that the structure of the industry has to be decided before privatisation, governments retreat into contemplation. The list of electric industry privatisations is very short. We believe this is because it is now almost impossible to consider the ownership questions in electricity without also considering the structure questions. These questions are difficult to resolve with assurance: experience is limited, and most governments have been unwilling to take a leap in the dark for a service of such great importance. Even where the industry is already private, changing the structure involves so many institutional changes that it is always slow.

For this reason, the rest of this book is devoted to explaining and evaluating the issues that arise when an electricity system moves horizontally across the matrix in Figure 2.1, by introducing more competition and choice.

3   INDUSTRY STRUCTURES

We now turn to the central theme of the book: restructuring the industry so that there is more competition among producers and more choice for customers. Throughout the book we are talking exclusively of competition in producing and selling the product electricity. We refer to generating companies as "generators" and to the actual or potential competing generators as "independent power producers" or IPPs, although competition can take the form of neighbouring utilities competing for each others' customers.

The basic functions of the integrated industry are generation (production) and transport of electricity, which contribute about two-thirds and one-third of the cost of the final product respectively. The operation and control of the transport system (the transmission and distribution wires) is viewed throughout the book as a natural monopoly in any area because of the requirement for central control of dispatch (the synchronisation of the generating plant to the system). The need for the system operator or dispatcher to be independent of the generators or of the retailers in the system is a question that has to be considered in each model we present.

From the point of view of competition in the product market, there are really only four fundamentally different ways of structuring the industry, although there are many possible variations on each. In this section, we introduce the four basic models which will serve us throughout the book. The models are defined on the basis of the extent of monopoly permitted or required in the industry. In the next section we define the models and the transitional issues. We then go into each model in more detail in Chapters 4–7.

STRUCTURES—THE FOUR MODELS DEFINED

The four models were chosen because they correspond to varying degrees of monopoly, competition and choice in the industry. The models are abstractions and do not describe particular systems. Although they correspond broadly to real electric systems, we have tried to explain the essential nature of the structures; particular systems may vary in their actual arrangements in ways we discuss in more detail later.

- Model 1—Monopoly at all levels. Generation is not subject to competition and no one has any choice of supplier; a single monopoly company handles the production of electricity and its delivery over the transmission network to distribution companies and/or final consumers.
- Model 2—Purchasing agency. This allows a single buyer, the purchasing agency, to choose from a number of different generators to encourage competition in generation. Access to the transmission wires is not permitted for sales to final consumers. The purchasing agency has a monopoly on transmission networks and over sales to final consumer.
- Model 3—Wholesale competition. This allows Distcos to buy direct from a producer and deliver over a transmission network. Distcos still have a monopoly over final consumers. There is open access to transmission wires.
- Model 4—Retail competition. This allows all customers to choose their supplier. There is open access to transmission and distribution wires. The distribution (delivery) is separate from the retail activity, and the latter is competitive.

Table 3.1 below summarises the important characteristics of each model.

Not by chance, the models have quite different types of trading arrangements. They require different sorts of contracting arrangements and have different regulatory requirements. They may require different ownership arrangements

Table 3.1 Structural alternatives

Characteristic	Model 1 Monopoly	Model 2 Purchasing agency	Model 3 Wholesale competition	Model 4 Retail competition
Definition	Monopoly at all levels	Competition in generation— single buyer	Competition in generation and choice for Distcos	Competition in generation and choice for final consumers
Competiting generators	NO	YES	YES	YES
Choice for retailers?	NO	NO	YES	YES
Choice for final customers?	NO	NO	NO	YES

for the companies operating in the sector. They also have different implications for stranded assets. These dimensions do not define the models. The defining characteristic which distinguishes the models from each other is competition and choice. The question which defines each model is "who may an independent generator sell to?"

In a Model 1 system, no one may buy from an independent generator, so none exists. All final consumers are supplied by the incumbent utility. The first step away from Model 1 is to introduce competing generators or IPPs. In Model 2, only the purchasing agency is allowed to buy from IPPs, which is why it is sometimes called the "single-buyer" model. The design of the power purchase agreements (PPAs) is a major feature of Model 2. The design of these contracts is the subject of Chapter 10.

In Model 3, Distos (companies which both own the low voltage wires and retail, i.e. traditional distribution companies) are given the right to buy direct from IPPs, but they retain a local franchise over retail customers. The IPP will therefore need access to the transmission network, and there will need to be trading arrangements for the network. The design of trading systems is the main feature in Model 3, and the subject of Chapter 11.

In Model 4, retail customers are given the right to buy from an IPP. This expansion of the list of customers who may choose their supplier, from retailers to "Mr Smith", means the trading arrangements and the access provisions may become more complex in practice. Access to distribution networks is required as well as access to transmission. The design of transmission access is the subject of Chapters 13 and 14.

Table 3.2 summarises the different models in terms of the IPPs' right to sell to customers, since most regulatory systems control trade in electricity by giving each generator permission to sell to named customers. The process of naming customers is the means by which choice is opened up.

Table 3.2   The defining characteristics

Who may an independent generator sell to?
If there are no independent generators, because no one is allowed to buy from them, we call this monopoly structure, or Model 1.
If only a single purchaser in an area is allowed to buy from an IPP generator, we call this a purchasing agency structure, or Model 2.
If an IPP generator may sell to any Distco, and the generator has access to the transmission wires, we call this a structure with wholesale competition, or Model 3.
If any IPP generator may sell to any retail customer, and the generators have access to the distribution wires, we call this a structure with retail competition, or Model 4.

Alternatively, we can look at it from the customer's point of view: who gets the choice? Figure 3.1 shows in a nutshell who gets the choice in each model. In Model 1, there is no choice at any level. In Model 2, the purchasing agency chooses which generator it will buy from. The purchasing agency is the wholesaler for any area. The choice may only be exercised when new plant is built if the purchasing agency works by signing long-term contracts with generators. However, it could also purchase spot energy from other generators or from other jurisdictions.

In Model 3, Distcos choose whom they will buy from. They can choose to buy from generators or aggregators or utilities or purchasing agencies outside their own area. To do this the Distco needs some form of contract with the transmission company and the generator needs connection to the system. These contacts are commonly called "access to transmission wires".

In Model 4, the choice filters down to the final consumer, who may choose to purchase from generators acting as retailers, or from independent retailers, or from other utilities. To do this, "access to distribution wires" is also required.

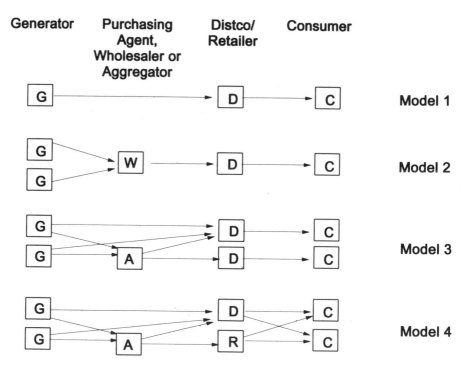

Figure 3.1   The choice moves closer to the consumer

THF

The   gh it is not the
inter   h of the issues
we   ments that are
the   e controversies
sur   of the key issues
ari   del. For ease of
ex   reas of interest:

- treatment of strange
- pressures for change.

At the end of each section we give some examples, and draw some conclusions as to the positive and negative features of the model. The following outlines some of the common concepts underlying our discussion of each of these issues in the following sections.

Transition Mechanisms from Model to Model

In Figure 3.2, we show the changes necessary for movements in the horizontal dimension of the matrix. Figure 3.2 shows the transition mechanisms which are the main focus of Part 2 of the book: contracts, markets and network pricing. Each is considered briefly in its turn when the model in which it becomes a necessity is introduced: here we show how they fit together.

A change from monopoly to competition in generation (Model 1 to Model 2) requires contracts for the purchase of power from independent power producers. These contracts are known as *power purchase agreements* (PPAs). They need to embody incentives for low-cost production, and have to be compatible with the dispatching arrangements of the purchasing utility.

The changes necessary to go from Model 2 (competition in generation) to Models 3 and 4 (wholesale and retail competition, with choice for some or all customers) are the development of *market trading arrangements*. These are necessary, even when most trading is carried out by contract between generators and customers.

Models 3 and 4 also require prices for using transmission and distribution

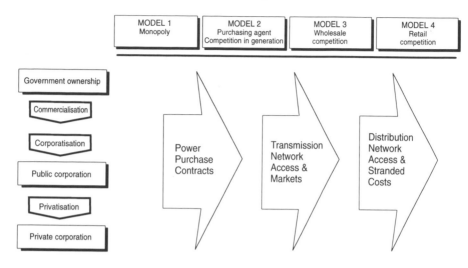

Figure 3.2   The features of transition: competition dimension

networks. In Model 3, the transmission provider must allow open access; in Model 4 distributors must provide it.

Trading Arrangements

The trading arrangements in a model are the set of rules buyers and sellers (collectively, traders) have to follow when they make transactions. The variable demand for electricity and the need for instantaneous response will mean that there will always be differences between what traders contract for and actual generation and consumption. The market mechanism must account for these imbalances and see that they are paid for.

Since all the power flows over a system according to the laws of physics, there is no way to tell whose power actually went to whom. There has to be a method of measuring and accounting for flows into and out of the network, or over interconnectors, if the transactions are to be invoiced and paid. There are many ways to do this, which vary in complexity with the number of traders who can use the network to make independent transactions.

Prices for using the delivery networks must give efficient location decisions and allow for the economic dispatch of plant. In Models 1 and 2, these decisions can be taken jointly with the decision to build plant, and there is no need for separate prices; but in Models 3 and 4, prices have to do the work of optimising location and dispatch.

Implications for the Structure of Companies

Many of the models will have implications for the structure of existing companies. Some functions will need to be separated to avoid conflict of interest. Large companies do not often willingly break themselves up into smaller ones, but reorganising the industry along the lines of the models described below often requires changes to the structure of companies. The restructuring decision involves consideration of the economies of scale and scope that originally led to the creation of integrated companies and which may still be important. However, conflicts of interest, self-dealing, cross-subsidies and market power create problems that offset or overcome the benefits of integration. Increased regulation or breaking up existing companies are common solutions to these problems.

Economies of scale mean that larger scale is cheaper than smaller. This used to be the case for generating plant and, as we noted earlier, this was a major reason for the historic monopolisation of generation. Economies of scope mean that different functions can be most efficiently performed by the same organisation. They often occur because of the transactions costs of setting up contracts for the tasks to be done separately.

Conflicts of interest and self-dealing problems arise when competitors find themselves in competition with the incumbent utility in situations where the incumbent can benefit itself at the competitor's expense, even if the competitor's product is better or cheaper. Cross-subsidisation is possible if a company has a subsidiary in the competitive sector and one in the regulated monopoly sector, particularly if there is cost-plus regulation: the company will have an incentive to load costs on to the regulated accounts. The solutions which have been tried in these situations are: separate accounts, policed by regulators; prohibitions on the incumbent engaging in the problematic activity; or divestiture.

Market power is the ability of a producer with a large share of the relevant market to raise the price and keep it there; or alternatively to keep competitors out of the market by barriers to entry, including predatory pricing. The remedies for market power include structural remedies, such as breaking up the company; behavioural remedies such as requiring advance contracting; or outcome remedies such as price regulation or profit regulation.

Economic Efficiency

Economic efficiency, the traditional concern of economists, is about giving the right incentives to use resources in the way that gives the "biggest bang for the buck" and that avoids waste. The concerns are usually divided into three types of efficiency:

- production and investment (efficient investment maintenance and closure decisions, the best choice of fuel, the right choice of investment type, location and timing, etc.);
- usage (consumers get the right signals to use electricity when their value exceeds the cost of production);
- allocation (prices should reflect the marginal cost of the resources at different times and locations to ensure that the correct amount is produced, that the most economic producers generate and that production is allocated to the consumers that value it most).

"Competitive markets" are generally assumed to have the advantage in that these types of efficiency are achieved simultaneously.

For regulated activities, incentives should be carefully structured so that the outcome is similar to the competitive outcome. Regulation must foster contracts, tariffs and trading arrangements that encourage efficient operation of the generators, network operators and customers. Ideally, these incentives would be provided with the absolute minimum of regulatory intervention. As the structure of the industry is unbundled into its separate components, more commercial agreements between companies are required to allow them to function as an integrated network industry. These commercial agreements must be designed to encourage companies to collaborate efficiently.

Social Policy Obligations

Social policy obligations are such things as demand side management (DSM) and conservation programmes, low-income assistance, fuel diversity (which may include subsidies to supplying industries), environmental issues, high local taxes and economic development. We can divide these into two sets: those that are connected with generation (DSM, fuel diversity and environmental issues) and those that are not (low-income assistance, economic development).

Whatever the market model under which the industry operates, the ability to impose and collect above-market costs depends upon the ease with which the customers can choose alternatives that do not have such costs attached. It will therefore be difficult to force the competitive functions to absorb above-market costs. However, since the regulated sector is a monopoly, these above-market costs can more easily be collected as distribution charges, for customers normally cannot bypass the delivery system. In each of our successive models, the regulated sector gets smaller and the competitive sector larger, reducing the scope for social policy obligations.

Economic development activities are local functions, and can be paid for locally, through a charge on the delivery of electricity. The same applies to low-income assistance. If the legislature wants, it can mandate the distribution business to pick up the costs. However, the costs of fuel diversity (windmills, nuclear, etc.) have usually been seen as simply high-cost generation. It is unlikely that these will be built under a competitive regime unless they are subsidised. There are non-distorting ways to subsidise these activities, but in a more competitive world it will need to be made explicit.

Treatment of "Stranded Costs"

Stranded costs are above-market costs, usually of generation, but also potentially of transmission and distribution, which cannot be recouped in a fully competitive market. They are usually costs which the customer is already paying. We examine these in Chapter 7 because they become most apparent in Model 4.

Pressures for Change

Each model has its own forces for stability and its own internal pressures for change. These are examined in each chapter.

At the end of each chapter we also review the positive and negative features of each model and summarise our conclusions in Chapter 8, before turning to the "agency issues" in Part 2.

4   MODEL 1—MONOPOLY

DESCRIPTION OF THE MODEL

Model 1 is a monopoly model, typically characterised by a vertically integrated system. In any area, one utility owns and operates all of the generating plant and the transmission and distribution wires used to transport the electricity, and is responsible for retailing the electricity to the final customer. The utility has a monopoly over production and over retailing in its service area. These service areas may cover a whole country, as in France, a single region or even a town. The model is shown diagramatically in Figure 4.1.

Optional features are separately owned "distribution companies" that own the low-voltage wires and have a monopoly in retailing in their service territory, but which can only purchase from a single generating/transmission company (Model 1b). The UK was like this before 1990. Model 1b is not importantly different in its economic characteristics from Model 1a because the distribution company monopolises the final customers and is in turn monopolised by the generator. This is sometimes called "vertical integration by contract".

In return for the monopoly the utility generally has an obligation to serve customers, i.e. to provide energy to everyone in the service area, at a tariff price which is regulated to the cost of service, somehow defined. The monopoly over generation may be enforced rigorously, so that literally no one else may generate, or it may permit self-generation, with very limited sales of excess energy to the utility at regulated "buy-back rates".

TRADING ARRANGEMENTS

Model 1 does permit trading between similar vertically integrated utilities across an interconnecter, and Model 1 utilities often coordinate their dispatch through pooling arrangements. This can provide back-up, increased security and help reduce costs by dispatching cheaper plant first. However, these Model 1 pools are generally short-term trading arrangements, based on comparisons of very short-run marginal cost. Model 1 utilities typically buy and sell to each

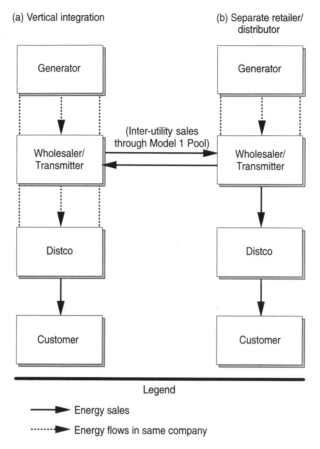

Figure 4.1   Model 1—monopoly

other at prices which split the gains from trade. The prices reflect the presumption that trading will be reciprocal, and are not intended to cover the full cost—the utilities own franchise customers pay for the rest of the costs of generation. There is no competition to generate or to build plant—each utility is expected to meet its own load needs. The agreements set up under a Model 1 system include elaborate arrangements to prevent free riding. Since this is the most usual type of arrangement found in current systems, it is reviewed in more detail in Appendix A at the end of this chapter.

TRANSMISSION ACCESS

In Model 1 the question of transmission access only arises as the question of access for traders to cross the network to get to the other side. For example, if France, Spain and Portugal all have Model 1 systems, but France wishes to sell to Portugal across Spain, then the conditions and price for access must be agreed. In the US, this would be called "wheeling across" a utility's transmission system; in Europe it is called 'transit.' (In Model 1 there is no wheeling or transit *into* a service area, since customers have no choice but the local utility, and no wheeling *out*, since there are no independent producers.) The issues here are about the traders' responsibility for the overhead costs and whether the transporting utility can capture the rents of the transactions (by charging a price equal to the difference between the cost of the power and its value in the receiving zone).

This question is addressed in the section on transmission pricing in Part 2 of this book.

SHOULD THE DISTCOS BE SEPARATE?

In a Model 1 structure, the most usual arrangement is the vertically integrated company. This company owns and controls the generating plant and the transmission and distribution systems, and reaps economies of scale by building bigger plant and covering the territory efficiently. It also can take important advantage of the economies of coordination, especially the coordination of the dispatch of the generating plant. The transmission system operator can command and control the operation of the plant. This ensures not only that the transmission system remains stable, but that the plants are dispatched economically, i.e. they are run in "merit order"—from lowest to highest marginal costs. This is the most economic method of dispatching plant since it minimises cost.

The structural question which most often arises in Model 1 is whether distribution should be separated from generation and transmission, and if so, what is the optimal area for the Distco to cover. These questions arise, even in the absence of re-structuring, as questions of internal organisation, and many companies go through cycles of de-centralisation and re-centralisation as they evaluate these issues.

The answer to these questions usually lies in consideration of "economies of scale and scope". Are there economies of scope (savings from performing two functions in the same organisation) in operating all the "wires" in one company; or is the low-voltage operation essentially different from the high-voltage transmission, requiring different skills and personnel? Can consolidation of retailing companies with networks into larger areas produce savings (economies of scale) in operation and maintenance of the assets, or of the billing systems; or is it better to be close to the customer, with management of smaller companies covering small areas able to make local decisions? Economies of scale and scope are reasons for having a single firm rather than several firms which contract with each other. Their presence would suggest consolidation, but lack of these economies does not necessarily require separating companies, or even creating separate businesses within an existing company. There is no universal answer to the question of separate distribution companies in Model 1, although the economies of scale in distribution seem to run out at a relatively small size. Electricité de France, a Model 1 company which has evaluated this issue more than most, runs its distribution business in a highly decentralised fashion, which would confirm this impression.

If a later move to Model 3 is contemplated (where Distcos compete as purchasers of electricity), distribution companies may be separated from generation as a transition mechanism. Several smaller sized distribution companies might also be created from a large one.

ACHIEVING EFFICIENCY

In Model 1, minimum-cost construction of generation is achieved through a planning process carried out by the utility, the outcome of which generally needs to be approved by the regulatory body or the government. The utility owns and operates the plant, although it may contract out the building construction. The costs of approved plant are passed to the franchise customers through the retail tariffs. Incentives for efficiency mainly arise from the regulatory lag between price settings.

In Model 1, most risk is usually passed through to customers under cost-of-service regulation. The customer pays for mistakes in investment, changes in demand, unanticipated technological obsolescence, and indeed virtually everything. This reduces the risk borne by the investors in the integrated company, which in turn may lead to a reduced cost of capital for investments by the company. However, this can also induce errors into the construction decision, since the cost of capital for investments as a whole is seen as low when the risk of any given project, and therefore the cost of capital appropriate for that project, may be high.

Passing on all costs, so that prices rise when costs rise, gives bad incentives to reduce costs. Various steps, generically known as "incentive regulation", can improve the incentives by shifting some risk to the owners or operators of the assets. The general notion is that prices should be, at least partially, unhooked from costs, so that there is an incentive to reduce costs. Even in cost-based forms of regulation, slowness of the regulatory process to adjust prices to costs (regulatory lag) can unhook prices sufficiently from costs. Other methods include explicit limits on the ability to pass increased costs on to customers, indexing prices to an independent measure of costs (for example an index of retail prices) or setting a price path in advance.[1]

The cost of putting the plant in the ground is a large element in final cost. The decision to build, and its accomplishment on time and to budget, has therefore been the area where there has been most pressure to substitute market mechanisms for the "planning process". This has led to bidding systems under Model 2, and a competitive market under Models 3 and 4.

SOCIAL POLICY OBLIGATIONS

One attraction of Model 1, which is carried over into Model 2, but is greatly reduced in Models 3 and 4, is the ability to accommodate social policy obligations. These are outcomes wanted by the government that would not appear in fully competitive markets. We may usefully divide these into two groups: those related to generation, and those that are not. The former group includes "obligations to supply",[2] environmental regulation of emissions, diversity of fuel sources and subsidies to the coal industry and to nuclear power. Social policy obligations not related to generation include uniform pricing across areas with unequal costs, rural electrification, discounts for customers who use a large amount of electricity, "lifeline rates" for poor people, conservation programmes and high local taxes. In Model 1 all can be achieved, but in the later models the generation-related policies come under serious threat.

The ability to achieve these objectives is made possible by the monopoly of the utility over its customers, which enables the utility to charge them the excess costs. High input costs and excess capacity can only be sustained if the customers have no other choice. Discrimination among customers is also feasible, since the tariff can be structured to sell to large users at a different price from small users.

Model 1 utilities are often the agents of so many social policies that they become effectively a tax collector. These policies are supported by above-market prices that the industry can charge because of its monopoly and because demand is so strong for a product which is close to a necessity. Examples include the coal industry in Germany and the UK, the engineering profession in France and the windmill industry in the US.

---

[1] The issues surrounding the correct form of regulation are various and a full treatment could not be attempted here. Interested readers are referred to Littlechild, S. C. (1983) *Regulation of British Telecommunications Profitability* (Report to the Secretary of State, February 1983) which provides a useful survey of the different forms of regulatory control.

[2] The obligation to supply is defined differently in different places. In general, we mean the obligation to offer service and/or the obligation to build sufficient capacity to guarantee some specified level of reliability.

IMPLICATIONS FOR ASSET VALUES AND STRANDED COSTS

Revenues and asset values in a Model 1 system bear a close relation to accounting concepts of cost-of-service rather than market valuations.

In Model 1, tariffs determine the utility's revenue. The regulatory body or the government will regulate tariffs to provide a return on assets and to keep prices in line with costs. Provided the tariffs are set at an adequate level, and provided the revenues are collected, the generators will be adequately remunerated. Model 1 relies upon the franchise customers to pay the capital costs of the plants, and ensure an adequate level of profits. Certainly, regulators do not always ensure adequate returns; sometimes they may permit too generous a return. "Regulatory lag" (slowness to adjust prices to costs) provides some deviation from full cost recovery. However, the regulatory bargain is that the utility gets reimbursed for prudent expenditures.

Customers in a Model 1 system not only pay all the costs of the utility,[3] they also take the risk of changes in technology which render existing plant obsolete. The customer takes the risk for mistakes made by the utility, if made in good faith. Often the customer also pays for social policy objectives that regulators or the governments deem wise, but that have little to do with provision of low-cost electricity. In return, regulators give the utility an obligation to supply that guarantees customers a supply of power.[4]

In a well-regulated and well-run Model 1 utility, the prices are set to deliver an adequate rate of return to stockholders, whether stockholders are private individuals or governments. The asset values (say, as measured in the stock market—if the company is privately owned) will approximate to the asset values recorded in the books of the company. This will be true even with past mistakes or government-imposed social objectives. As long as the form of price control permits the company to recoup an adequate return from customers, it can maintain the value of its assets.

PRESSURES FOR CHANGE

Model 1 (monopoly and monopoly service) begins to break down most spectacularly when the marginal cost of competitive generation, or the price that new entrants could charge, is less than the price charged by the utility.

---

[3] "The customers pay all the costs"—of course, in some countries, social policy dictates that the customers pay well below cost, and the utility runs a continuous deficit.
[4] In developed countries, the obligation to supply is often interpreted as absolute. In poorer countries the obligation is more nearly not to discriminate in allocating shortages.

This price may be higher than under competition because:

- the depreciation policies of the regulatory regime do not adequately capture technical progress;[5]
- past capacity acquisitions have been poor (nuclear plants have often been excessively expensive);
- the incumbent's choice of plant must meet social policy objectives but similar requirements do not apply to competitors;
- large quantities of a fuel (such as gas) may become available at low prices, making a different technology a cheaper option. (This appears to have been a major factor in many cases.)

Model 1 utilities also create dissatisfaction by refusing to offer reasonable terms when customers install their own equipment and need back-up provisions. Utilities have sometimes refused to purchase excess energy from self-generators, and have refused access to their wires. The UK had a law requiring open transmission access for independent generators for six years before it implemented a radical restructuring. There were no takers because of the terms offered for transmission by the incumbent Model 1 utility, the CEGB. In the US, litigation over access has been extensive and costly.

EXAMPLES OF MODEL 1

Most countries start with monopolies covering their entire electricity supply industry. Sometimes there is one monopoly for the whole country, sometimes local monopolies. Almost all countries had this form of organisation up to 1980, and most still do. Electricité de France (EDF) owns the entire industry in France. The UK was an example of Model 1a until 1990; the CEGB owned all generation and transmission and there were separate monopoly distribution companies. Italy, Malaya and Japan all follow Model 1.

The US had almost complete monopoly until PURPA was passed in 1978. Investor-owned utilities served most of the country and had a monopoly from generation to the final customer. (There were also some publicly owned power

---

[5] "Economic" depreciation would measure the reduced economic value, in terms of future streams of returns, of an asset over time. Since technological progress has an impact on future expected returns, this would automatically be factored into the depreciation calculation. Regulatory and financial accounts, however, only approximate to this notion of depreciation. The regulatory and financial accounting values of particular assets may therefore differ considerably from the economic value.

companies eligible for tax-free financing, and some separate retail/distribution-only companies that bought from a single supplier.[6])

Despite having multiple generating and distribution companies, some privately owned and some publicly owned, Venezuela also has a Model 1 system. Only utilities may generate, and no one has any choice over whom they buy from and sell to. The list of Model 1 countries is almost as long as the list of countries, since the movement to competition is quite recent, and other models are the exception.

CONCLUSIONS

Model 1 has been the paradigm for a century, for good reason. This form of vertically integrated organisation has enabled the development of large-scale transmission systems and has enabled introduction of larger plants. These "economies of scale" arguments that were persuasive for many years, and still apply in some developing countries, justified monopoly arrangements.

The total monopoly has also allowed subsidies for poor areas, rural electrification, development of indigenous fuels, and other government policy objectives. These objectives may continue to require a monopoly in electric production and retailing.

---

[6] The pressures of these distribution-only companies to get the freedom to go to alternative sources of supply led to costly litigation, although most of the pressure was for lower prices offered by a supplier which had lower sunk costs, not lower marginal costs.

APPENDIX A
PARTIAL-COST POOLS

Vertically integrated utilities have a monopoly over sales to final customers in their jurisdiction, but they frequently have coordination or pooling agreements with neighbouring utilities. These can be called "spot markets" since a spot market is defined as a market for immediate delivery of the product. These may initially be for short-term emergency support. They may evolve into mechanisms for more regular short-term energy transactions, to reduce overall short-run costs. They may eventually develop into medium-term trading arrangements.

An Example of a Model 1 Pooling Agreement

The Joint Operation Agreement in Sweden states that:

Every company must meet its power and energy consumption, principally with generation capacity it owns or power purchased against long-term agreements.[1]

For joint operation to perform correctly, the pricing of the temporary power interchanges must be based on variable costs only. From the fairness aspect, it must then be demanded that all power utilities participating in joint operation should meet, to an adequate degree, the fixed costs incurred in their generation systems.[2]

These two paragraphs are the marks of a Model 1 pool. The requirements are for each company to hold capacity to meet its own load, and for trading to be based on variable costs. Key words are fairness and joint operation—the hallmarks of cost-sharing arrangements.

In Model 1, pools operate in a variety of ways: they may settle through automatic pooling transactions, governed by previously agreed rules, or they

---

[1] Nutek (1992) The Swedish Electricity Market—From monopoly to competition, Swedish National Board for Industrial and Technical Development, Stockholm, p. 44.
[2] Nutek (1992) The Swedish Electricity Market—From monopoly to competition, Swedish National Board for Industrial and Technical Development, Stockholm, p. 45.

may have opportunities for continual negotiation. Prices may be set according to a "split-the-difference" rule or according to a complicated dispatch simulation to calculate and divide the gains from trade. The price for these transactions need only cover the running costs: each trading partner has its own service territory, and its own franchise customers, who are responsible for paying most of the utility's costs.

The major characteristic of a Model 1 spot market price, therefore, is that it is not designed to cover all the costs of owning and operating plant. (See Box.) Rather, it is designed to split the gains from trade for very short-term transactions, where the other costs of the system have already been covered. This is why we refer to them as "partial cost pools". The spot market is therefore part of a much wider contract between its members, which covers obligations to construct, maintain and commit plant. This explains the reluctance of US pools to admit distribution companies as members.

How can you tell what type of system is in operation in a particular place? As an example, consider Sweden. In the Swedish system, individual utilities are required to demonstrate that they can deliver electricity with a small probability of failure, to all of their contracted customers.[3] The pool price is then based on short-run avoidable costs.

The short-run avoidable costs, which are appropriate for very short-run dispatch, do not incorporate the previously incurred costs of commitment, maintenance or construction. This is why we refer to these types of pools as "partial-cost spot markets". The big danger in these spot markets is free-riding, otherwise known as "leaning on your neighbour". Spot markets that set prices based on the dispatch costs therefore need supporting rules to ensure that other costs are covered elsewhere. *Membership must also be strictly limited* to those who have agreed to cover the rest of the costs—you cannot allow just anyone to purchase at the trading price.

There are two requirements, which we return to later when we consider other types of pools, for an electricity trading arrangement to result in economic dispatch. One is that the system operator knows the marginal costs of the plant, so that they can dispatch them in order. The second is that generators are paid more than the marginal cost of the plant so that they have an incentive to run it. In the end, they will not run plant unless all their avoidable costs are covered. They will also not build new plant unless all the capital costs are covered.

Partial-cost pools expect the owning utility to take care of the capital costs and the maintenance costs, but arrange to meet the other conditions by two rules: they require truthful disclosure of marginal costs, and they have pricing arrangements typified by "split-the-difference" pricing, so that the gains from trade are shared between the buyer and the seller, with a small payment to the pool taken out of the trading gains.

---

[3] They must demonstrate this capability to the Joint Operating Committee, Svenska Kraftnät (SvK).

However, the incentive is to cheat. The seller, with the low marginal cost, has an incentive to overstate his cost, because he gains more from splitting the difference that way. (The seller's costs are 2, the buyer's are 4, and the split-the-difference price is 3. However, if the seller says his costs are 3, the price is 3.5—the seller makes 1.5 by cheating, whereas he would have made 1 by telling the truth.) The buyer, with the high marginal cost, has an incentive to understate his cost for the same reason. If both cheat, they will eventually get to a negotiated price, the trade will take place and the outcome will be efficient. But the dispatcher will not know who is lying and who is not, and an uneconomic dispatch will result.

"Tight pools" such as the New York Power Pool, which enforce this type of trading arrangement, break down under the economics of the situation. Selling companies may find more lucrative opportunities; buyers may find better deals than they get splitting the difference. They first make long-term contracts to meet their needs, and later they make short-term deals outside the pool and schedule the transactions through it. Finally, the market forces prevail over sharing arrangements. Looser arrangements for trading, which do not require the price to be based on the notified marginal costs, do not give the dispatcher the information needed for economic central dispatch, and therefore require active and transparent trading outside the pool to achieve minimum cost.

In the US, regulators have become less inclined to prevent transactions at market prices, instead of at costs, if both parties agree. So we see the advent of looser forms of bilateral trading arrangements. The pressure is to move towards market prices, determined by negotiation. This may be via a broker system (as in Florida) or a bulletin board (as in California). Trades within these systems move towards market prices if there are many transactions. They will move quickly to these prices if arbitrage is allowed. The 1992 *Energy Policy Act* (EPAct) permitted arbitrageurs into these markets. The buyers and sellers are still regulated utilities. But there is obviously pressure to allow final consumers to take advantage of the low prices found in these markets.

It must, however, be remembered that these markets in the US are still loose forms of the partial-cost pool. The utility sellers have captive customers who pay all the costs of the plant, so that the marginal sales need cover the marginal cost by a small amount to be remunerative. Under the most usual form of US regulation, which is based on a rate of return to plant in service, there are incentives to overbuild.[4] The pooling agreements often enhance these incentives by requiring excessive reserve margins. Moreover, plants are not closed when they become uneconomic to maintain: most regulators require that a plant be "used and useful" if the captive customers are to pay for its sunk

---

[4] See "Behaviour of the firm under regulatory constraint", *American Economic Review* (1962), by H. Averch and L. Johnson. This is a classic article in regulation. The idea is that if utilities are regulated by limits on their rate of return and that this rate exceeds the cost of capital, then they will have incentives to make their production too capital intensive.

costs. This leads to excess capacity. When there is excess capacity, the prices in these loose pools, even those not subject to split-the-difference pricing, will be lower than the true free market price. (Conversely, when capacity is tight, constraints on new building would lead to prices higher than the "true" market price with free entry.) If the trading is to be freed up then decisions to build and close plants should also be liberalised. This is essential to avoid uneconomic decisions.

The further operational problem of expanding directly from loose pools into a decentralised trading arrangement is the question of system control. While trading is a marginal activity, so that the utility serves most of the load, the dispatch can accommodate the marginal trades without physical problems on the system. The operator is still in charge of the plants that provide frequency control, reactive power and reserve, and can deal with transmission constraints by backing off plant. If all the transactions were done as bilateral trades, the operator could lose control of the transmission system unless the market provides the services formerly provided by the controlling utility. A change to a more complex form of trading, such as Model 3 or Model 4, requires a rethinking of the Model 1 pooling arrangements.

5 MODEL 2—PURCHASING AGENCY

DESCRIPTION OF THE MODEL

In Model 2, shown diagramatically in Figure 5.1, independent generators (IPPs) are allowed. These may be created from existing utilities by divestiture, or they may be new producers who enter the market when new plant is needed. The IPPs compete to construct and operate plant and carry the construction and operating risk. (This distinguishes this model from a Model 1 utility that may contract for new plant if it does not have a construction division to construct its own plant.) IPPs sell their output to a purchasing agency. In turn, the agency sells the output on to Distcos that have a monopoly over their customers.[1]

While Model 2 allows *competition in generation*, all power must be sold to a purchasing agency; so the purchasing agency is a monopsony, buying the output from the generators. Generators compete to sell to the purchasing agency. This introduces competition at the level of new construction and for generation operation. Generators will typically compete for contracts to supply the purchasing agency.

The purchasing agency can in principle discriminate between generators; either bidding procedures or some other provision will be needed to prevent this. Sometimes, however, the purchasing agency is created precisely so that it can

---

[1] A feature sometimes found in Model 2 is the provision for "competing retailers". Retailers are only able to purchase from the single purchasing agency at the standard wholesale price; they do not have a choice of anyone other than the purchasing agency supplying them. They can compete only on the mark-up in the retail tariffs. They do not have the opportunity to find a new supplier and by making profitable choices put pressure on the suppliers to lower their costs. They cannot take the market risk of new plant construction, and make a profit doing so, because the purchasing agency has already taken the market risk. Governments value the possibility of offering choice to customers, and many include this "retail competition" in Model 2, but in practice this choice may not be operative in Model 2 because the profits to be earned in such a retail business are small. Despite this there has been some entry into the market in Northern Ireland for retail competition along these lines. However, since full retail competition is expected in Northern Ireland in the next few years, the decision to enter the market now may have more to do with establishing a reputation and other first-mover advantages for the future, than the desire to exploit the limited opportunities available at the moment.

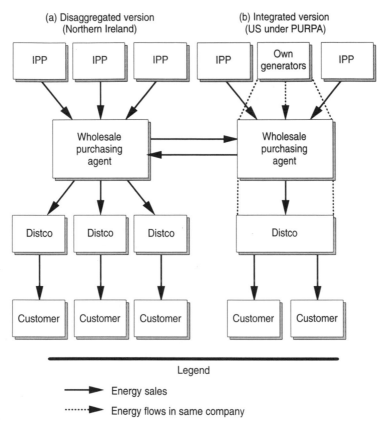

Figure 5.1   Model 2—purchasing agent

exercise monopsony power and discriminate between generators, offering lower prices to lower cost generators, and in this way appropriate the "economic rents" from low-cost sources or sources for which the customers have already paid.

For example, in a transition to competition, a government or regulator may face an industry where private ownership of low-cost hydro resources has been regulated to provide low-cost power to consumers. A move to market prices would ensure windfall gains to the owners. At the same time there may be high-cost nuclear plants where windfall losses would result from competition. The regulator can perhaps see virtue in introducing competition, but is unhappy with making some owners millionaires while bankrupting others. A purchasing agency model would avoid this problem, since it would bear both the windfall gains and the losses. It could provide existing power at some average of the high and low costs, while purchasing new power at market prices.

TRANSITION MECHANISMS

When a government-owned industry moves to Model 2, existing plant may be sold by tender to private buyers, complete with contracts for power sales to the purchasing agency. This is what was done in Northern Ireland. Alternatively, a regulator could order a Model 1 utility to purchase new power requirements by competitive bid from IPPs. This method is fraught with potential conflicts (see below). In the US, a Model 2 system was introduced by PURPA, which required utilities to purchase at "avoided cost".[2]

TRADING ARRANGEMENTS

In Model 2, the purchasing agency model, generators typically have contracts with the purchasing agency, known as power purchase agreements or PPAs. Normally, these contracts have an availability payment, designed to cover fixed costs, and an energy payment, set to cover the variable costs of generation in order to dispatch the plant. The contracts are called in order of their variable costs of generation to achieve short-term efficiency in dispatch.

Economic dispatch requires that the energy payment be designed to match, as accurately as possible, the marginal cost of running the plant. However, setting energy payments to actual costs incurred gives the generators poor incentives to reduce those costs. One solution to this is to track costs closely, but independently of actual costs, by linking the energy payment to an index of costs. Consequently, we see many PPAs with clauses that link energy payments to fuel price indices.

Full payment of costs requires that the overheads also are paid, and this is usually done through an availability payment (usually paid for each kilowatt of generating capacity). If the plant is to have an incentive to be available to generate, this payment needs to be linked to the actual availability of the plant. However, short of an army of engineers on motorcycles, the availability of a

---

[2] The history of this fiasco would take a whole book. The problem was not so much in the concept, which was designed as a counterweight to the utilities monopsony power. In purchasing from heat and power (cogeneration) plants and other small producers, utilities could beat the price down to the producers' marginal costs, since they were the only purchaser. PURPA enunciated the rule that the utilities should pay what it was worth to them, i.e. the costs they avoided by buying the power. Regulators attempted to estimate avoided costs (an exercise which of course they undertook constantly for the purpose of approving utility construction plans) and required the utilities to offer long-term contracts at these prices. However, in the early 1980s when this was taking place, the price of oil was at its height and, with hindsight, many of the contracts signed under PURPA look exceedingly generous. Moreover, in some states there was no appreciation of the fact that as the supply increases, the avoided costs are reduced. Unlimited contracts were therefore offered at inflated prices, greatly increasing excess capacity.

plant is difficult to monitor directly if the plant is not actually running. As a result, we usually see availability payments together with "penalties" for not being available. Plants incur these penalties if the dispatcher calls them to generate, but they are unable to do so. Ideally, these penalties would relate to the market value of energy, so that there are incentives to be available at the times of highest value. Design of the availability penalty is a major consideration in IPP contracts that we consider in more detail in Part 2 of the book.

In Model 2, sales from the purchasing agency to Distcos often take place at preset wholesale tariff prices. Efficiency considerations suggest that this tariff should follow the marginal costs of the system. Also, the tariff should cover the total costs to the purchasing agency of purchasing power. Multi-part tariffs, with fixed and variable charge elements are often used to meet these objectives. Variable elements of the tariff can be set to mirror system marginal costs. Fixed components can then be set to recover any remaining costs. The tariffs should then be differentiated appropriately by time of day or season. Retail tariffs would inevitably reflect the cost of purchasing at the purchasing agency's wholesale tariff.

Such a wholesale tariff allows the introduction of interruptible rates, allowing the purchasing agency to cut off demand, usually from large industrial customers, at times of system stress. These customers usually provide this service in return for lower rates. Interruptible rates offer more opportunity to adjust the system to demand and supply conditions. It is possible to calculate a spot price for this system at the wholesale level, broadly similar to that in the England and Wales Pool price, to provide spot incentives for load management and plant availability.

TRANSMISSION ACCESS

The question of crossing the system, discussed in Model 1, is still an issue here, and continues to be in all the models. The additional issue in transmission access in Model 2 is the question of how to reflect transmission costs in the location of generation and the dispatch of plant. The bidding process for obtaining new plant must allow for the actual and potential transmission constraints and losses and handicap the bids accordingly.

Clear terms and prices for transmission access must also be laid down. These terms of access will determine how independent generators are treated if they cannot run because of transmission constraints. For instance, the purchasing agency may guarantee a generator access to the system. If the generator was then unable to deliver power because of a transmission constraint, the purchasing agency would have to compensate the generator.

The issues surrounding generator access to the grid are discussed further in Part 2.

SHOULD THE PURCHASING AGENCY BE SEPARATE?

A structural question in Model 2 is the identity of the purchasing agency. The purchasing agency has to make long-term contracts with generators, so it needs to be credit-worthy. The government or a well-established utility is therefore a primary candidate, but either of these creates other conflicts.

The purchasing agency should in principle be independent of the owners of the generation, or conflicts will inevitably arise. The agency needs to be seen not to discriminate in favour of its own resources, either in procurement or in operation. In procurement, it might seem a simple matter to devise bidding procedures that make it clear which is the lowest cost producer, but in practice it is often difficult to compare plants with different cost structures providing power at different times and at different locations. The fact that the purchasing agency takes the market risk means that IPPs can be financed with high proportions of debt, "leaning" on the purchaser's equity. If the purchaser is also a generator, its "costs" are bound to be higher than the competition, if evaluated at the overall company cost of capital including the larger equity requirements.

In the US, there has been constant tension during the Model 2 phase about the utilities acting as the purchasing agency. There have been calls for the utilities to divest themselves of generation, and pledges by utilities not to build any more plant on their own account. As with all structural issues, the benefits of independent operation need to be weighed against the costs of reduced coordination and increased transactions costs.

A further conflict arises if the utility is also the system operator, responsible for dispatch of the contracts. In a mixed system, where running the operator's own plant may be more profitable than running a competitor's, the conflicts are likely to be substantial. One solution would be carefully-drawn contracts that give the system operator the right incentives to dispatch the least cost plant, irrespective of ownership. In the US, these potential conflicts were often resolved by permitting self-dispatch of small generators under PURPA, so that they could not accuse the dispatcher of discrimination. This has resulted in some cases in high-cost IPP plant being dispatched while low-cost plant belonging to the utility was backed off, in complete disregard of merit order.

The purchasing agency in Model 2 could in principle be a completely separate stand-alone company, but it could also be part of a separated transmission company. It makes no substantive difference whether there is a separate transmission company, or whether the purchasing agency and the wires are in common ownership. In Northern Ireland, the wires company owns the purchasing agency.

ACHIEVING EFFICIENCY

A crucial aspect of Model 2 is that generating plant procurement, which is arguably the most important area to control costs, has been opened to competition. The capital costs of generating plant are a large fraction of total industry costs. Alone, this makes it important to induce efficiency in investment. The investment decision also dictates fuel type, which affects running costs for years to come.

The decision to build, and its accomplishment on time and to budget, has therefore been the area where there has been most pressure to substitute market mechanisms for the "planning process". This has led to bidding systems, under Model 2, and to competitive markets, under Models 3 and 4. Minimum cost generation in Model 2 is achieved through competitive bidding for construction and operation of plants, on long-term contracts.

An asserted advantage of Model 2 over Models 3 and 4 is that the long-term contracts reduce the risk that new technology will cause the generators to lose their market. This means that the cost of capital for generation projects, a substantial component of the final price of electricity, is likely to be lower here than in Models 3 and 4, which can lead to overly capital-intensive production. Both the IPPs and the purchasing agency are insulated from the technology and other risks associated with the market. (Model 2 has this in common with Model 1 and cost-based regulation generally.) Insulation from these risks undermines the superior incentives to innovation inherent in a more market-driven situation. The Model 2 generator does not compete with new entrants whereas the Model 3 generator does. The Model 2 generator does not take the market risk and decide when new plant is necessary but the Model 3 generator does.

Efficient dispatch in Model 2 is achieved by careful design of the IPP contracts so that the marginal cost to the dispatcher (the energy payment) is the marginal cost of running the plant. The marginal revenue to the generator, the availability payment plus the energy payment, is higher than marginal cost and this gives the plant the incentive to run. (The design of contracts is considered further in Part 2.) Efficient location decisions require some pricing of transmission at the bidding stage, while efficient dispatch of the contracts needs some adjustment for marginal losses.

Finally, efficient consumption decisions depend on how well the purchasing agency's wholesale tariff reflects marginal costs, and in turn on how well retail tariffs reflect wholesale tariffs.

SOCIAL POLICY OBLIGATIONS

One attraction of this model, which is shared with Model 1, is the ability to accommodate social policy objectives. Discrimination among new plant can occur if the government (or regulator) instructs the purchasing agency to diversify fuel sources. The purchasing agency can ask for bids for a particular type of fuel, or for plants in a particular location. It can also ask for windmills or other non-conventional types of plant for environmental purposes, and roll the cost into the tariff.

In this structure, the purchasing agency will have an obligation to ensure there is sufficient generation, because it has either a direct or an indirect monopoly over customers. To meet this obligation, it must ensure sufficient power is available from IPPs under contract or from IPPs bidding for dispatch.

The utility's monopoly over the Distcos makes it possible to achieve these objectives, since it enables the purchasing agency to charge the excess costs to them. The purchasing agency can sustain high input costs and excess capacity if its customers have no other choice.

IMPLICATIONS FOR ASSET VALUES AND STRANDED COSTS

In Model 2, the existing plant can continue to be remunerated at historic cost: the feature of the customer absorbing all the costs can be maintained, thus obviating the problems of stranded costs. The purchasing agency has a monopoly over all Distcos, and can therefore pass on costs to customers. Regulation is necessary to give it incentives to purchase prudently, and to allow it to pass on some approximation of its purchasing costs to consumers.

A contract, however, does not guarantee payment. Some countries have tried to introduce IPPs as a solution to capital inadequacies of their existing utilities. However, they have foundered on the lack of a suitably credit-worthy purchaser of the power. In Model 2, revenue adequacy for the independent generator (the IPP) has three steps: the customer must pay the Distco; the Distco must pay the purchasing agency; and the purchasing agency must pay the generator. The PPA is the last step in the chain. The first is to ensure that the tariffs are set at an adequate level. This can be a substantial problem in poorer countries where the provision of electricity is viewed as a social service, and where theft is tolerated as a fact of life. The retail tariffs must be set to cover the payments under the IPP contracts.

Given adequate tariffs, Model 2 provides substantial assurance to new generators. Moreover, changes in asset values (stranded costs) consequent on the move to a more competitive system can be minimised. For example, low-cost generators can be given contracts entitling them to fixed payments, while high-cost generators get higher fixed payments. Thus, the incentive properties of the contracts can be maintained, while reducing total costs to the purchasing agency. Or, if the government sells a plant that it owns, it can ensure that it recoups its investment by providing above-market contracts.

In a Model 2 structure, therefore, the asset value can be maintained, for the purchasing agency has a monopoly on Distcos in its territory.

PRESSURES FOR CHANGE

Pressures to move on from Model 2 (competition in generation) to Model 3 (wholesale competition) come from various places. One source is wholesale customers—Distcos or large industrial customers who feel they could do better elsewhere in systems where there are multiple purchasing agencies, as in the US. In some cases, this needs to be resisted, since it is not a pressure derived from more efficient production or lower marginal costs. It often has more to do with tariff differentials created by cost-of-service regulation. For example, two utilities may be facing similar marginal costs, but one company has older or more depreciated assets, and therefore lower tariffs. Customers of the high-priced utility may wish they could get hold of lower prices. However, allowing them to do so would not reduce total costs—they may even increase. This is simply a problem of wishing to avoid carrying a share of the historic investment obligations.

Pressures for freeing "access to the wires" will also come from IPP generators or utilities earning less than the market value of power under their contracts or under regulation. It may also come from generators who could produce from new plants at a total cost below the sunk costs reflected in the tariffs of the purchasing agency. These generators may be able to bypass the system by selling to nearby purchasers using their own wires. (Model 2 may allow some generators this option, but usually only in restricted circumstances.) On-site generation is also a pressure on Model 2.

By contrast, in some countries where the growth of demand is enormous, a central purchasing agency can act as a bottleneck. Some localities would be prepared to pay for independent power production, even at market prices that are above cost, rather than ration demand and lose productive opportunities.

EXAMPLES OF MODEL 2

Northern Ireland introduced an example of a Model 2 system in 1992, with an independent purchasing agency combined with the transmission.

The US has been using a variant of this model since 1978, with the incumbent utilities acting as purchasing agents for IPPs.

The Spanish system, although it is complicated by financial compensations between separate companies, is in essence a Model 2 system.

China has many regional and provincial companies, and some separate distribution companies. Monopoly relationships were continuous throughout the system, at least until 1985. Since then, there has been some experimentation with alternative ownership of generation, and this has been very successful in getting new plant built.

CONCLUSIONS

This model introduces competition in generation, which is arguably the place where the pressures of competition can do most good in reducing costs. It can also be a useful model in tapping new sources of capital. At the same time, this model avoids some of the costs of later models: the transactions costs of spot markets and transmission access and an increased cost of capital that arises when generators bear technology risk. The model may also make it easier for governments to achieve social policy objectives such as rural electrification, subsidies to producers and diversity of generating plant.

In small systems where there are very few generating plants, each plant may effectively have a monopoly at some point in the load curve, and Model 2 may be chosen as an effective form of regulation by contract.

On the whole, Model 2 is a good transition model in places where the more sophisticated arrangements needed for a more complete market structure are not in place and would be hard to establish. For example, in countries where there are as yet no reasonable accounting systems in the industry, proposing the type of settlement system required for Model 3 and the metering required for Model 4 might strain credulity. There are some housekeeping chores that must take precedence, such as corporatisation and commercialisation. Procurement of new plant from competitive sources under a PPA is a step that can mesh well with tariff reform and other requirements of commercialisation.

However, Model 2 also provides insurance to the independent generators against market risk and makes it easier for them to raise capital. Since the IPPs are not dependent on market prices for their revenues and do not have to compete against later entrants, they can finance with a very high proportion of debt, which reduces the prices they have to charge. The risk is passed, via the purchasing agency, to the captive customers.

By insulating the owners of the plant from the effects of technical change and market forces, Model 2 does blunt the dynamic benefits of competition, leaving many aspects of the choice of when to build and what to build in the hands of central planners rather than entrepreneurs. Moreover, the cleansing effect of competition is sometimes overlooked. Market prices make it difficult for participants to hide excess costs in payments for power. Market prices also make self-dealing and even plain old corruption less likely. There are millions of dollars at stake in each new IPP contract, and the opportunities for corruption are large and cannot be adequately counteracted by incentives and regulation. This of course is also true under Model 1, where the procurement of fuel and plant can also be corrupted in a way that is much more difficult under a competitive model, where the test is the market price.

6

MODEL 3—WHOLESALE COMPETITION

DESCRIPTION OF THE MODEL

Model 3 which is shown in Figure 6.1 is characterised by choice of supplier for Distcos together with competition in generation. This is sometimes called wholesale competition to distinguish it from retail competition (Model 4) where final consumers rather than Distcos have a choice of supplier.[1] In Model 3 there are separate Distcos. These can purchase energy for their customers from any competing IPP generator. The Distcos maintain a monopoly over energy sales to the final customers (they each have a franchise to serve a given set of customers).

In one sense Model 3 moves the purchasing agency down to the low-voltage level, rather than keeping it at the high-voltage level, but it is no longer a "single buyer" model. Since Model 3 permits open access to the transmission wires, it gives the IPP alternative buyers. It is not therefore necessary for the buyer to take all the market risk, and the form of contract for power can change from the Model 2 contract to a contract which simply hedges price risk. We examine the different contracts in Chapters 9 and 10. With free entry to the market, a Model 3 generator competes against entrants. However, final customers within a service area still have no choice of supplier. With this structure the "obligation to supply" moves to the retail company, which still has a monopoly over final customers.

---

[1] Wholesale and retail in ordinary language are only loosely defined. They are both merchant functions, but the distinction is not absolute. Wholesalers and retailers are middlemen in the merchant chain—they aggregate supplies and rebundle them into larger or smaller lots for further sale. They take possession of (i.e. take the price risk on) the product, unlike a broker who simply matches buyers and sellers for a fee. A generator may be its own wholesaler in Model 3 or its own retailer in Model 4. For the purposes of clarity we have adopted the following convention: the difference between *wholesale and retail transactions* is defined by the identity of the *buyer*: if the buyer is a final consumer, the transaction is a retail transaction; if the buyer is a retailer the transaction is a wholesale transaction (a "sale for resale"). However, in the text, the term *a wholesale market* (for instance, a power pool) is used more loosely as regards the identity of the participants: it is a market (many buyers and sellers, a single product, a time, a place) in which the sellers are predominantly producers and the buyers are predominantly retailers, but not exclusively so. In this chapter, the definition of *wholesale competition* is that the purchasers of power in the wholesale market are exclusively Distcos who have a monopoly over the final customers.

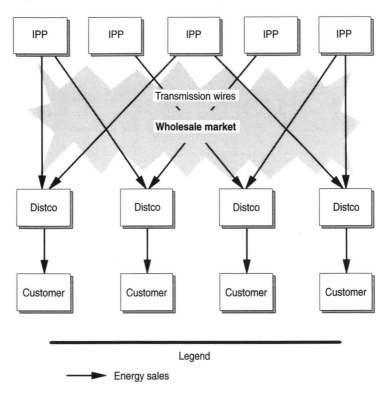

Figure 6.1 Model 3—wholesale competition

The arrival of wider competition does not eliminate the role of regulation. The monopoly providers of the wires must still be regulated, and the structure of the competitive parts of the market still need to be overseen.

TRADING ARRANGEMENTS

Whilst we discuss the trading arrangements for competition in Models 3 and Model 4 more fully in Part 2 of this book, it is useful to lay out the main requirements here.

● A dispatch function, which should be independent of the traders. The job of the "system operator" is to keep the frequency and voltage of the transmission system stable. To do this the operator requires access to wires, voltage support, frequency support, and reserve energy.

- A spot market or power exchange for electricity into which buyers and sellers of electricity bid to establish a spot price for electricity (on an hourly or half-hourly basis).
- Transmission prices which reflect the marginal costs of transmision, and which prioritise and manage the use of congested paths in an economically rational manner.
- A forward market in which the parties can contract bilaterally with each other. (This will develop naturally if not inhibited by bad regulation or protocols.)
- Last, and often overlooked, is the requirement that there be freedom of entry and exit from the market, i.e. the freedom to open and close plant in response to market forces. The market must be left free to provide the necessary reserves. This may require changes in legislation and custom.

The trading mechanism that we prefer—which we investigate more fully later—is a form of spot market or power exchange which we have called "full-cost pooling". Full-cost pooling is so called because all generators' costs could, at least in theory, be recovered at the pool's spot market prices. The generators' costs include "capacity costs", and the market price will be allowed to rise to quite high levels to signal the need for new capacity. This differs from partial-cost pooling where native load customers bear the fixed costs, a specific level of reserve is required to be held by all customers, and trades are made at avoided cost only. Prices in full-cost pools should be allowed to vary freely to the market levels. This ensures that sufficient generation is constructed, made available and operated at any time. In practice, full-cost pools are supplemented by bilateral contracting arrangements between customers and generators to hedge the price risks of operating in the spot market alone. Traders settle the imbalances between these contracts and actual flows at market prices. The market for energy trading therefore consists of a spot market, organised by the Market Operator, and bilateral contracts.

It is possible to get by in Model 3, where there are relatively few traders, with a system known as "wheeling". In this customers and generators make bilateral contracts; an existing utility opens its wires to competitors to deliver contracted power (usually under compulsion) and sets regulated prices for imbalances on contracts. The utility therefore acts as the Dispatcher, the Transmission Provider and the Market Operator. This form of operation requires extensive regulation because of the intrinsic conflicts of interest in a transmission owner opening his wires for his competition to steal his customers. "Full cost pools" can enhance efficiency in Model 3, and provide a platform for the move to Model 4; because of the greater number of players in Model 4 markets, a workable "full-cost pool" or spot market becomes essential.

TRANSMISSION ACCESS

Competing generators in Model 3 may sell directly to Distcos. These still have a franchise over their customers and may be associated with the distribution function, owning the low-voltage wires. However, they are not required to provide open access to the low-voltage wires. This model therefore only requires transmission prices for the high-voltage wires. These prices must provide the right economic incentives for plant location and dispatch, and sufficient revenue for the transmission owners.

IMPLICATIONS FOR THE STRUCTURE OF COMPANIES

In Model 3, a set of conflict, self-dealing and market power issues arises. Many of these issues have already arisen in the UK. It is worth fleshing out the description of the problem with a few words about the solutions, or non-solutions, adopted in the UK and elsewhere.

Transmission

In Model 3 the functions surrounding transmission need to be redefined. First, consolidation of transmission networks (if there are many of them) may be called for, since there are economies to be had. In Model 3, contractual agreements between networks become vastly more complicated. The more networks there are, the more agreements have to be negotiated and enforced to deal with the operation and settlement of flows at the interfaces between networks. The costs of doing this may indicate network consolidation as the most effective alternative.

Second, the question of whether the transmission functions need to be separated into separate companies, because of potential conflicts, becomes acute. New functions related to trading over networks need to be identified and assigned to someone. We have identified at least three functions, those of: Dispatcher, Transmission Provider and Market Operator.

A Dispatcher is required to keep the transmission system stable and act as traffic controller. To avoid self-dealing concerns, it is best if the Dispatcher is independent of the buyers and sellers of electricity. Systems where an integrated utility acts as Dispatcher are also feasible, but they may require extensive regulation to avoid the reality and perception of self-dealing.

A transmission provider (TP) must be identified to set the terms of users' access to transmission and to collect revenues to pay for the use of the transmission assets. This provider is often the owner of the transmission assets, but this is not necessarily the case.[2]

A Market Operator (MO) must also be identified to police an arrangement to settle imbalances between contracted amounts of energy and actual flows. Although most trades will be made by contract, it is inevitable that the contract amounts will not match the amounts actually generated and consumed. This will be true even if the seller and buyer try to match load to supply. (In practice, there is no reason to try to do this anyway, since it is much more economic to dispatch plants in merit order and settle the imbalances later.) An MO needs to be identified to run the market for spot imbalances.

These functions should often be performed independently of the traders in the market, or they will have to be heavily regulated. It may also be necessary for these functions to be performed independently of each other, due to potential conflicts of interest.

In many industry models the company that acts as TP also acts as Dispatcher and MO. These functions need not be integrated and sometimes integration of these functions creates self-dealing concerns. Provision of transmission services often involves some financial risk to the provider, which may be conditional on the market prices for energy. As a result, there may be conflicts between the functions of TP and Dispatcher and MO. The Dispatcher's decisions set energy prices and the MO's actions calculate and settle the payments due for energy and transmission. Both functions could affect the transmission provider's revenues.

In the UK, the Dispatcher and TP functions are performed by the National Grid Company, while the pool is the MO.[3] The separation has produced difficulties of coordination, some of which have been solved by changing the rules. In this model the TP lacks suitable incentives to maintain and expand the grid in an efficient manner. A more radical restructuring would have vested the three functions in entirely separate companies.

A further option is to combine the MO and the Dispatcher in a single body since there are no obvious conflicts between them.[4] However, this is not necessarily a desirable pairing. The two functions are often thought to go well together because of the benefits of sharing information between dispatch and settlement of the system. However, the skills involved in dispatching a

---

[2] Proposals by Southern California Edison and San Diego Gas and Electric in the restructuring debate in California have separated these functions. An independent system operator ("Poolco") would be responsible for operation of the transmission system, market operation and the provision of transmission services. This organisation would then pay transmission owning utilities for the use of their assets. See *Comments of Southern California Edison in Response to the Inquiry Concerning Alternative Power Pooling Institutions under the Federal Power Act, before the Federal Energy Regulatory Commission*, Docket No. RM94-20-000.

[3] While the pool actually determines the settlement rules, NGC Settlement Ltd (a subsidiary of NGC) actually collects the settlement information and calculates the required payments.

[4] This combination has been instituted in Victoria, Australia.

transmission system are very different from those required for settling a large number of transactions. The latter skills are abundant in industries such as banking and commodity trading. As a result, the benefits of employing a separate MO may exceed the cost of separating the functions.

Generation and Retailing

The role of Distco, the purchaser of power in Model 3, involves retailing and may conflict with generation ownership. The conflict is caused by potential self-dealing. A Distco affiliated with a generator might prefer to purchase from the affiliate, even if the price is higher than other sources in the market. The fact that the Distco has a monopoly over the final consumer in Model 3, means that the excess costs can be passed on to customers (subject of course to regulation).[5] An existing integrated utility may therefore find itself under pressure to sever the retail business from the generation business, either through accounting separation, or by divestiture.

In the UK, this conflict was recognised early, and not fully dealt with. The Distcos, Regional Electricity Companies or RECs were granted a monopoly over smaller final customers for eight years after the 1990 restructuring. Immediately after privatisation they entered the generating market and took equity positions in new gas-fired plant. The regulator was obliged by his charter to review the purchasing policies of the RECs, which he did. It proved almost impossible to make relevant price comparisons (due to differences in load mix, duration, index provisions, etc.) but in the end he gave the RECs a clean bill of health. However, there are those who have argued that the incentives to self-deal in these circumstances are irresistible and impossible to police, and that the conflict should be resolved by divestiture.

Market Power in Generation

Questions of appropriate market share and potential market power in generation also arise in Model 3. Obviously enough, a generator who has had a legal monopoly is likely to have a large market share of an unregulated market. Market power can be limited by *structural* remedies, including breaking up existing companies and removing barriers to entry; by limiting the *results* of exercising market power, for example by instituting revenue or profit caps; or by regulating *conduct*, for example by limiting prices which can be charged.

In the UK, the market power problem was initially resolved by breaking the existing company into three smaller generating companies and encouraging

---

[5] This conflict actually goes away if Model 3 transitions to Model 4 because, with retail competition, a retailer cannot afford to indulge in self-dealing. In fact, in Model 4, retailers and generators are likely to be integrated, since there is not a great deal of profit for middlemen.

entry—a *structural* remedy. Although there were eight competitors in the spot market on the first day, there were two large fossil generators who between them had most of the power to set the market price. Since the price never dropped to the level that the excess capacity would have suggested, it is generally assumed that they exercised their market power to raise the price. There are those who argue that three companies are insufficient for competition, and feel that there should have been at least five fossil generators created.

The market power of the generators was limited in the first three years of operation by the existence of "vesting"[6] contracts, which constrained *results*. These contracts virtually fixed the revenues of the fossil generators over this period. However, they still allowed the spot market to give price signals at the margin for efficient operation of plant, and for closing and opening plant. When the contracts expired, generators started to make real revenues directly in the spot market. When the spot market price subsequently rose, the regulator stepped in and forced an agreement with the generators that they would set caps on the pool price, a *conduct* remedy. He also told them to take steps to divest themselves of some generating plant.

ACHIEVING EFFICIENCY

In Model 3 the choice of generation assets, both in quantity and fuel type, is left to the market. A generator will construct a plant if the market price is expected to cover the cost of construction and operation, as in any other market. In Models 1 and 2, the generator had no access to wider markets. As a result, it needs a contract (either implicit as in Model 1 or explicit as in Model 2) before constructing a plant. Model 3 generators are also likely to seek contracts. However, the existence of an organised spot market, in which they can sell their power, means that the contract is not essential. A Model 3 contract is used to share price risk, whereas a Model 2 contract is necessary to ensure performance on both sides.

A pool of the type described more fully in Chapter 12 is a real incentive to generating efficiency, even with a limited number of buyers, and even if all the market is covered with forward contracts. A low-cost generator can sell power at spot and, in effect, sell its power to a higher-cost generater to enable it to meet its contracts. The high-cost generator can even decide to close its plant and meet its obligation through the spot market. This is a powerful tool for achieving generating efficiency.

---

[6] "Vesting day" was the day on which the parts of the former CEGB were vested as limited companies in the public sector, and on which the UK pool began operation. The "vesting contracts" were the contracts instituted at vesting, many of the contracts were designed to carry subsidies to the coal industry, and were hence above the market price. However, since they fixed generators' revenues, they effectively limited the rewards from the use of market power.

The spot market price is also a strong incentive to efficiency in usage. A true spot market always clears—there can be no "shortage" because the market price will always rise sufficiently to match demand and supply. Since short-term supply is limited, demand response to short-term pressure on the system offers a major improvement of efficiency over tariff rates, or even interruptible rates. Access to the spot market for purchasers can therefore enhance efficiency. In England and Wales, there is already evidence that large firms can respond to the pool price by rescheduling operations. At least one firm has calculated its marginal value of electricity in order to cease consumption when the price exceeds this value.

SOCIAL POLICY OBLIGATIONS

The ability of generators to accommodate social policy obligations connected with generation virtually disappears in Model 3. The purchase of uneconomic inputs (high-cost coal, excessive environmental standards, technologies favoured for national security reasons) cannot be sustained in a competitive market. The generation market in Model 3 has become competitive, and high-cost sources will not have a place unless specifically subsidised. Specific subsidies can of course be designed to encourage windmills or coal-burning plant, or whatever the favoured technology is, but the market will not provide the funds by itself.

However, non-generation-related social policies can be continued, if regulators decide they are appropriate for the retail monopoly. For example, discrimination in favour of large consumers can continue so long as there is no mechanism for the customers to resell their low-cost power. The same is true of sales to poor people at below cost. The markets required in Model 4 will effectively permit resale. But in Model 3, the final customer cannot resell.

Subsidies require someone to bear the costs. Customers who have been monopolised and who are highly inelastic usually fit the bill, although taxpayers could bear the costs directly. In Model 3, the customers are still monopolised and can bear the weight of higher local taxes, or of subsidies to the poor citizens.

IMPLICATIONS FOR ASSET VALUES AND STRANDED COSTS

The introduction of wholesale competition is the beginning of the potential erosion of the asset values of generating assets in systems where accounting costs result in prices above market value. Market prices could not be expected to cover the cost of past mistakes and social objectives. Furthermore, they will only by the merest chance be equal to the "accounting costs" of existing capacity. If the accounting costs are higher than the market prices, the introduction of competition will encourage movement to low-price sources. This of course is what competition is intended to do.

The problem of stranded costs is discussed more fully under Model 4, retail competition, in the next chapter.

PRESSURES FOR CHANGE

In Model 3, wholesale competition, Distcos may purchase directly from competing IPP generators or from a utility of their choice. It requires "access to the transmission system". Once Model 3 is in place, and generators are allowed to compete for sales to Distco, definitional problems creep in: what exactly *is* a Distco?

If a Distco is defined as being a wires company, purchasing for resale, does a large industrial company with its own network count? How about an industrial park? Can a group of large customers declare themselves a Distco? Can a town become a Distco? Can a shopping centre?

Model 3 simply limits customer choice by defining the customers who can exercise it. This definition will inevitably be ragged. If customer choice is limited to consumers with an aggregate load larger than a certain level, are they allowed to aggregate loads over several buildings? Can they form a joint purchasing company to aggregate loads over several firms? Must the loads even be in the same location, or supplied from the same network?

These definitional problems cause Model 3 to turn into Model 4. If some customers are able to make their own arrangements they will be able to purchase market-price electricity. The rest of the utility's costs will then be left to others. This is the "stranded cost" problem. However, since large consumers very often face tariffs which are close to marginal cost anyway, the cream skimming, and the consequent problems of stranded assets, may not be too extensive. Model 3 may survive for some years on its own or as a mixture with Model 4. Some retail customers may get Model 4 style "direct access" while others do not.

EXAMPLES

Model 3 is close to the UK system as it operated immediately after it was privatised in 1990. The transmission system was separated and provided open access. However, the Regional Electricity Companies (RECs), who owned the low-voltage wires, had a monopoly over all but the largest consumers (over 1 MW). In the UK, this structure was viewed as a temporary situation, in transition to Model 4. Open access was provided to large customers from the beginning, so the UK is a mixture of Models 3 and 4.

In the US, "wholesale wheeling" was permitted by the 1992 *Energy Policy Act* (EPAct). This allows separate Distcos to choose their suppliers, and requires open access for these customers to the transmission. In the US, however, separate "distribution companies" do not account for a high proportion of demand. Those that existed at the time of the EPAct were mainly municipally owned. There are also a few suppliers who are not already contracted to a utility. The EPAct specifically prohibited the federal authorities from ordering a move to retail competition, or Model 4. However, some states have subsequently taken steps to introduce it.

CONCLUSIONS

Model 3 expands competition by providing more customers for IPPs. More buyers make the market more competitive and more dynamic than the single buyer in Model 2.

The benefits of competition in generation are enhanced by pushing the market risk and the technology risk back to the generators. Generators are usually in a better position to judge the benefits of new technology than a regulator. When their own cash is at risk, they are also likely to give new investments more careful thought! In Model 3, an existing company has to compete against new entrants; in Model 2 it does not.

However, Model 3 increases the transactions costs by requiring markets and network agreements. Allocating new technology risk (the risk of stranded capacity) to the generators also increases their cost of capital. It removes the ability of governments to direct the choice of new generation technology, other than by direct subsidies or directives. However, it leaves some monopoly in the industry, since customers have no choice of supplier. This allows some subsidies and public service obligations to be maintained, although it limits the form in which they can be imposed. It does introduce the problem of stranded generation costs, but by keeping all customers monopolised as franchise customers, it provides at least a potential solution.

Model 3 certainly appears to have all the virtues. Yet we believe that this is an unstable model, mainly a way-station to Model 4. Way-stations can be useful, if they provide platforms for testing new market institutions such as pooling and transmission access. Model 3 could therefore be thought of as a testing stage. Our reason for doubting that Model 3 can survive is that we observe that both in the UK and in the US, when some types of customers are granted choice, while others were excluded, the definitional problems become acute. In the UK, there was a phased transition, in which customers were granted access to competitive markets in order of their size. Nonetheless, the bulk of the UK regulator's work for a year was to define the exclusion. Nor does the monopoly over final customers guarantee that the stranded asset problem will be resolved. In the US, the large consumers threatened to "municipalise the hell out of the country" i.e. to persuade friendly municipalities to declare themselves independent retailers so that they were eligible to buy and resell (to the large industrial customers, of course) and by implication avoid paying for the sunk costs of their suppliers. We believe that once the markets are opened, it becomes very difficult to limit who may purchase from them, and that trying too hard to limit choice only invites uneconomic bypass, and uneconomic self-generation.

7

MODEL 4—RETAIL COMPETITION

DESCRIPTION OF THE MODEL

Model 4 is called retail competition or direct access; it is shown diagramatically in Figure 7.1. In Model 4 all customers have access to competing generators either directly or through their choice of retailer. Model 4 differs from Model 3 in that it is characterized by choice for all customers, not just distcos who have a monopoly over their final consumers. The basic case of Model 4 would have complete separation of both generation and retailing from the transport business at both transmission and distribution levels. There is no monopoly over retailing, and competing retailers can perform the same roles as they do in other markets. The distribution wires provide open access or common carriage, just as the transmission wires do in Model 3.

With this structure there would also be free entry to generation markets and free exit. This means there should be no regulation over "need for new plants" and no requirement to maintain capacity in production when it has passed its economic life. There would also be free entry for retailers. Retailing is a new function in Model 4. It is a merchant function which does not require ownership of the distribution wires, although in many cases the owner of the wires will also compete as a retailer.

It needs to be emphasized that Model 4 is not a "single buyer" model. Model 4 pools are not purchasing agencies, they are auctioneers. They never own the power, they do not take the market risk; they cannot price-discriminate. Model 4 is of necessity a single transporter model, moving power to facilitate bilateral trading. The trading arrangements we discuss for Model 4 involve a method for the physical delivery of power. Inevitably this means that all trading has to be done over an integrated network of wires. The operator of the wires has to measure and account for the trades. In the pooling arrangements, there is provision for bidding into a spot market to facilitate merit order dispatch (calling of plants in the order of their short-run costs). The pool acts as auctioneer, matching supply and demand and determining the spot price in each half hour. It collects money from purchasers and distributes it to producers. This is sometimes referred to in the UK as "selling to the pool and buying from the pool", which is misleading. The producers and retailers sell to

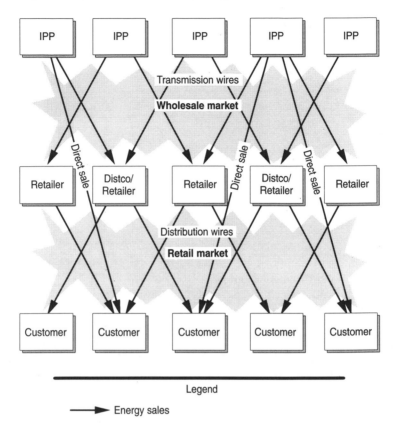

Figure 7.1 Model 4—retail competition

each other, not to the pool. Model 4 trading arrangements are completely different from Model 2.

TRADING ARRANGEMENTS

Model 4 needs open access to all wires, both high voltage (transmission) and low voltage (distribution). A mechanism needs to be introduced to permit extensive bilateral trading across the network. This will be similar to the pooling mechanism we described briefly under Model 3 and this is the subject of a chapter in Part 2 of this book. Model 4 requires prices for access to both high- and low-voltage wires. These prices must, of course, provide the right economic incentives for location of plants and dispatch of plants. They must also provide sufficient revenues to the owners of the wires.

In Model 3, with relatively few customers, all of them regulated retailers, we noted that a spot market was preferable but not essential. We indicated that it might be possible to get by with some form of regulated open access across a utility's system, with imbalances settled at a tariffed rate.

However, in Model 4 a spot market becomes essential. A spot market, in our view, is always required when contractual arrangements between customers and producers are carried out over a network owned by a third party. The network owner must ensure that there are commercial arrangements that allow for the settlement of imbalances between contracted amounts and actual flows. If different parts of a network are operated separately, inter-area payment schemes will also have to be devised.

In Model 4, metering becomes a major problem. Metering by time of use is no longer merely a useful way of promoting efficient usage; it is a commercial necessity. Each customer needs to be metered half-hourly, if this is the settlement period. Since the price changes every half hour, it is necessary to know how much the customers of each competing retailer used in each settlement period, in order to be able to bill the right customers and to settle accounts properly. Problems have emerged in the UK with the metering necessary to extend choice to smaller customers. Initially, only 400 customers (over 1 MW) had direct access, and since these customers had adequate metering there were no problems. When choice of supplier was extended to 40 000 customers over 100 kW in 1994, there was a great deal of confusion. The full extension to 22 million customers in 1998 will be a major logistical problem. In the absence of metering capability for all customers, some profiling of demand will be needed, but this will always provoke disputes.

Trading arrangements for Model 4 i.e. pools and transmission prices, are the subject of Part 2 of this book.

IMPLICATIONS FOR THE STRUCTURE OF COMPANIES

Generation and Retail

In Model 3, there was a conflict between being a generator and being a Distco, because of the potential self-dealing. However, in Model 4 there is no longer a self-dealing issue.[1] In Model 3, if the retailer purchases from his own generation,

---

[1] That is there is no self-dealing issue arising from vertical integration *per se*. However, horizontal concentration in generation and/or retailing could lead to self-dealing problems and, as with other industries, these restrictions may be more a matter for the competition authories than a specialist energy-sector regulator.

it is hard to persuade the retailer to minimize costs since they could be passed on to captive customers. In Model 4, the customers can choose other generators, so self-dealing is no longer a problem. In fact, there is reason to suppose that there is a natural integration of generation and sales to final customers. The reason is that there appears to be very little value added in retailing *per se*. The retailer in other industries performs various functions such as displaying goods in a store, making preliminary choices among different manufacturers as to the style and quality its customers will want, taking the risk on purchasing unsold amounts, quality control of manufacturers and unbundling large shipments for sale as smaller bundles. These are all value-added activities that earn the retailer a return. In electricity, the retailer takes risks and unbundles services: the retailer buys bulk electricity and repackages it in tariffs or other forms of contract. These are useful functions, but ones which generators can as easily perform. Retailing as a stand-alone business appears to be a high-risk and low-return business. Of course, the potential existence of independent retailers, who can hit and run if the profits are too high, introduces a useful discipline in the market.

Distribution and Retail

The integration of distribution with retailing is another optional feature. The basic model assumes that the distribution wires are operated separately from the retailing function. The retailer may make arrangements with the distribution company for them to send customers in their region a bill covering all costs including transmission, distribution and the product itself. Alternatively, the customer could be sent separate bills for transport and for product.

There is a real trade-off between the potential for self-dealing and the potential benefits of allowing the owner of the distribution wires also to retail. The conflict problem is evident: for the same reasons as the Dispatcher needs to be independent in Models 3 and 4, the distribution system operator should arguably be independent in Model 4. For instance, if bad weather damages the wires, Distco has great incentives to fix its own customers first, and so on. It will require regulatory policing to avoid problems. On the other hand, in all cases we are aware that the companies being restructured own the wires and retail the electricity. Customers are used to going to that company for service and most customers are likely to prefer not to have to bother with changing their ways; in particular they do not want to have to call several different places to get service if things go wrong. For such an essential commodity as electricity, there may need to be a local entity that has some obligation to offer a tariff even to customers who, because of their load characteristics or payment record, are not sought after by the entrant competitors. This is a complex issue; in the UK the RECs in each area have a licence that gives them responsibilities different from those of the competing retailers who do not own the wires in that area.[2]

Transmission and Distribution

There is no obvious reason of conflict or self-dealing why the distribution and transmission should not be in the same company. They are in the same business at different voltage levels, and all the wire functions are likely to remain monopolies. Whether there are economies of scale in running them jointly may depend partly on the institutional history of the systems, for instance, whether the systems have been jointly operated in the past and on how much congestion there is on the low-voltage systems. In most of the systems we are familiar with, distribution is operated separately from transmission. One reason for keeping it separate would be to provide some sort of "yardstick competition" for the distribution companies, a notion which has proved easier in principle than in practice. However, whichever body regulates the distribution function would have better data if several distribution companies "compete" for regulatory treatment based on service to customers, innovation and price.

ACHIEVING EFFICENCY

Why bother to go to all the trouble of introducing direct access and retail competition? The transactions costs of negotiating all the required contracts are not negligible. In addition, as we have pointed out, many monopoly companies have had fine records in supplying reliable service at low cost. What additional efficiency does competition bring? One big bonus is on the supply side; as prices of new technologies fall, the urgent demands of independent entrants become more difficult to resist. Competitors only want to compete when they can supply at prices below the prices of the incumbent. The march of technical progress, combined with the load of social obligations borne by the utilities, means that entrants can often beat the *prices* of existing service. Entry would not necessarily be efficient. Many systems with high prices have excess capacity and low marginal costs, so entry would be inefficient. The cheapest way to increase output would be by running existing plant more intensively. Some pressure for competition comes from customers who (obviously

---

[2] The "first-tier supply licence" (retail licence) is granted to the local owner of the wires, whereas competing retailers are granted "second-tier supply licences". The difference is that first-tier companies may supply the franchise market and the non-franchise market, while the second-tier companies can only supply the non-franchise market.

enough) want lower prices, even if this means avoiding whatever obligations they have to pay the sunk costs of the franchised utility. Utilities counter by making access to the transmission wires as difficult as possible. Regulation becomes more contorted as it tries to square the circle of fair allocation of sunk costs with the pressures of suppressed competition.

If the entrants cannot get through the regulatory maze, they will find physical ways to bypass the system, even at higher cost than the marginal costs of the producers they seek to supplant. Thus, there are examples of on-site generation, physical bypass by means of new physical connections, superfluous transmission wires built to meet badly drawn criteria for access, and so on. Making a clean break for competition, and solving the stranded cost issue by making it explicit, is itself an antidote to these inefficient investments.

The general arguments for competition (i.e. efficiency in production, investment and consumption) favour Model 4, although as we have pointed out, some of them can be achieved in Models 2 and 3 or even under Model 1 with good regulation. Competition should improve both short- and long-term incentives for efficient production and consumption. On the supply side, the market price signals which plants to close and which to leave open. Plants should be closed if the market price cannot cover all the avoidable costs, including maintenance and staffing. If misguided regulation does not offset the economic decision with hold-over rules from the old regime, uneconomic plant will close, and there will be savings. When the price in the market rises high enough, then new plant will enter, again provided that entry is not hampered by hold-over rules from central planning.

Also, because of the visible spot market, the value of availability becomes explicit—it is the spot price of electricity less the short-run operating cost of the plant. Managers can make decisions about how much it is worth investing to make the plant available, and many decisions can be decentralized. A bid price pool of the type we describe in Part 2 of the book induces economic dispatch of the entire system. It also offers the right marginal incentives to build, to maintain, to run and to close plant.

These supply-side incentives also operate under Model 3. It is on the customer side that Model 4 produces additional competitive pressure. Many customers make a more competitive market than few customers—they will search out new suppliers and put pressure on incumbents. The Model 3 retailer with a monopoly over customers does not face the same incentives to purchase at minimum cost. Furthermore, if customers are free to respond to a real-time price, they will make changes in consumption. For example, the UK pool price has varied within a single day by as much as 28:1 between peak and off-peak. Even utilities with time-of-use tariffs must set them based on expected costs, and will have to average over the peak period; typical tariff ratios would be up to 5:1 within a day. When the peak actually occurs, it is under-priced, while the rest of the time it is over-priced. This is what induces "needle peaks"—periods of 20–40 hours per year in which load exceeds normal levels by 5–10%.

These peaks require capacity that cannot possibly cover its cost. In a competitive situation, with customers able to respond to real market prices, these peaks disappear. In England and Wales, there is already evidence that large firms can respond to the pool price by rescheduling operations. Firms have calculated their own *Value of Lost Load* in order to cease consumption when the price exceeds this value.

A third virtue of introducing full competition is that it can be the pivot to get rid of many inefficiencies of the previous system. Among these may be procurement policies that favoured certain national or local industries, social policy obligations or just an old bureaucracy used to doing things a certain way. A radical change may do this better than an evolutionary change since, in moving to competition, a re-think of nearly all the existing institutions is necessary and desirable. In the UK, the biggest saving to consumers was one they never had to pay for: the plans for four new nuclear plants and three new fossil plants were dropped when the move to competition was announced. In California, the mere thought of direct access saw the end of the Biennial Resource Procurement Update—the process that had induced many thousands of megawatts of excess capacity in the name of environmental protection.

SOCIAL POLICY OBLIGATIONS

There can be no obligation to supply in this model since there is no monopoly franchise. Social policy programmes connected to generation can only be imposed by specific subsidy mechanisms or by an overall sales tax. Subsidies should be tailored so as not to impede efficient operation of the markets. For example, governments can encourage "renewable technology" by arranging to purchase such power on a contract similar to the IPP contracts discussed under Model 2. They would then sell it back into the market at market price, taking the loss.

Model 3 still permitted discrimination between customers, for example by providing special deals for large customers or lifeline rates for poor people. This can no longer be accomplished indirectly in the tariffs. Since the market will obey the law of one price, retailers cannot offer special deals and stay solvent. As a result, explicit provision by other means will need to be made for these programmes. This usually requires legislation to charge a non-avoidable levy on all retail sales and/or a charge via a monopolised sector of the industry, the distribution or transmission wires.

Other social programmes such as conservation, high local taxes, some sorts of research and development, could still be collected by the monopoly wires company at least up to the point where they induce self-generation. By the time pressure for Model 4 has built up, and especially if it is new technologies that have created the pressure, the ability to collect above-market rates may be severely strained by the economics of the potential by-pass. Explicit (legislated) levies designed to be non-bypassable are potential solutions to this problem.

IMPLICATIONS FOR ASSET VALUES AND STRANDED COSTS

Under Model 4, the stranded asset problem if it exists becomes much more acute. This is not a minor issue: in the UK, when the generating industry was privatised, generating plant that had been carried on the books for £25 billion was sold at an implied value of £5 billion. This re-distribution of asset values (or obliteration of asset values) consequent on introducing open access to a Model 1 system, has been alluded to in previous models.

In a competitive market with many competitors the price of energy may fall to "avoidable costs". This does not mean simply the very short-run avoidable cost of fuel. Generators will close plant if the expected prices for the coming years do not cover all the costs they can avoid by closing. Avoidable costs have a time dimension—costs are avoidable day-ahead, month-ahead, year-ahead or many years ahead. The market price must sustain all the costs the generators will incur, or the generators will close plant. If there are big players with some market power, even with excess capacity the price will not drop as low as the avoidable cost. Large players can keep the price up by relinquishing some market share. The price, however, may remain below entry level, as indeed it should if new entry is not to be induced in the face of excess capacity.

Introduction of competition will change the revenue of virtually every plant and company in the industry. Even if there is no excess capacity, the market price will only cover the costs of new entrants: there is no guarantee of a remunerative price (covering costs already sunk) for existing plant. Some plants will earn much less than their book costs; some plants may earn much more than their book costs.

In a move to Model 4 this issue must be analysed and assessed. When the owner is the government (as in the UK), and the government decides to open the sector and suffer the hit on generation asset values, it is the government that takes the loss. If the sector is already private, and has been operating in a legal framework which was thought to guarantee revenues, opening the markets can involve major windfall gains to some owners of generating plant. For other owners there may be serious losses to stockholders and costly litigation. As we have pointed out, Model 2 avoids these problems, and for that reason is often preferred.

Although incumbents are understandably more worried about stranded costs than a windfall gain, there are occasions and countries where the problem presents itself in the opposite guise, as follows: much of the generating plant has a book value which is well below the market price. This may be hydro plant that was cheap to construct or depreciated old plant, but is still economic. A move to market prices for generation would give big windfall gains to the owners of these assets, and raise prices to consumers who may in some sense have "already paid for" the assets. Conceptually, these opposite problems could be similarly resolved.

It has been suggested that investors faced with stranded costs are bleating too much—they are wimps. The wimp argument goes as follows: investors have been buying utility stock for years. Each time the regulator allows a rate of return, he/she looks at the price of the stock, and through such analyses as the Capital Assets Pricing Model (CAPM) or dividend growth models, estimates the rate of return investors require to invest in the industry. This is the basis for the allowed rate of return. The investors cannot have been blind to the coming of competition. Industry analysts have been writing about it for years. The rates of return investors have been getting included the risk premium for increased competition and its consequences, and they should not bleat now that it has happened.[3]

This argument, of course, weakens the basis for all regulatory agreements, since it implies that no investor can rely on any regulatory guarantees that might be overturned by the introduction of competition. When windfall gains rather than windfall losses occur from restructuring, the concepts adopted should be applicable in both cases; just as it seems hard to argue that the customer should pay twice if the plant is already depreciated, so it becomes hard to argue that they should not pay once if it is not. Normally, regulators are keen to provide some continued support to the shareholders of existing companies, if only to maintain their reputation for providing a stable commercial environment in the future. However, while regulators may grant permission for existing companies to recover stranded costs, they sometimes underestimate the difficulty of doing so in a competitive market. Design of appropriate cost recovery mechanisms—and the appropriate regulatory support—is therefore an issue worthy of detailed discussion.

---

[3] For a response to the argument that investors have been getting a return on their assets, see William J. Baumol, Paul L. Joskow, Alfred E. Kahn, "The Challenge for Federal and State Regulators: Transition from Regulation to Efficient Competition in Electric Power", prepared for Edison Electric Institute, Washington, D.C., December 9, 1994. They argue that the methods used by regulators did not in fact remunerate investors for the risk of major changes in the regulatory system.

Netback Pricing

Netback pricing (also known as efficient component pricing, or top-down pricing) must also be mentioned as a way of recovering stranded costs. Netback pricing takes the existing bundled price and subtracts out the monopoly provider's avoided cost of providing the competitive service. If the competitor can provide power more cheaply than the avoided cost of the incumbent, then they should do so. If they can only beat the bundled price, including the stranded costs, then entry is uneconomic. Netback pricing is conceived of as a way to ensure only efficient entry. There are many objections to it, on a dynamic basis, which we will not go into here, but it is proposed as a way to recover stranded costs. Virtual direct access (which we review in Chapter 8) is a form of netback pricing.

The UK government found many ingenious ways to limit the hit on the Treasury implied by the initial sale price of the generator companies. First, it imposed a levy that amounted to a sales tax of 10% on all final sales: this raised £1 billion per year for eight years, which went mainly to Nuclear Electric to pay off sunk costs. It kept the small consumers captive long enough to dismantle the coal industry subsidy and to pay for the excess generating capacity on the system: the small consumers paid much more than the "pool price" for their electricity for the first eight years. Third, the prices set for the distribution wires were very generous. This enabled the government to sell those companies for a tidy profit to offset the losses to the Treasury on the generation side. Finally, the government itself kept 40% of the stock in the generator companies. When it sold this stock after five years, the value was three times as high as the original sale price. This was in all probability due to the market power of the original generators. By closing inefficient plant they kept the market price from sinking to very low levels.

If the potentially stranded costs are to be reclaimed by the owners, it requires careful design of the mechanisms of recovery so as not to interfere with the emerging market prices. The UK mechanisms were not without their problems. However, they proved that the owner could avoid taking too much of a drop in profits, while still introducing a competitive market with positive results for efficiency.

EXAMPLES

The UK, Norway, Chile, Argentina and Victoria, Australia have systems that approximate to this model, or are in a phased transition. In each of these countries, the transmission system is owned separately. In none of them have the low-voltage wires been separated from the retailing function, although separate accounting is always required. In the UK, the question of separation of retailing and distribution has been raised as the introduction of retail competition for all customers (a full Model 4) approaches.

CONCLUSIONS

Model 4 expands competitive pressures by making final consumers part of the equation. It also greatly increases transactions costs by requiring more complex trade arrangements and metering.

For the large users, the transaction costs are relatively small per unit of electricity, and meters are already in place. For small users, the costs may easily outweigh the benefits. Not only are metering costs comparatively higher for small customers but the benefits of "one-stop shopping" are lost, a problem which has also arisen in the telephone industry. Precise responsibility for poor service may be difficult to pinpoint when the local distribution company is not also the retailer.

The world of electricity has changed radically in ten years. Our overall view is that Model 4 is the world of the future. However, the institutional questions are as important as the technical ones. In some countries the major problem is to get accounting systems in place, to get adequate tariffs and to get people trained to run control rooms, not open access to networks. Open access may be a frill. In other countries, the use of the electric industry as a vehicle for social policy will be hard to replicate if the policies have to be reenacted as specific legislation or subsidies—that is why they were hidden in the electric industry in the first place! Direct access may in practice be limited to only a few large consumers who threaten to leave the system, while the bulk of consumers stay effectively monopolised.

8

WHICH MODEL?

In this chapter we review the structure question, and introduce the analysis in Part 2 by considering the apparently opposed paradigms used to describe trading.

FINAL THOUGHTS ON THE STRUCTURE QUESTIONS

Is there a conclusion to be drawn about appropriate structures? On the whole, being economists, we tend to the view that competition, absent specific indications to the contrary, is the preferable form of organization for efficient production, since market prices give the right signals for both consumption and production, and (if the rest of the economy is competitive) give the right allocation of resources to electricity production. The most obvious contra-indications are scale economies, which might lead to unregulated monopoly power or destructive competition; or substantial transactions costs, which would render competition inefficient.

In small systems there may still be scale economies to be reaped, which would indicate continuation of monopoly, or at most a Model 2 system where the potential monopoly power of generators is restrained by contracts. Even in large systems, it has been argued that the benefits of standardization and a centralized nuclear program constitute scale economies of sufficient significance to outweigh the benefits of competition.

In many developing countries the transactions costs of competition are a significant problem. Countries where the electricity system is not yet on a sound commercial footing may reasonably choose first to get the tariffs in order, persuade people to pay their bills, and get the accounting system in place, before introducing the further complications of spot markets and open access. Countries where the entire legal framework of commercial activity is lacking may reasonably choose to enact company law, property law and bankruptcy law before moving to any form of non-monopoly organization.

If there is to be a Model 1 monopoly, should it be government-owned or should it be privately owned and regulated? The US experience from the 1940s to the 1970s of regulated monopoly is often adduced as an example of independent regulation of private monopolies which worked to bring low-cost plentiful power to the whole population. Yet in the same period, the government owned monopolies in Europe were able to perform much the same feat: demand was growing and mistakes were swamped by the continual improvement in technology. After the technology stopped improving, and fuel prices rose, demand growth fell off and both systems were slow to react; they all continued to overbuild plant; governments in both places prohibited gas burning long after it was reasonable to do so, slowing the advance of technology, and unleashing an avalanche of low-cost generation when the prohibitions were removed. The effect of the monopoly was to insulate the producers from the advance of technology and the risks of the market place. Private producers fully exposed to the demand risk might well have chosen a different path; in fact, the first casualties of impending competition, both in the UK and in California were the additions to capacity planned by the government on the one hand, and the regulators on the other.

Model 2 does not solve these problems, although continual bidding for new plant might uncover lower-cost sources, provided the purchasing agency does not limit bids to specific technologies or fuel sources. Model 2 can be used to invite alternative sources of capital into government-owned systems, without forcing the entrants to take the market risk, and may therefore be more successful in inducing investment in emerging economies. However, some emerging economies are so starved of power that the purchasing agency, with its bidding procedures and standard tariffs (and rationing procedures in many cases) can become a bottleneck. China, where in the early 1990s some provinces were on a reduced work-week because of power shortages, has had some success with Model 2, but the shortages persist. Some limited form of open access would allow new entrants to compete to sell directly to hungry manufacturers or townships at what the market would bear, without waiting for the cumbersome procedures of the purchasing agency.

Are any of the alternative models more amenable to maintaining an existing system of vertically integrated companies? Conflicts are not simply theoretical problems: they can result in prolonged litigations, or wasteful and suboptimal palliatives being adopted. Model 2 was instituted in the US with the built-in conflict of the incumbent utilities acting as purchasing agents while also owning competing generation and the transmission system. Perhaps as a result, many of the IPP contracts are non-dispatchable, resulting in seriously suboptimal dispatch. A Dispatcher independent of the competing generators would have been preferable. Again in the US, where limited versions of Model 3 exist in the form of municipalities which could exercise choice over suppliers, the utility which owns the transmission is also the competing supplier, and operates under different rules as far as risk and obligations. This has resulted in a decade of litigation over open access. Model 2 really required separation of the purchasing agency and the transmission from the incumbent utility for it to work well. In theory, properly structured PPAs (power purchase agreements) and bidding systems could resolve the potential conflicts, but this seems seldom to happen. Setting up a Model 2 system with independent transmission would be a step towards full competition at a later date. This is a major step requiring substantial reorganization.

Problems of conflict of interest, self-dealing and market power in Models 3 and 4 may require more extensive breaking up of existing companies. This is not a pleasant thought for existing vertically integrated companies; it is complicated and expensive to do, and absorbs much management time. Alternative methods for avoiding conflict, such as creating different business units with separate accounting, may be tried. Not all conflict and self-dealing situations are lethal: there may be offsetting advantages in terms of economies of scale and scope which should be balanced against the potential problems. Furthermore, the conflicts which exist in one model may disappear in the next; this implies that careful thought should be given before making large and dislocating changes.

The most obvious example of the problem changing with the model is the question of divestiture of generation. In Model 2, the purchasing agent should not be a competing generator, nor should one of the competing generators control the transmission; therefore in a Model 2 system there will be pressure to divest generation to avoid conflict of interest problems. In Model 3, there will be pressure to divest generation from the Distco, because of perceived self-dealing problems; a Distco who has a monopoly over captive customers will prefer to purchase from an affiliated company so long as he can pass the costs on to the captive customers. Controlling this tendency may require such intrusive regulation that divestiture, to ensure arms-length dealing, is a better idea. However, in Model 4, the self-dealing conflict disappears; if the retailer is facing competition, he would be foolish to favour his own subsidiary if cheaper power is to be found. In fact, in Model 4 there seems to be a natural vertical integration of generating and retailing, and the problem becomes horizontal market power—the ability to raise prices because a single entity has substantial control over a local market, and there is insufficient transmission to permit competitors from outside. This problem may indeed require divestiture if other remedies cannot be found, but it did not exist in Model 3 because the Distco had a 100% monopoly over the customers and was therefore regulated.

In Models 3 and 4, the operation of the transmission system needs to be independent of the traders; we have discussed the different functions and possible conflicts. Model 3 in any event seems to us to be unstable, although it may persist for some years, because of the difficulty of defining who is entitled to choose their supplier once some entities may do so, and because of people's ingenuity in redefining themselves into the favoured category.

The experience of the pioneer countries has shown that Model 4 is feasible, and that trading arrangements can be introduced which allow customers to choose their suppliers. This has unleashed a veritable earthquake of interest in restructuring the electric sector and introducing direct access. While Model 2 is preferable in some instances, particularly where the institutions are immature, or the systems so small that competition is inherently limited because of too few generating units and consequent market power problems, we believe that Model 4 is likely to be the model of choice for developed countries with sophisticated systems. However, the case is still undecided: the UK system at the time of writing has not yet completed the transition to full retail competition, and there may still be pitfalls in enlarging the numbers of customers eligible for competitive supply so dramatically, and in maintaining adequate capacity.

It could be the case that, ten years hence, the question of whether to revise and re-issue this book will arise, and we will be amazed that we had ever thought that Model 4 was the end of the line. The major source of pressure will be, in our estimation, the remarkable changes in technology alluded to in the Introduction—the scale economies in generation may have reversed themselves so far that we will be looking not at how to accomplish economic dispatch and market trading over a central network, but rather at the advent of cheap dispersed generation, fed by gas. The technical advances of recent years in materials technology have made turbines much more efficient (this is due to harder steels and ceramic coatings, combined with computer-aided design) so that visionaries are seeing the move to retail access as the last dying gasp of a central-station industry, rather than the beginning of a new era. If small-scale combined heat and power (co-generation) or the gas-fired fuel cell become the technology of choice, and if back-up becomes unnecessary or very cheap (as televisions have become virtually free of defects) we could see a power sector very different from the one we see today.

Nonetheless, with our vision limited by the existing possibilities, we now move to discuss the institutional arrangements and the technical matters that need to be understood before Models 2, 3 or 4 can be introduced in practice.

INTRODUCTION TO TRADING ARRANGEMENTS, TRANSMISSION PRICING AND RETAIL ACCESS

In this final section of Part 1 we attempt a synthesis of what is to follow, and explain as simply as possible two new paradigms which are quite important for understanding the growing literature on trading electricity. A paradigm is a conceptual model of what is happening; it is a "convenient fiction". The old paradigm was one of allocating the costs of the utility. The new paradigms both recognise that we are now in a market world: electricity is a commodity; it has a market price. It is standardised as to voltage and frequency, and one unit is indistinguishable from any other. It is of absolutely no importance to the final consumer which generating plant produced the power being used. The paradigms used to envisage the trading system may be unimportant, or they may in fact have unintended consequences.

Convenient Fictions: Two Paradigms

One paradigm is a "market" model derived from observing most markets, even commodity markets, where producers, wholesalers and retailers take possession of a physical product and transport it from place to place in various ways. Thus this paradigm applied to electricity envisages producers who schedule sales over networks to retailers, paying for transport (transmission) as they go, and retailers who sell to final customers over distribution networks, paying for the use of distribution wires as they go. Those who use this paradigm observe that if the trading system is set up to accommodate bilateral energy trades, competition will ensure that arbitrage and entry to the market will push the market price for all these services to the competitive level, which we take to be:

> the marginal cost of providing service if there is excess capacity, or the value of service if there is not.

If there is no competition, for example in transmission, the job of the regulator is to determine the marginal cost so that it can be charged to the customer.

The other may be called the "optimisation" paradigm. It works from the final result of these proposed markets: after everyone has bought and sold, if there are many buyers and sellers, generation prices will equal local marginal cost, if there is surplus, or the value of power if not. Transport prices separate the prices in geographically separate markets, and if there is competition in transport, transport prices will likewise equal marginal cost if there is excess transport, or congestion rents if there is not. Retail prices will likewise equal wholesale prices plus the marginal costs of distribution. But there is no need to pretend that the electric system is like other commodities; it is fully and instantaneously connected. All that needs to happen is for the (independent) system dispatcher to act as an auctioneer. The dispatcher must receive bids to dispatch the system, and must dispatch at minimum cost, given the network characteristics: the right spot prices will fall out at each node on the system. The system operator buys and sells at the nodal prices. The transmission prices fall out as the difference between the prices at the nodes. The market clears without messy arbitrage and buying and selling of wholesale power, retail power, transmission services and distribution services. In this paradigm, the buyers and sellers are free to make financial deals to offset the risk of the spot market, which they do through swap contracts or contracts for differences.

	"Optimisation"	"Market"
Market mechanism	Pooling	Bilateral
Transmission pricing	Locational pricing	Explicit transmission price
Retail arrangement	Virtual direct access	Direct access

Figure 8.1 "Convenient fictions". Two paradigms

Three apparent dichotomies in the literature can be explained by reference to these two ways of looking at the world. The first is the apparent dichotomy between "bilateral markets" and "pooling".[1] The second is the apparent dichotomy between "transport models" and "nodal pricing". The third is the apparent dichotomy between "direct access" and "virtual direct access".

These three pairs—bilateral markets and pooling, transport and nodal pricing, and direct access or virtual direct access, all rest upon the same two paradigms. The first of each pair is the optimisation model and the second is the market model. This is shown in Figure 8.1. Each of the pairs, properly defined and operated, is equivalent, but the paradigms used to envisage what is going on have a different flavour and appear to be different. In the discussion below we show that, in each case, the result of setting up a "market" can be reached directly by setting up an "optimisation" market.

In this book we have set out to explain how the "market" can be set up and administered: thus in Part 2 we explain how to set up markets for bilateral trading, and how to set efficient transmission prices. While the "optimisation model" is a beautiful and internally consistent way of looking at an idealised system, it is not yet practical for most countries because of its computer requirements. In our practical work we have been asked to develop trading systems which are founded on bilateral contracts; we have been asked to develop

---

[1] This is the US term. In the UK the same dispute is about "trading outside the pool".

appropriate transmission prices for various systems. This way of looking at things also makes more explicit what has to be done, by whom, at each stage. It is also easier for most people to understand, since it makes an easier transition from a system (such as the US) where transmission prices have been separately regulated. None the less, the optimisation model with central dispatch of bid prices, and financial contracts, is what we helped develop for the UK pool. It has the distinct advantage of going directly to the minimum cost solution, and of separating the financial markets from physical delivery.

What is important is that the system adopted for trade ensures that the lowest-cost producer produces it, that the right amount is transported and that the accounting systems are set up so that the customers pay for what they use and the producer gets paid for what is sold.

We now explain the dichotomous pairs individually.

Bilateral Markets and Pooling

The dispute between "bilateral contracting" and "pooling" is sometimes expressed as whether spot markets will arise "naturally" (the invisible hand) or whether they have to be helped by instituting a "pool" (a visible hand)—this is sometimes expressed as the choice between whether everything has to be sold to "big brother" or whether the parties can just do what comes naturally and sell to each other.

The bilateral contracting model envisages traders making deals for physical delivery of energy, scheduling those trades with the transmission system operator, and having the operator deliver the scheduled power. If trading is to occur, it will occur outside the transmission system. The pooling approach envisages that sellers will bid to have their product dispatched, buyers will bid to purchase and that the system operator will dispatch the generating units in order of the bids. The price will be set at the highest bid dispatched in each hour, or the lowest demand bid. Contracts will be financial instruments, "swaps", or "Contracts for Differences", which "substitute" the pool price for a fixed price, on terms agreed bilaterally. The system operator neither knows nor cares what the contractural arrangements are.

The proponents approach the trading problem from different angles. The pooling people come mainly from the system operating side and are concerned initially with the physics of getting the system dispatched and how to substitute market signals for the operations which are now done by command and control. Pooling market solutions therefore derive from the operating solutions. The proponents of a bilateral system on the other hand, many of whom have had experience in the gas industry, start from the markets which they assert will develop naturally, and worry about the operations later.

However, although the descriptions look remarkably different, the operational details of the solutions are remarkable similar. If contracts are to be scheduled across an electric network, some provision has to be made for the fact that what is scheduled and what is actually dispatched will be different— there will be imbalances, which will arise because customers change their electric use at will, or because generating plant breaks down, or because of transmission constraints. The system operator may try to discourage imbalances, and set a penalty price. This is what happens in the US gas markets, and participants do indeed attempt to avoid the penalties by buying make-up gas to meet their contracts. But in electricity, imbalances require the system operator to make good the imbalance in real time—the electricity grid cannot store electricity, as the gas grid can; neither can it give busy signals as the telephone grid can. It must make up imbalances in seconds, and to do this the system operator must have incremental price bids from all participants, and choose the cheapest source. If the price of imbalances is set at a "market" price, which matches supply and demand bids instantaneously, a spot market is effectively created. Then, with a spot price in existence, the participants have the choice as to whether to use the spot market, or whether to schedule physical contracts. They may choose to do both or they may choose to buy at spot and hedge the price risk with financial contracts. This mixed system requires the transmission settlement system to settle the contract amounts as well as the spot purchases, which is what the Norway pool does. The alternative is to treat all sales as spot sales, to schedule only by bid, and to force all contracts to be financial hedges, which is what the UK pool does.

In our analysis in this book we have stayed with the bilateral markets model, since it reduces to the pooling model if scheduling is not permitted; the scheduling and settlement problems are worth going over, since many systems will choose to schedule trades, and the complications should be understood. The advantage of the bid-only pool (as in the UK) is that there are fewer transactions going through the settlement system and fewer occasions for dispute. The advantage of the bilateral markets system is that it is easier for traders to understand, at least initially. It is also easier for arbitrageurs to make a profit, which appeals to the arbitrageurs. The disadvantage is the increased number of transactions the system operator is responsible for clearing, which increases the potential for dispute and litigation.

Transport and Nodal Pricing

The second dichotomous pair is the transport/nodal pricing paradigm. In this pair the regulator takes the place of the "market" in the transport model. The "optimiser" in nodal pricing is still the system operator. The two views of the world start out with similar descriptions of transmission.

In any geographically dispersed commodity market system, the price of the commodity at any place differs from the price at any other place by the price of the transport between the two places. The price of electricity can be quoted at a central place for trades between two other places if the price of the transport is known. Free entry into transport activities tends to push the cost of transport to its marginal cost, so that we can further assert that the price of the commodity differs by the marginal cost of transport. The seller at point A gets the local price for the commodity; the buyer at point B pays the local price. The difference is the shipping cost, and in fact it matters not one bit if the same shipment arrives directly at B, or if the shipper sold it at point C and arranged for some other shipper to deliver an equivalent commodity to B.

If there is a shortage of transport, the price of transport rises, pushing down the price of the commodity in the export-constrained area to the marginal cost in that area, and raising it in the import-constrained area to the marginal cost in that area. The cost of transport then includes the "shadow price" of constraints, i.e. the difference in price between the zones. If the transport company makes a lot of money from the constraints, new entrants will come in to cream off the "congestion rents". If there were a transport monopolist, efficiently regulated, we would say that the efficient transport price should be the marginal cost of transport, and that when constraints occur, the transport price will rise until it is economic to add capacity rather than accept the congestion costs.

In our analysis of transmission pricing in Part 2 of the book, we have started from this view of the world: transmission is just another form of transport. The transmission system may be complex and difficult to operate, and energy may flow in all directions, but it has the same economic characteristics as other transport systems. The price of electricity at two locations will differ by the price of the transport. If this price is badly set, by poor regulation, then the amount of transport will be sub-optimal. If it is set at the marginal cost, including the shadow price of constraints, and if the system is expanded when the cost of constraints exceeds the cost of relieving them, then the transport system will be optimal. This is the job of the regulator of the monopoly transmission system.

So our analysis concentrates on setting proper prices for transmission, which is the question the Federal Energy Regulatory Commission (FERC) in the US and the EU in Europe have been concerning themselves with. Whereas in the past, the problem has been seen as how to allocate embedded costs of transmission "fairly", we assert that the proper prices for transmission are the marginal costs of transmission. These we define as marginal losses, constraints and, eventually, the net cost of building, after taking credit for reduced losses and constraints. We demonstrate our proposals on a two-node system. Losses and constraints are measured by reference to the actual (marginal) losses between the two points plus the cost of the constraints; this is measured as the difference in marginal costs. These marginal costs are used to set the price, which may be a tariff, or a contract, or a spot market price. This analysis works well for two nodes and for interconnectors between networks, but it becomes more complex on the networks themselves to identify directly the losses and constraints between any two nodes. One way to do it in advance is to increase the load at any point and to compute the consequent increase in losses and congestion costs on the system. This relatively unsophisticated method of computing expected marginal costs and charging for them, is quite similar to standard methods of computing marginal costs for tariff making.

There is, however, another much more sophisticated way of looking at it, which comes to the same thing, analytically,[2] but requires much more complex software to institute. This "optimisation" view relies again on the system operator. On a multi-node electricity network, the system operator's job is to minimize total costs, subject to system constraints. In minimizing losses, constraints and generation costs simultaneously, the operator implicitly derives transmission prices from the difference in price between nodes. (In a no-loss system, the price at each node would be the same, regardless of the underlying cost of a generator at that node, since prices rise to the system marginal cost—the cost of providing an additional unit at *any* node.) Looked at this way, traders can buy and sell at their local nodes, and the transmission cost is the difference in the price between the nodes. So the price can be quoted nodally, or it can be quoted at a single point with transport to that point equal to the difference in price between each node and the central node, just as in other commodity markets. This obviates having to compute losses and constraints directly, and changes the paradigm from "setting transmission prices" to "reading off the transport cost from a minimum cost dispatch" or nodal pricing.

The advantage of transmission pricing over nodal prices is that prices (tariffs or contracts) can be set in advance, rather than in real time, obviating the need for large-scale on-line load flow models. This problem, acute at the time of writing, may be overcome with large computers. Nodal spot prices, if they can be computed, can be hedged with financial contracts, giving the same price protection as tariffs.

The second problem with nodal pricing is the incentive problem. The transmission system sets a spot price and collects spot revenues which is antithetical to the notion that a regulated monopolist should not be allowed to both set the price and charge it, because it creates incentives to create constraints, or incentives not to relieve constraints when they occur. The incentive problems with nodal pricing can be solved by having

---

[2] The paradigms of nodal pricing and virtual direct access have been associated in the 1990s with Professor Bill Hogan, whose writings on the subject are too numerous to list, and his colleague Larry Ruff. We are immensely indebted to their insights, and have no basic quarrel with their work, just a small quibble. Their writings emphasise that the actual flows on an electric network depend on physical laws—"electricity flows where it will"—and constraints can arise on lines carrying well below the rated capacity, because of problems elsewhere in the network. This of course is true, but it does not mean that electricity is not amenable to analysis as a form of transport. It is not magic, or peculiar to electricity, that the price of transport is what separates the prices of a product in two markets. Road transport can be risky and constrained, too!

the transmission company issue the financial contracts for hedging the spot price.

Direct Access and Virtual Direct Access

"Direct access", "retail wheeling" or "retail competition" use the paradigm of the retailer purchasing electricity, repackaging it into tariffs and contracts, and selling it on. In the UK, the retailers actually buy out of the pool on a retailing licence, and sell the power on to customers. This is the "market" method for retailing. It requires a fair amount of settlement software to clear the central accounts.

The alternative, as the reader may be able to guess from the previous discussion, is for the distribution company to deliver power to the customer and charge the spot price, with the delivery charge separate, and permit or encourage the customer to make his or her own arrangements for insurance and hedges against the spot price, which will be equivalent to a tariff or contract. This approach has been called "virtual direct access" and is analogous to the Contracts for Differences described in Part 2 for the wholesale contracts around the pool.

As with the contracts for differences around the pool, which do not have quite the same flavour as bilateral contracts, so virtual direct access does not have quite the same flavour as "choosing your supplier" from among competing retailers. Getting a bill and sending it off to your insurer to turn it into a fixed price may not appear to be "customer choice of supplier". At the wholesale level, these problems have been overcome, as traders realised that the financial contracts have the same effect as the physical trading they previously envisaged. With final customers it may be necessary to preserve the more familiar paradigm, and it may therefore be necessary to integrate the settlement of the financial contracts into the billing made to final consumers, as if the bill came from a competing supplier.

Summary

These two ways of looking at the world of competitive trading lead to different descriptions of what is going on, and may lead to different commercial institutions. In the "optimisation" versions, the central auction sets a spot price, and all trading proceeds from that spot price. In the market models, trading (or regulation, in the transmission case) brings the prices to the market price equivalent. If the market institutions are set up to minimise friction in the multiple transactions that need to take place, they will come to the same result as the optimisation institutions.

Part 2

AGENCY PROBLEMS:
CONTRACTS,
MARKETS AND
TRANSMISSION
PRICING

9   SOLVING PROBLEMS WITH CONTRACTS

Part 1 of this book set out the ways in which electricity sectors are being disaggregated into their constituent parts. Obviously, these constituent parts must continue to cooperate in the production, transmission and distribution of electricity, as the industry will remain physically interconnected. The industry will therefore be held together commercially by the contracts signed between electricity companies. Part 2 of this book takes a close look at these contracts, as the basis for maintaining efficient and integrated operation.

We begin, in this chapter, by describing the purpose and form of contracts in general, and their role within the electricity sector. Chapter 10 looks at a very common form of electricity contract, the Power Purchase Agreement (PPA) signed by individual generators. Chapter 11 examines wholesale and retail contracts. Chapter 12 sets out the special requirements for settling contracts which involve trade across a network and Chapters 13 and 14 discuss the costs incurred by and contracts required for use of a transmission network. Together, these contracts make up the "matrix" which ties together a disaggregated industry.

However, the purpose of contracts is not only to allow separate companies to deal with one another. Contracts can also be used to solve particular problems, such as how to manage risk in a decentralised system and how to provide incentives for efficient behaviour. These two problems may be called the "agency problems" of the electric sector, i.e. they arise when one person (the "principal") wants to influence or control the actions of another party (the "agent"). They represent some of the most serious considerations when writing a contract.

Generally, it is not sufficient to draft a contract consisting of simple commands ("Thou shalt generate electricity"). The agent will only fulfil the contract if there is an incentive to do so. Actions must therefore be linked to rewards (or penalties). The electricity sector faces a number of specific problems when designing contracts to provide incentives for efficient behaviour.

First, the physical attributes of an electric power network make it impossible to match physically any particular seller of electricity with any particular buyer of electricity. Electricity does not flow in a direct path from seller to buyer: rather, generators put the electricity into a big tub and the buyers take the electricity out. Without a special set of contracts, the seller ("principal") would have no means of ensuring that the buyer ("agent") has any incentive to pay, since any buyer could simply take electricity off the system as required. This is why we examine not just contracts for physical delivery of electricity at a generator's point of connection (Chapter 10) but also contracts for electricity delivered to a buyer on the other side of the network (Chapter 11).

Second, supply and demand must be in instantaneous balance to maintain the frequency, voltage and stability of the network. In theory, this could be achieved economically by a system of bilateral spot trading between buyers and sellers, combined with full contingent claims contracts on the capacity of the transmission network. However, in practice it is difficult for any economic mechanism to achieve the speed required for instantaneous equilibrium. The function of some electricity contracts is therefore to provide the *ex ante* agreements about who pays *ex post* for the maintenance or restoration of equilibrium when the spot market does not work fast enough on its own. We examine the settlement contracts which support electricity markets in Chapter 12.

Finally, a major feature of electric networks is that one person's use of the network influences the ability of another person to use the network. For example, the use of a generator at one location can limit the use of a generator at a nearby location. This means that efficient operation of electric networks is subject to the classical "commons" problem.[1] Property rights must be established so that scarce transmission capacity, for example, is allocated efficiently and to ensure that the providers of the capacity can recover their costs. The costs of transmission are discussed in Chapter 13 and their relation to property rights over transmission networks is considered in Chapter 14.

The chapters in this book do not amount to a complete manual for writing perfect legal contracts, but they do set out what kind of contracts are required in a disaggregated electricity sector, and also what they should look like in general. We hope they will assist industry participants in designing their own contracts.

THE PURPOSE OF WRITING CONTRACTS

Before we examine how contracts are used to buy and sell electricity, it is useful to understand what a contract is for. A sales contract is simply a document (or

---

[1] In medieval England, most villagers were allowed to graze their cattle on the common lands. Each villager exploited the commons as much as possible, without considering the effect on others. The result was a gradual degradation of land quality which was only solved by the Enclosure Movement, a major land reform.

even a set of verbal statements) in which one trader agrees to deliver a product or service to another trader, on certain conditions and in return for a certain amount of money (or for other products or services). If one trader is required to hand over money, we can say that a purchase or sale has taken place; the trader handing over money is the "buyer" and the other trader the "seller".[2] The contract provides an opportunity for the buyer and the seller to agree in advance the terms of the sale.

In theory, the buyer and seller could simply agree the terms of each sale at the time of delivery. One must therefore ask why consenting adults go to the bother of constructing detailed and long-lasting contracts, often with the assistance of expensive lawyers. Since no one is forcing them to sign a contract, the buyer and the seller must benefit by doing so. The benefits of contracts come in various guises. Achieving these mutual benefits is the justification for contracts (and for lawyers' fees). The main forms of benefit which explain the desire for electricity contracts are:

- savings in transactions costs;
- relocating risk; and
- providing better incentives.

Each of these benefits is so important for the design of an electricity contract that they deserve closer inspection.

Because we are used to seeing contracts in operation for large projects and long-term agreements in many industry sectors, it is sometimes difficult to identify the benefits of contracts, because we cannot imagine how else business might be done. We therefore need to contrast the use of contracts with some alternative. A contract is a long-term agreement between two "legal persons" (individuals, firms or public agencies) on terms for a sale from one person to the other. The basic alternatives are: short-term agreements (spot trades); or vertical integration (organisation within a single firm or agency).

Savings in Transactions Costs

In a spot market, traders have to agree the prices and conditions of each sale just before delivery. Consumers of a product must buy more or less as their consumption rises and falls. Imagine having to phone up the electricity company (after agreeing with the telephone company a price for the call), every time you switch on the television (assuming that you have already agreed a price for the

---

[2] In "barter contracts", where products and services are exchanged for other products and services, there is no distinction between buyer and seller.

programme you want to watch), to negotiate for some more electricity. It would cost the electricity, telephone and television companies a fortune to make the necessary deals. No consumer would bother to carry out this time-consuming process. The world would have to operate without electricity, telephones or television.

To solve this problem, we agree with the relevant company to pay a certain price over the next year for each kWh of electricity, telephone call, and year (or hour) of television viewing. This is a much simpler process than arranging spot market transactions. People obviously want to consume electricity, telephone calls and television. The long-term agreement with each company has therefore made it possible to enjoy the benefits of such products (and made them cheaper to provide) by reducing the "*transactions costs*", i.e. the costs of negotiating, executing and enforcing payment for each purchase.

Contracts are a particularly good way to reduce transactions costs when someone is likely to buy a large amount of a very similar product from a single seller, in small lots over a long period. The contract allows the buyer and the seller to standardise terms, based on expected conditions in the future. This is mutually beneficial when the cost of standardising terms (and maybe getting them wrong) is less than the cost of negotiating different (but correct) terms at each individual transaction.

The alternative way to reduce transactions costs is to carry out two businesses within one firm, so that there is no need for a spot market trade between the businesses. This argument has been used to explain vertical integration in a number of industries for many years. However, it is not usually possible for an individual to become vertically integrated with a company, so the provision of labour services and purchases by consumers always require some kind of contract.

Furthermore, vertical integration brings problems of its own, as discussed in Part 1 of this book. The choice of vertical integration or contract depends on the cost of these problems relative to the cost of making transactions. Recently, the fall in the price of computers has reduced the transactions costs of contracting and the case for vertical integration has therefore become weaker.

Relocating Risk

Contracts not only help to reduce predictable costs, such as transactions costs, they are also used to handle uncertainty—i.e. the problem that the future is unpredictable. Uncertainty becomes important when it translates into a risk for someone—i.e. a variable net income. Contracts allow someone to pass financial risk to someone else, in conditions where there is a benefit from doing so. A potential benefit can be realised either:

- when another person is more willing and able to bear the risk; or
- when another person has more control over the source of the risk.

Some of the most familiar contracts deal with "two-sided" uncertainty, i.e. cases where the buyer and seller are both unsure of something and so both are exposed to risk. Contracts allow the risk to be passed to the most suitable person, either by "sharing" the risk, or by "spreading" it.

Risk Sharing

To take an example, suppose a farmer wants to sell a tonne of wheat in six months' time; no one can be sure what the spot market price will be then. If the farmer is unhappy at the prospect that the price might drop, he can sign a contract to sell wheat at a fixed price, for example, to a miller. In doing so, the farmer has transferred the risk to the miller; this is called "sharing risk".

The miller is now committed to buying wheat at a fixed price, and is therefore exposed to the risk that the market price of wheat (and hence flour) will fall in the future. If this risk is related to general economic trends, the miller may simply have to bear it as part of his business. The miller will make sure that the fixed price offered to the farmer is low enough to provide a margin or "premium" that can be saved up in "good" times (when the price of flour is high) as a reserve to call on in "bad" times (when the price of flour takes a tumble). In general, these "undiversifiable" risks will be transferred to the people who demand the lowest premium as an incentive for bearing the risk. (Sometimes this will be the miller and sometimes the farmer.) This type of risk can also be shared by vertical integration along the supply chain (i.e. if the farmer acts as his own miller).

Risk Spreading

Some risk in the wheat market is "diversifiable", in that fluctuations in the wheat price are uncorrelated with other prices in the economy. If this is so, the miller may be able to go to a commodities broker who will arrange for a speculator to sign a fixed price contract in return for a premium. The speculator will sign a large number of such contracts, in a variety of different commodities. Some will turn out to be profitable and some loss-making. Overall (taking several periods together), the speculator expects the profits and losses to cancel out (or to average out to some predictable level). The speculator is left holding the premiums (or a predictable share of the premiums) as net revenue.

By signing the fixed price contract for wheat, the miller eliminates his exposure to the uncertain spot price. The speculator deliberately takes on the risk, because it will offset other risks. This is called "spreading risk" and it is the basis of most insurance schemes.

Risk can also be spread by "horizontal integration", i.e. by combining a variety of activities within one company. However, most recent experience with "corporate diversification" suggests that the management problems outweigh the benefits. Investors can diversify their risks much more cheaply by holding a portfolio of shares in different, specialised companies.

As we shall show in subsequent chapters, a large number of contracts are signed by producers, traders and consumers of electricity, with the intention of sharing risk. However, there are signs in competitive electricity markets that electricity speculators are beginning to emerge. These speculators use electricity contracts to broaden the range of products over which they spread risk.

Relocating Risks and Improving Incentives

Sometimes uncertainty is "one-sided", in that one party to a transaction understands the risks better than the other.[3] For example, suppose that a "principal" (e.g. an investor) is trying to encourage an "agent" (e.g. a manager) to carry out some task, in conditions where costs or profits can vary either because of exogenous factors (e.g. changes in market prices) or because of the agent's behaviour (e.g. slackness in cost control). Often, uncertainty over the source of profit variation is one-sided, because the agent knows more than the principal about his own behaviour.

In these cases, the principal can use a contract to provide better incentives for the agent to behave in an efficient manner. Increased efficiency in the agent's behaviour will eventually reduce the principal's costs or increase his or her profits. The main task in contract design is to ensure that the structure of contract payments allocates exogenous or two-sided risks in an advantageous way, and also provides an incentive for the agent to behave efficiently.

This is done by trying to separate the effects of exogenous factors from the effects of the agent's own behaviour:

- the agent pays the additional cost of any inefficient actions, so that he or she has an incentive to behave efficiently; and
- extra costs due to exogenous risks are shared by the agent and the principal in the appropriate manner.

If the contract achieves the first of these aims, it is said to be "incentive-compatible". The difficulty arises in trying to combine this aim with the second.

For example, consider a three-year contract to supply fuel oil to a generator. The simplest type of contract would specify a fixed price for the oil. However, the owner of the generator knows that the price of fuel oil varies considerably on world markets, even within a year, and that no supplier will want to bear the risk of such exogenous price variation. The owner of the generator could

---

[3] For those that like them, the technical term for one-sided uncertainty is "informational asymmetry".

therefore pay an agent a fixed fee to find fuel oil and deliver it to the generator, at which point the generator would pay the agent the actual cost incurred to purchase the fuel oil.

The trouble with this type of contract is that the agent would have no incentive to seek out the cheapest source of fuel oil. Any escalation in the actual purchase cost could be presented as the inevitable result of rising prices on the world market and the generator would be in no position to refute the claim. The generator would not be able to tell whether costs had increased because of exogenous factors, or because of inefficiency on the part of the agent.

Faced with this situation, the agent could give up trying to find the cheapest source of fuel, and might even be tempted to engage in corrupt business practices which earn the agent a profit (such as accepting bribes from expensive, but favoured suppliers). The result is bound to be an escalation in costs for the generator.[4]

To solve this problem, most fuel contracts contain complex indexation clauses, under which the price paid by the generator depends upon an independent indicator of true world market prices, i.e. a "posted price" for fuel oil (or some near equivalent). As the posted price rises and falls, so the agent is allowed to charge more or less. The agent is therefore protected against the exogenous risk of market price variation—which is equally observable by both the agent and the generator. However, if the agent can reduce the price he pays for fuel oil, through his own effort, he will make more profit. Similarly, if a lack of effort leads to higher purchase costs, the agent will make a loss. The generator cannot tell how much effort the agent is making, but it does not matter; the generator's price is determined irrespective of the agent's effort.

Within the period of the contract, only the agent benefits from increasing the effort to locate lower cost supplies of fuel oil, so the agent can decide how much effort to make. Since the agent captures the full extent of any cost savings, and bears the full brunt of any cost escalation, the agent has the proper incentive to decide on the efficient level of effort, i.e. the level where the extra cost of seeking out lower-cost suppliers (time, phone calls, publication of tenders, etc.) begins to exceed the reduction in purchase costs that he expects this effort to achieve.

Although benefits within the period of the contract accrue to the agent, the principal can capture the benefits during contract negotiations before the contact is signed. The principal must anticipate the actual level of effort that

---

[4] The temptation to succumb to these practices is limited by the generator's ability to choose another agent at the end of the contract. The agent may try to retain the contract by demonstrating an ability to keep fuel costs down. The success of such tactics (and the incentive to act efficiently) depends upon whether the agent can show he or she is acting efficiently.

the agent will make to cut costs and set prices low enough to cover this anticipated level. Trying to forecast the cost level after efficiency savings is not always simple, but the principal can capture the cost savings anticipated by potential agents by auctioning contracts to the highest bidder.

Contracts, Risks and Incentives

From the above, it can be seen that a primary purpose of contracts is to move risk around between different traders. An industry based exclusively on spot markets would start with a certain allocation of risk among the players. Contracts allow the risk to be passed to others. Vertical and horizontal integration can achieve some of the same results. However, integration is not always possible and often causes other problems which more than offset the benefits.

In the case of "two-sided uncertainty", traders reallocate the risks inherent in any project to those who are most willing to bear them. Unavoidable or "non-diversifiable" risks tend to be "shared" with the trader who demands the lowest premium for bearing the risk. "Diversifiable" risks, on the other hand, can be passed outside the industry by signing contracts with speculators and brokers who maintain a balanced portfolio of risks, like an insurer. "Spreading risks" over a portfolio is sometimes a cheaper way to handle risk.

In the case of "one-sided uncertainty", a "principal" uses a contract to allocate the risk inherent in some project to an "agent", so that the agent has an incentive to manage risks and to achieve an outcome which is better for the principal. Usually, the contract encourages the agent to adopt the minimum-cost method of completing the project and therefore removes some of the risk of cost escalation.

The final allocation of risk in any industry depends on the cost conditions and the nature of uncertainty. In general, risks are passed to (a) those most willing or able to bear them, or (b) those who are in the best position to control them. In many cases, these rules conflict and it is necessary to adopt a compromise. Finding the most beneficial compromise is the stuff of contract negotiation. However, these general rules often help to suggest or explain how contracts will be used in any industry.

THE BASIC TYPES OF CONTRACT

Electricity can be bought and sold in a number of different ways, using standard forms of contract. Since the terminology can be confusing, the following sections set out the basic forms of contract, as used in every commercial sector, and explain how they work.

We begin by examining a spot contract, perhaps the simplest form of transaction, to identify the basic terms of any sale. We then investigate ever more complex forms of contract, by varying the terms for:

● time of delivery;
● conditions of delivery; and
● method of settlement.

Spot Contracts

Spot transactions are sales of an asset for immediate delivery. Spot sales are often not accompanied by the creation of any formal contract. Money is passed from the buyer to the seller, and the asset changes hands in the opposite direction. However, the terms of the deal are clear and can be specified whether there is a formal contract or not.

Spot transactions, like any transaction, involve a specified *quantity* of a defined asset. The key characteristic of a spot transaction is that delivery is *immediate* and *unconditional*.[5] However, several other terms must also be defined to make the transaction possible, such as the *place* of delivery. Some spot transactions involve sales of commodities, such as oil or foodstuffs, which are located miles from the market itself.[6] The financial terms of a spot contract include not just the *price* per unit of the commodity but also the *method of settlement*. The contract may be settled by an immediate cash payment, but may also allow a grace period of 30 or 60 days before payment is due.

These terms must all be agreed before any spot transaction can be completed. Sometimes the terms are agreed informally, but often a formal contract is in fact drawn up. One of the roles of a spot market is to provide standardised contracts which can be drawn up quickly and easily to minimise transactions costs.

Time of Delivery: Forwards and Futures

Not all contracts require immediate delivery like spot contracts. Many buyers and sellers want to fix the terms of a contract in advance of the time of delivery. Forward contracts and futures contracts have both emerged to fulfil this need.

---

[5] What qualifies as immediate delivery varies from industry to industry. The delay between agreeing a deal and making delivery may be anything from a few seconds up to several days. In the electricity sector, the cut-off point for a spot market trade depends upon the scheduling and despatch timetable. Beyond a certain time, trades are effectively arranged by the system operator—although they may be recorded and settled as if they were spot trades between two other parties.

[6] The place of delivery in an electricity contract is particularly relevant to the arrangements for pooling and transmission. We return to this issue in later chapters.

Forward contracts

A forward contract is also a contract for delivery of some asset at an agreed price and in a defined location, but at a specified time in the future. No cash is paid initially. The contract price is paid only at the time of delivery, when the asset is received.

Any difference between the market value of the asset and the contract price at the date of delivery represents a profit or loss for the holder of the contract. For example, if the forward contract has a price of $100, but the spot market value of the asset rises to $110 on the date of delivery, the *holder* of the contract makes a profit of $10 by taking delivery of the asset and immediately selling it again. The level of this profit defines the value of the forward contract. The *issuer* of the contract, who has to deliver the asset, makes an equal and opposite loss.

Futures contracts

A futures contract is similar to a forward contract, in that it specifies a price and a future date for delivery of an asset. However, futures contracts are highly standardised contracts offered by and traded on a futures market; changes in the value of the contract are settled in the market daily; and futures contracts do not normally result in physical delivery of the asset. These features combine to make futures contracts easy to trade. The creation of a liquid *forward* market is only possible if some traders are really able to absorb large deliveries of the commodity concerned. Liquid *futures* markets can emerge among any traders with the financial resources to meet liabilities in cash. Once a deeply liquid market emerges, traders can use forward and futures contracts for cancelling out previous delivery obligations, as well as for creating new ones.

Each futures contract is issued by a particular financial exchange. The contract usually provides for buyers and sellers to lodge a standard *security margin*, or deposit, with the exchange, to insure against default. The place of delivery is often specified as the exchange. Only the contract price is negotiable.

When a futures contract reaches its maturity date, the holder may pay the stated price to the issuer of the contract, in return for the asset. Usually, however, holders of futures contracts sell them immediately prior to their maturity, and issuers buy back futures contracts to offset their obligations. These transactions take place at the spot value of the asset and eliminate the transaction costs of delivering the contracted item to the exchange.

The profit on the contract, which accrues to the holder of the contract, is the difference between the price paid for the contract and the market value of the asset at the maturity date (as for a forward contract).

Conditions of Delivery: Options

Spot, forward and futures contracts are all agreements to deliver a fixed quantity at a defined time and place. However, many traders prefer to retain a degree of flexibility over future deliveries. Option contracts allow for a trader to decide whether or not the commodity should be delivered at a later date.

Call options

A call option gives the holder the *right to buy* an asset at a specified exercise price, at some time in the future. Unlike a forward or futures contract, an option contract does not *oblige* the holder to buy the asset.

The price of an option contract is comprised of two elements.

1. The *exercise price* (or "basis" or "strike" price) is the price paid when the option is exercised, i.e. when the buyer "calls" for the contract to be fulfilled. This may differ greatly from the spot market price of the asset which is expected to prevail when the contract is called. If it does, the contract holder will normally have to pay an option fee or *premium*;
2. The *premium* (or "option fee") is the sum of money paid by the *holder* (buyer) of an option contract and received by the *issuer* (seller). It reflects two differences between the basic exercise price and the expected future spot market price: the "intrinsic value" and the "time value". The intrinsic value is the difference between the *exercise price* and the *current spot market price of the asset*. The intrinsic value varies in line with the spot price of the underlying asset and determines the daily settlement payments referred to earlier. The "time value" reflects the difference between the *current spot market price* and the *spot market price which is expected to prevail* when the contract is called. The time value is normally expected to reflect the rate of interest and may be observable by examining the price of forward and futures contracts with a similar maturity date.

The period in which an option contract may be called can be defined in different ways. A *European call* can only be exercised on one particular day (e.g. the last trading day of August); an *American call* can be exercised at any time on or before that day.

The following example provides an illustration of how a call option might work. Suppose a call option with an exercise price of $100 is just about to expire. If the asset price is, and is expected to remain, at the level of (say) $90, then nobody will want to pay the exercise price of $100 to obtain the asset via the call option. The call option is therefore valueless. On the other hand, if the spot market price of the asset is (say) $110, it is worthwhile *exercising* the option to obtain the asset. The option is worth $10, i.e. the difference between the spot market price of $110 and the $100 that must be paid to buy the asset under the contract.

If the market price of an asset exceeds the exercise price, a call option is said to be *in the money*, and the call option holder will exercise his option, earning the difference between the two prices (the exercise value). If, on the other hand, the market price of an asset is below the exercise price, a call option is *out of the money*, and the option will not be exercised. (When the market price exactly equals the exercise price, the option is said to be *at-the-money*. Whether or not it is called is then immaterial.)

Put options

The holder of a put option has the *right to sell* the underlying asset at a pre-specified exercise price at some time in the future; an option fee or premium is paid for this right, just as for a call option.

Another illustration may help to explain the workings of a put option. Assume that a put option gives the holder the right to sell an asset for $100. The circumstances in which the put option is valuable are the opposite of those in which the call option is valuable: if the spot market price of the asset is greater than $100 immediately before expiration, nobody will want to sell the asset at the exercise price and the put option is valueless. If the asset price is less than $100, it would be worthwhile producing the asset (or even just buying the asset on the spot market) and then taking advantage of the option to sell it for $100. The value of the put option at expiration is the difference between the $100 proceeds of the sale and the market price of the asset.

Combinations of options

It has been said that "Calls and puts are the basic building blocks that can be combined to give any pattern of payoffs".[6] This means that combinations of call and put options can be used by traders to limit any risk.

For example, suppose an investor *sells* a call for $105, but is worried in case the spot market price rises very high. The investor then faces the risk of having to pay a high price to fulfil the contract. He can limit the risk of such losses,

---

[6] Brearley, R. and Myers, S. (1991) *Principles of Corporate Finance*, 4th edn, McGraw-Hill, New York.

by *buying* another call at $110. The investor will then never need to pay more than $110 to fulfil the first call option.[7]

Most usefully for our purposes, the combination of put and call *at the same exercise price* is called a two-way option, and is equivalent to a fixed price contract. These types of contract are very common in the UK electricity market, where the aim is to replicate the fixed price power purchase contract. When the spot price rises above the exercise price, the call option will be exercised by the buyer; when the spot price falls below the exercise price, the put option will be exercised by the seller; the contract will therefore be exercised in all conditions, just like a forward contract.

Method of Settlement: Financial Contracts

To settle a conventional contract, the seller must deliver the commodity at the time and place specified in the contract; and the buyer must hand over the requisite sum of money in return. However, arranging for physical delivery according to the terms of a standard contract is not always convenient to the buyer and seller concerned. Many contract markets have therefore adopted more convenient methods of settlement, using cash.

Swap contracts

A commonly used form is the "swap contract", in which two parties agree to exchange the future incomes from two assets (e.g. the interest earned on two loans), rather than the assets themselves (e.g. without having to reassign the

---

[7] Some of the combinations of option contracts are well known as risk-limiting instruments and have been given specific names. The most common are spelled out below.

- A *spread* is a combination of put and call options in a single contract with the exercise price of the put usually less than the exercise price of the call. For example, suppose an investor owns a stock currently priced at $100. If this investor then sells a call valued at $105 and buys a put at $95, he has ensured that the value of the portfolio will never rise above $105 or fall below $95.
- A *straddle* is a combination of put and call options in the same contract where the exercise price and maturity date are identical for both options. A straddle loses money for small changes in the asset price (because of the costs involved in buying the contracts) but it earns money for large changes. It is also known as a *two-way option*.
- A *strangle* is similar to a straddle except that the trader buys a call and a put with different strike prices; both call and put options are "out of the money" and therefore demand low premiums. The strangle will be profitable if the underlying futures price moves far enough beyond either strike price. It therefore provides protection against extreme price movements.
- The *fence* or *collar* comprises the purchase of an option, involving premium expenditure, simultaneously with a sale, bringing premium income. The example given above, of selling a $105 option and buying a $110 option, is one such combination. This strategy is relatively inexpensive (and popular with the oil industry, for example).

loans). This form has even been used in England and Wales for some power purchase agreements (PPAs). An independent power producer (IPP) must sell all its output to the Electricity Pool and receives in return a variety of payments at pool prices. To avoid the risk associated with pool prices, the IPP signs a swap contract with a buyer, who hands over agreed contract payments (i.e. the income from the contract) in return for the IPP's earnings from the pool. Settlement of this contract is a financial transaction, divorced from the actual delivery of energy.

Contracts for Differences

"Contracts for Differences", or CfDs, are a variant of swap contracts which are more convenient because they are settled by handing over the net cash value of the item sold (after deducting the exercise price), rather than by handing over the item itself. A CfD is normally structured as a call option with a specified exercise price (although other forms are possible). The buyer normally calls a CfD when the spot price is higher than the exercise price. When the contract is called, the buyer must pay the exercise price for the item sold in the contract. However, instead of handing over the item itself, the seller is liable for handing over the cash value of the item, as defined by the spot market price at the time.

Contract settlement is then a purely financial matter:

- the buyer owes the seller an amount equal to the contract price;
- the seller owes the buyer an amount equal to the spot price;
- the seller transfers to the buyer an amount equal to the difference between contract price and spot price.

Contracts can only be written in this way if the spot price is clearly and unambiguously defined at all times. CfDs therefore tend to grow up only some time after a liquid spot market has been functioning smoothly enough to allow the market organisers to publish "the" market price at any time.

How Contracts for Differences Work

Given the widespread interest in this novel form of electricity contract, it may be useful to consider how a CfD works by taking a simple example. Suppose someone holds a call option (in the form of a CfD) for 50 units at $100 per unit. Suppose also that the spot price rises to $110 per unit. The holder will call the option to buy 50 units at the exercise price:

- the buyer owes the seller $5000 (i.e. the value of 50 units at the exercise price of $100);
- the seller owes the buyer $5500 (i.e. the value of 50 units at the spot price of $110);
- to settle the contract, the seller transfers $500 to the buyer (i.e. the difference between $5500 and $5000).

CfDs are so named because settlement involves transferring the difference between two prices. Normally, a call option is called when the spot price is higher than the contract price and the seller must transfer the difference to the buyer. However, a CfD structured as a put option would be called in the reverse situation, when the spot price was less than the exercise price, and the buyer would transfer the difference to the seller. A "two-way" CfD which combined call and put options would be exercised under all conditions, and is therefore equivalent to a forward contract.

CfDs are particularly important in the electricity market of England and Wales. Here, the Electricity Pool does not arrange for physical delivery of contracts, rather it runs a spot auction for physical delivery and sets a spot market price. This price is used as the numeraire for CfDs. Although the CfDs are financial instruments, they have the same economic effect as a contract for physical delivery. They simply allow contracts to be settled bilaterally, outside any pooling arrangement.[8]

Summary

Every time an asset is sold in exchange for money, there is a contract. It may be a formal written document or an "implicit" agreement. Every contract must specify:

- a buyer and a seller;
- the form and quantity of the commodity to be sold;
- a price per unit to be paid on delivery; and
- a place for delivery.

The contract may contain additional terms which determine what type it is. There are relatively few basic types of contract and they are distinguished largely by:

---

[8] This point is explained more fully in Chapter 12.

● time of delivery:

  —immediate; or
  —at a specified date in the future;

● conditions of delivery:

  —in any given set of defined circumstances (forward or futures contract);
  —at the buyer's request (call option); and/or
  —at the seller's request (put option);

● method of settlement:

  —by physical delivery (most forward, futures and option contracts); or
  —in cash (swaps or CfDs).

These basic concepts can be adapted to fulfil the requirements of a restructured electricity sector.

CONTRACTS IN THE ELECTRIC SECTOR

The scope for using contracts in the electric sector can best be described in terms of the supply chain, from the primary generator, all the way through the system to the final consumer. The supply chain is shown schematically in Figure 9.1, which assumes that the electricity industry has been fully disaggregated into its constituent trading functions.

Bulk electricity is produced by a *generator*, who sells it to a *wholesaler* (or "aggregator"). Wholesalers buy and sell bulk electricity on their own account, both by contract and in spot markets. Wholesalers sell electricity by contract to *retailers*, the parties responsible for selling electricity to consumers. Retailers may sell to *consumers* on a tariff or an individually designed retail contract. Any of these deals may be arranged by a *broker*, who does not take title to electricity, but merely charges a commission for bringing a buyer and seller together.

The supply chain shown here represents a general form, although in practice many industries combine several functions within large companies. The role of wholesaler may be performed, for example, by a generator, by a transmission or distribution company or by an independent "aggregator". To the extent that functions are carried out by separate companies, contracts are needed to tie the industry together into one integrated whole, as explained below.

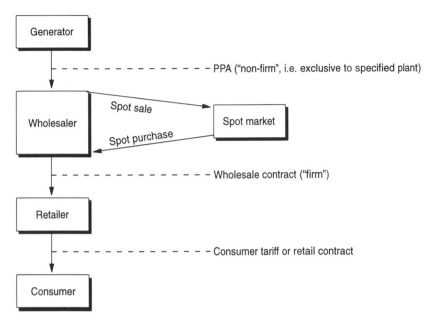

Figure 9.1 The electricity supply chain

1. Power Purchase Agreements (PPAs). The chain begins with the sale of electricity from a single generator to a wholesale company, in this case acting as a buyer. The wholesale buyer signs a PPA, which is a bilateral contract between the generator and the wholesaler, for the purchase of the generator's output (measured in kWh). A wholesaler may buy the output of many generators, under many different PPAs. In Model 2, PPAs are the main form of contract between generators and the central purchasing agency. In Models 3 and 4, PPAs are optional, as generators can act as their own wholesalers.
2. Spot Sales. Electricity from wholesalers can be sold in a spot market. Standing on the other side of the market, the wholesaler can also make spot purchases. These trades allow wholesalers to balance their total purchases and total sales on a short-term basis (since electricity cannot be stored). Spot markets emerge in Models 3 and 4 as wholesale markets.
3. Wholesale Contracts. The wholesaler sells to another wholesaler or to a retailer via a wholesale contract. The ability to call on the spot market allows the wholesaler to offer firm contracts. Typical wholesale contracts include bulk supply tariffs, "full requirements contracts", firm sales for a defined quantity of electricity at a fixed price and (in some countries) financial option contracts. In general, competition at this level tends to encourage innovation in the terms offered to retailers.
4. Retail Contracts or Tariffs. Lastly, the electricity is sold to final consumers, sometimes on an explicit contract but often in a "tariff" (a published schedule

of prices). Some people distinguish between contracts and tariffs, but a tariff can be viewed as a call option for an unlimited quantity. The tariff offers the buyer a fixed price, for a certain period, and the seller often undertakes to provide tariff customers with a certain standard of supply. The rest of this chapter will discuss tariffs as a type of contract.

The importance of these different types of contract depends largely on the structure of the industry. In Model 1, electricity is only sold at the retail level, through consumer tariffs or retail contracts. In Model 2, IPPs can sell electricity to the purchasing agency and will require PPAs to do so. The central purchasing agency continues to sell electricity through contracts and tariffs. In Model 3, the introduction of wholesale competition leads to the creation of a wholesale market, so that wholesalers can balance their purchases and sales. Model 4 allows the possibility of competing retail tariffs (and contracts) for sales direct to consumers, instead of regulated consumer tariffs.

Consumer tariffs are a component of electricity pricing in conventional (Model 1) electricity systems and the science of tariff design has been analysed at length. Given our focus on the requirements for restructuring, we will not repeat that discussion here. Instead, we will focus on the two major types of contract needed when an electricity system is restructured: PPAs and wholesale contracts.

PPAs are needed for the efficient implementation of Model 2, but they may remain important as a way to limit risk in Models 3 and 4, even after customer choice has been introduced. PPAs are discussed in Chapter 10.

The main consequence of introducing customer choice, even if it is limited to wholesale customers in Model 3, is the creation of a spot market, as explained in Part 1. The existence of a spot market allows traders to offer firm wholesale contracts which are backed by their own generators *and* by supplies purchased from the market. The introduction of competitive, firm contracts represents a radical innovation for electricity contract design, since the ability to fulfil a contract no longer depends upon the performance of any individual generating plant. Wholesale contracts are therefore considered at some length in Chapter 11.

10 POWER PURCHASE AGREEMENTS

A power purchase agreement (PPA) is a contract for the sale of energy, availability and other generation services from an independent power producer (IPP). In Model 2 systems (competition in generation), the buyer is the central purchasing agency, who may be the operator of a transmission grid performing the roles of dispatch and network control, or alternatively an integrated generating company. However, PPAs may also be used in more competitive systems such as Model 3 (wholesale competition) and Model 4 (retail competition), for sales of electricity from a single IPP to an electricity wholesaler or aggregator. The wholesaler would combine purchases under a number of PPAs with spot purchases and sales, to assemble the volume of electricity required to service wholesale or retail contracts. PPAs may therefore be found in any system where it is possible to establish an IPP (i.e. a separate generating company).

This section explains the main elements of a PPA, in particular payments for energy, for availability and for other services provided under a PPA.

ENERGY PRICES

The energy price, in $/kWh, is the price paid per unit of incremental output. Early attempts to design contracts for IPPs relied heavily on the energy price to cover all the costs of the plant. The contract fixed the energy price equal to the IPP's average cost at some predetermined level of output or to the buyer's avoided cost. Provided the IPP achieved this level of output (or higher), its costs were covered (and a profit earned). However, this is a bad way to structure a contract and will lead to huge inefficiency if it is applied generally.

The energy price is a key determinant of the pattern of dispatch. Ideally, generators should run in "merit-order", i.e. only the generators with the lowest running costs (i.e. variable costs per unit) should be generating to meet demand. If an IPP has a contract in which the energy price lies above its variable cost of output, the incentive for efficient dispatch is lost. The owner of the IPP will want to run at all times, regardless of the cost of other generators on the system and even if the IPP displaces other, cheaper generators. On the other hand, the dispatcher will be reluctant to dispatch the IPP except at times when the marginal cost of other generators is very high; the dispatcher may hold the IPP off the system, even when it represents a cheaper source than some generators who are currently on line.

For efficient dispatch, the dispatcher needs to know (and pay) the IPP's actual variable cost of generation. Energy prices in PPAs should therefore be set as close as possible to the costs of fuel burnt in generating 1 kWh, plus some allowance for operation and maintenance costs which depend on the level of energy production. The dispatcher will then dispatch the IPP only when it is cheaper than other sources. The owner of the IPP will be indifferent to the pattern of dispatch, as it will have no bearing on total profits. However, since the IPP has no particular incentive to run, the IPP's earnings must be made partially conditional on availability, to which we return below.

The energy price may take a simple form, i.e. just a single price per kWh. However, it is possible for the PPA to specify different prices for the different stages of operation, e.g. a price per start-up, and a different price for different levels of output. Sometimes penalties are charged if generators fail to generate according to the instructions of the dispatcher, to encourage them to generate exactly as instructed.

Energy prices may be fixed, or set by a formula which includes separate terms for the cost of fuel and the assumed rate of conversion into electricity ("thermal efficiency"). It is usually possible to estimate the likely level of efficiency in combustion. However, the cost of fuel can vary widely. Fixing the unit cost of fuel in the PPA would expose the owner to risk, in the event that actual fuel costs rose. Whenever actual costs rose above the figure in the PPA, the IPP would make a loss on every kWh generated and its owners would be unwilling to let it be run at all.

One way to limit the risk is to include the actual purchase costs of the generator's fuel and its actual thermal efficiency. However, energy prices in PPAs do not usually reflect the full actual costs of generation incurred by the generator, since this rule would remove any incentive for the IPP to seek out lower cost fuels, or to increase efficiency of operation. Instead, energy prices in PPAs are usually tied to external indices, of fuel prices, thermal efficiency and other variable costs, which are not influenced by the decisions of the IPPs themselves. The owners of the IPP then have a profit incentive to operate more efficiently and to find cheaper fuel sources because, by doing so, they cut their costs but leave their revenues unchanged.

Indexing energy prices in this way provides a strong incentive for efficiency, but still imposes some risk on IPPs, since the index may fail to reflect some special factor which increases the IPP's fuel costs (such as an increase in local transportation costs). Some fuel price indices therefore include an allowance for the IPP's actual fuel costs, where they can be observed. The more heavily the index reflects the IPP's actual fuel costs, the lower the risk faced by the owners, but the weaker the incentive for the IPP's owners to minimise costs. The owner of the generator and the buyer of the generator's output therefore have to negotiate an index, which achieves an acceptable balance of risk and incentives.

PAYMENTS FOR AVAILABILITY

Availability payments in PPAs perform two main roles.

1. They provide extra revenue to the generator, to cover the capital and other fixed costs which are not covered by the energy price per kWh.
2. They provide incentives for generators to be available at times when the system needs generation capacity.

The second of these roles is particularly important for mid-merit and peak generators, which need to be available at specific times of the year, when the value of generation is particularly high (e.g. owing to high levels of demand). However, even baseload generators need to be given representative signals about the value of their output to the system, to ensure that they time their maintenance outages to coincide with periods when the system is in surplus and the value of output is low.

The first step in negotiating availability payments is to agree a *target level of availability*, T, in terms of a MW level and a number of hours per year. (The target can be made more complicated, for example if MW availability varies from season to season or when maintenance is carried out.) The target level of availability may be specified for the year in total (T_y), or it may be defined differently for each hour (h) in the year (T_h).

Next, the PPA must specify the *fixed annual payment* to be paid if the generator achieves the target level of availability. The fixed annual payment (F) would normally be expected to cover the non-variable costs of the generator, including a normal rate of profit.[1]

Finally, the contract must specify a system of *availability bonuses and penalties*

---

[1] In the case of an existing facility, there may be some disagreement over the level of depreciation and profit to be earned. The seller will accept no less than the minimum amount necessary to keep the generator in operation, i.e. without any contribution to the sunk cost of past investment. The buyer will pay no more than the cost of building and operating a new generator, including all investment costs. In between these two bounds there is considerable scope for negotiation. However, some government policies require generators to be kept in operation (e.g. to maintain employment or for environmental reasons) at a cost which lies outside these bounds. Buyers will only sign up for high-price contracts if their ability to choose other sources is limited. When governments adopt this tactic, the additional cost of the generator should be recovered through the fixed annual payment, to avoid distorting operating incentives.

for availability (A_h) above or below the target level. These bonuses and penalties give the generator a continuous incentive to ensure that the generator capacity is maintained and available. However, the buyer should not pay more than the capacity is worth to the system. These simple statements immediately raise two important questions: how much is availability worth? and what is the availability of a plant that is not running?

THE VALUE OF AVAILABILITY

Availability is measured in MWh, i.e. a MW of availability for an hour. The value of a MWh of any generator's availability, to the system as a whole, is the difference between:

- the *value* of the generator's output to the system, and
- the *price* paid for the generator's output under the PPA.

In any hour, the value of a generator's output is equal to the cost incurred by the whole system if the generator decreases its output. If the generator's output is replaced by output from another, more expensive generator, this value is called the "System Marginal Cost". The System Marginal Cost varies from hour to hour. However, if a reduction in output from the generator can only be accommodated by shedding load (cutting off some customers), then the value of the generator's output is not well represented by the cost of other generators. On these occasions, the value of electricity on the system rises to the "Value of the Lost Load" of the consumers who are being cut off.

The concepts of System Marginal Cost and Value of Lost Load (VOLL) are discussed further in Chapter 12, as the basis of spot market prices. Since not all systems will have a spot market (e.g. Model 2 systems), we shall refer to the value of electricity as the *economic value* (V_h), whether it is determined in a market or not.

A typical time-series of the economic value can be seen in Figure 10.1, where it rises and then falls over a certain time period. The price paid for the generator's output is the energy price fixed in the PPA, which reflects the variable costs of the generator (E), in $/MWh. This price is normally constant from hour to hour, but may be indexed from month to month, or year to year. Between the time T_1 and the time T_2, the generator's variable cost is lower than the economic value of electricity and, ideally, the plant should be generating. The value of having the plant available to generate during these periods is the difference between the economic value and the plant's variable cost:

Value of availability (per MWh) $= B_h = V_h - E$ (subject to a minimum of 0)

The value of availability therefore varies from plant to plant, depending on

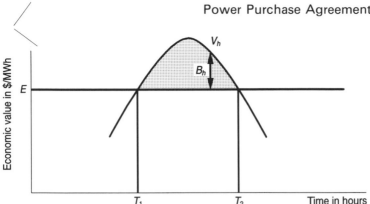

Figure 10.1 The economic value of electricity

its energy price. The vertical arrow on Figure 10.1 measures the value of B_h for one plant in one particular hour. Note that the value of availability (B_h) varies from hour to hour, in line with the economic value of electricity (V_h). Sometimes, the value of availability will be very high, especially in cases when V_h rises to extreme levels. However, in Figure 10.1, the value of availability is zero outside the period T_1–T_2, since the variable cost of the generator is higher than the economic value of electricity. The total economic value of the output of the plant over the whole period shown is indicated by the shaded area.

Availability bonuses (penalties) are paid when the generator exceeds (falls short of) the availability target in the hour concerned. Under this form of contract, an IPP's total annual revenue to cover fixed costs (i.e. before revenues from generating any output) equals the following sum of fixed payments and availability bonuses and penalties:

$$\text{Availability payment (in \$ per annum)} = F + [\sum_h B_h(A_h - T_h)]$$

where F is a figure in dollars, $\sum_h$ is the sum over all hours in the year, A_h and T_h are availability figures in MWh and B_h is an availability bonus in \$/MWh.

Contract prices for availability (B_h) should provide good incentives for efficient operation, which means that they should be derived as much as possible from the actual economic value of electricity at the time. In Models 3 and 4, where there is a spot market, the economic value is best represented by the spot market price. In Model 2, where there is no actual market price, the economic value might be derived from an estimate of the market price calculated and published by the system operator. Alternatively, availability penalties might equal a forecast of V_h which should reflect short-term variations in V_h—if not hourly, then at least between summer and winter, between weekday and weekend, and between day and night. Most investors in generation prefer to limit their financial risk by setting down in the PPA the size of any availability penalties, to avoid heavy penalties for being unavailable at times when V_h is exceptionally high.

Sometimes, both the availability target (T) and the fixed annual payment (F) are set equal to zero. The generator's only revenue is then derived from the energy price and the availability bonuses. However, agreement on targets and fixed payments helps to stabilise the generator's revenue from year to year. Without such agreements, investors may find IPP projects too risky.

Hence, just as with the indexation of fuel costs in energy prices, the main task facing contract designers when setting the value of availability is to find the optimal balance of risk and incentives.

AVAILABILITY TESTING

The best test of availability is to pay a generator for running at times when the value of its output, V_h, is higher than its energy price, E, and not otherwise. However, many PPAs contain availability bonuses based on the forecast level of V_h, rather than its actual value (not least in Model 2, where the value of V_h cannot be observed in a spot market). Such contracts will occasionally offer an availability bonus when the generator is not running (because V_h is actually less than E). For this type of contract, availability bonuses and penalties are normally calculated by comparing the availability target (T_h) with the level of availability *declared by the generator* (A_h). If the generator's actual level of availability is shown to be lower than the declared level, the contract should impose a substantial penalty, because the generator has been receiving unearned availability bonuses. The main problem is to determine the actual level of availability independently of generator declarations. The actual level of availability is usually checked, either:

- by monitoring the performance of the generator when it is dispatched up to the level of declared availability, in the course of normal operations; or
- in a special "availability test".

The PPA will normally define various standards to be met by the generator and the penalties imposed if the generator fails to meet these standards. For example, the generator may be required to generate at the level of declared availability for three continuous hours, in order to prove that the declaration is true.

The penalties for failing this test may be defined in financial terms—e.g. the generator may have to hand back recent availability payments. Alternatively, the PPA may state that the generator will in future receive availability bonuses only for availability that has been *demonstrated* by actually producing output. These rules are encapsulated in the form of complex algebraic expressions for "monitoring availability".

SUMMARY OF AVAILABILITY CONDITIONS

The treatment of availability is one of the most complex parts of any contract. A PPA will specify an availability target, for a year or for particular periods. The generator will normally be entitled to a fixed annual payment in return for meeting this target. The PPA will then set out how variations in availability around the target will be (*a*) valued and (*b*) monitored.

In principle, the value of availability in any hour (*h*) is defined by $V_h - E$, the difference between the economic value of electricity and the energy price of the generator concerned (subject to a minimum value of zero). This value varies from plant to plant, in inverse relation to the energy price.

Availability is monitored by comparing the generator's "declared" value with the target, subject to occasional tests by the dispatcher. Large penalties are imposed if the generator is found to have declared an incorrect value of availability.

ANCILLARY SERVICES

As well as the energy price and payments for availability, a PPA should also contain clauses on the following matters, which are sometimes referred to as "ancillary services":

- performance of frequency control;
- provision of short term reserve generation (spinning or standing);
- provision of voltage control (reactive power);
- payments for emergency generation (incremental output above normal levels, or "black starts" after a system outage).

The exact terms in these clauses will depend very much on conditions in each electricity system. Important considerations include: the cost of providing the service; the value of the service to the system (in the time and place where it is supplied by the generator concerned); and the ease with which output can be monitored. The terms of PPAs will also be affected by the terms implicit in any other technical agreements which impose obligations on generators or others. For example, all generators may have to provide frequency control as a condition of connecting to the network; further payment will not be required, unless the system operator wishes to encourage some generators to act more responsively than others.

There are very few systems where detailed contracts for ancillary services have been developed. Most systems, even competitive ones, retain a high degree of integration between the system operator and major generators. For example, even in the UK, where the electricity sector is highly commercialised and competitive, payments for ancillary services originally took the form of lump-sum payments for a willingness to perform certain duties and are only gradually being refined to reflect actual performance. However, as competition develops, the generator portfolio owned by any system operator is likely to shrink and new entrants will be less willing to provide ancillary services unless they receive some explicit remuneration. It is therefore likely that future PPAs will contain more specific incentives for providing ancillary services than current ones.

OTHER TERMS AND CONDITIONS

Finally, any PPA must include provision for a variety of other eventualities. A checklist of important technical issues might include:

- any constraints on the flexibility of operating the generator;
- procedures for maintenance scheduling;
- treatment of forced outages.

In addition, the PPA must allow for adjustment of the terms in the light of unforeseen events caused by others. Apart from a general *force majeure* clause, a PPA would normally refer to:

- changes in the regulatory regime and any other documents (such as a grid code) which would materially affect the costs of the IPP;
- the length of contract and conditions for contract termination;
- conditions for renegotiating the contract if any other conditions change.

Given the rate at which electricity industries are being restructured, it would be unwise of any investor to imagine that PPAs will remain in force, untouched, for 15–20 years. The contract must therefore anticipate the need for renegotiation and should, at the very least, set out a procedure for it.

CONCLUSION ON PPAs

The main economic elements of PPAs are the clauses relating to energy prices and payments for availability.

The energy price (E) should cover the variable cost of output when requested by the dispatcher. This provides the information that the dispatcher needs to ensure an efficient dispatch. The price should therefore reflect as closely as possible the actual variable cost of generation, but should be tied to external indices of fuel prices to give the generator an incentive to minimise fuel (and other) costs.

Availability payments are needed to cover the non-variable costs which are incurred to keep the generator available, whether or not the generator is required to produce energy. Each MWh of availability is worth the difference between the economic value of the generator's output (V_h) and the incremental variable cost of its output (E). Ideally, the incentive for availability ($V_h - E$) should reflect the actual economic value of energy on the system as a whole in any hour, but investors may prefer to limit their risk by defining contract availability payments which reflect prior estimates of the economic value.

If the sum of energy payments, availability payments and earnings from the sale of ancillary services is not enough to cover the costs of the generator, then the case for building it is rather weak. The sum of energy, availability and ancillary service payments represents the plant's total value to the system. If the payments do not cover the plant's costs, the plant is not economic. However, government policy may require some additional cost to be incurred, e.g. for environmental reasons, or to support generators who use domestic fuel, or to locate generators in a particular region. The additional cost should be added to the fixed charge, so that it does not distort decisions about availability and output.

In summary, negotiators must ensure that a PPA is designed in a way which encourages efficient operation and dispatch of the generator. Without the clear market price signals provided in a competitive system, this is a difficult task and many PPAs have been badly designed in ways which lead to gross inefficiency. However, the task is not impossible and examples of good (if not perfect) PPAs are now to be found in a number of countries. The benefits of designing PPAs efficiently have frequently been shown to justify the effort involved.

11 WHOLESALE CONTRACTS

BULK POWER CONTRACTS

In this chapter, we examine the role and design of wholesale contracts. In particular, we explain how bulk power contracts can be used to manage the risks faced by individual generators. We also examine the incentives offered by bulk power contracts, as opposed to PPAs.

Bulk power contracts are different from PPAs in a number of respects. PPAs specify the generating plant which will supply the power; if the generator is unavailable, or simply not operating, the buyer cannot use a PPA. In contrast, bulk power contracts specify a node on the network where power will be delivered, but allow the seller to choose from a range of possible sources. This allows the seller to offer the buyer a "firm" supply.

Under a bulk power contract, the seller has a great deal more flexibility than under a PPA and will normally select the lowest cost source of supply. In Chapter 12, we show how a spot market run by the Market Operator is one such source. Sellers of bulk power contracts therefore decide whether to generate electricity from their own plant, or to buy power from the market, depending upon which is cheaper.

In the short term, this encourages efficient dispatch, as the seller will only run a generator with costs below the market price. In the longer run, it will encourage efficient decisions about maintenance and plant shut-down. A seller will only keep a generator operational to service a bulk power contract if its future costs are less then the costs of buying power from the market.

Bulk power contracts are therefore ideally suited to Models 3 and 4, where a wholesale market exists. In Models 3 and 4, an aggregator may still buy the output of a single generator by signing a PPA, but it is almost impossible to serve multiple independent customers at different points on the network with a PPA tied to the specific characteristics of a single generator. When no single buyer takes the entire output of the plant, there will be fruitless negotiations over which buyer is responsible for start-up costs, maintenance, no-load costs, etc.[1]

---

[1] The development of the UK pool was delayed nearly a year while this lesson was painfully learned!

Instead, aggregators will offer bulk power contracts with terms which are better suited to the needs of the customer. The aggregator is then responsible for choosing the source of supply.

Many people feel nervous about offering bulk power contracts which can be used by the buyer, regardless of whether a particular generator is operating. In this chapter, we will explain how traders in a wholesale market can use bulk power contracts to manage their risks. In doing so, we will draw extensively on the discussion of contract types set out in Chapter 9. We will then be ready to explain (in Chapter 12) exactly how bulk power contracts interact with the wholesale spot market.

WHOLESALE MARKET PRICES

To begin with, we consider the pattern of wholesale market prices and their relation to the operations, revenues and costs of typical generators. Figure 11.1 shows the time path of wholesale market prices, as a representation of the economic value of a generator's output. (See Chapter 10 for a discussion of the economic value.) The market price moves up and down over the course of several periods. Generating plant with a variable cost of generation equal to E (in \$/MWh) would expect to generate during the lightly shaded periods, when E is less than the market price.

When the plant is running, the owner would expect to capture the full value of its output, i.e. the market price. This could be done quite simply, by selling the plant's output into the market in a number of spot transactions. If this

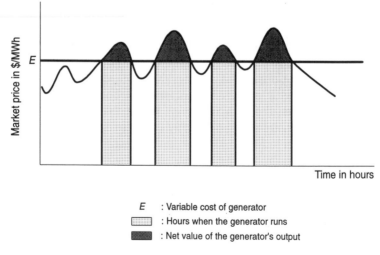

E : Variable cost of generator

▨ : Hours when the generator runs

▰ : Net value of the generator's output

Figure 11.1 Wholesale market prices

were done, the plant would recover not just the variable cost of operation but also the revenue indicated by the darkly shaded areas, when the market price is greater than the plant's variable cost. This extra revenue would be used to cover the fixed costs of building and maintaining the plant.

However, the generator will then be subject to four different kinds of risk: market price risk; sales quantity risk; fuel price risk; and availability risk.

1. *Price risk* is a risk associated with the market. In any single hour when the plant is running, the market price may be higher or lower than expected, as a result of variations in supply and demand to the market. The generator cannot therefore be sure what price will be achieved. This will affect the revenues earned by the generator in excess of variable cost, and could therefore undermine the ability of the owner to recover the fixed costs of construction and maintenance.
2. *Quantity risk* is due to variations in market conditions which affect the output of the generator. Changes in market prices in some periods may require the plant to run for more or fewer hours than expected. This will affect not only the revenues of the generator, but also its variable costs of fuel, operations and maintenance.
3. *Fuel price risk* lies outside the electricity market, but affects the ability of the generating plant to supply the electricity market. Rises and falls in fuel prices will affect E, and therefore change both the number of hours that the plant runs, and the net revenue earned in each of these hours.
4. *Availability risk* is again due to factors outside the electricity market, but is an all too familiar problem to most generators. Even if the generator knows the pattern of electricity and fuel prices (and hence the number of hours in which the plant is required to run), there is no guarantee that the generator will always be available to run. Availability problems may cause the generator to miss periods in which they expected to earn some revenue. The random nature of availability problems therefore injects some risk into total revenues.

Chapter 9 provides a general discussion of risk management and the next section explains how risk is managed by generators and consumers of electricity. In the electricity sector, it is useful to divide the above list into "market risks" (price and quantity) and "plant risks" (fuel cost and availability). Market risk is exogenous and observable. It raises questions about the ability of traders to share (or spread) risk. Generators often sign contracts to share market risks with consumers (or even to pass them over to speculators). On the other hand, plant risks are partly under the control of the plant managers, in ways which cannot be observed by electricity consumers. They raise questions about risk sharing, but also about the incentives on plant managers to behave efficiently ("agency problems"). The next section explains how efficient contracts handle these problems.

SHARING MARKET RISK

To understand how contracts handle risk, it is first necessary to develop a more convenient formulation of market price variation. Figure 11.1 showed market prices varying through time. To simplify analysis, the order of trading periods (hours) can be rearranged, so that they are shown in order of market price.

Figure 11.2 shows all the hours in a year put in order of market price, beginning with the highest price hours on the left. For each hour, the market price in that hour is shown on the vertical axis. The market prices trace out a line which slopes downward from left to right, as we move from high-price hours to low-price hours. This concept is similar to the "load duration curve", a tool familiar to most electricity system planners, and will be referred to here as a "market price duration curve".

Once again, the variable cost of the generating plant is shown as E. If the plant runs in every hour where the market price is higher than E, it will be dispatched for H_1 hours per annum. In practice, the ability of the generator to run plant in all these hours will be limited by availability problems, but we will ignore these initially and return to them below.[2]

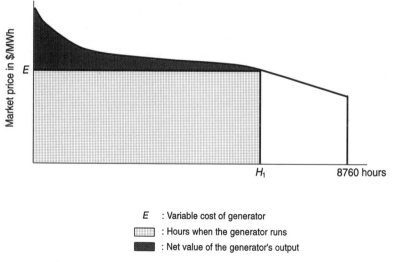

E   : Variable cost of generator

▭ : Hours when the generator runs

▪ : Net value of the generator's output

Figure 11.2 Market price duration curve

---

[2] The ability of some generators to exploit all high-price hours is also limited by their flexibility. Many generators take several hours to run up to and down from full output. They would therefore find it difficult to exploit the opportunity represented by a high market price in one hour which was preceded and followed by hours where the market price was very low. Such complications can safely be ignored for the purpose of this exposition, but can be very taxing to real generator companies.

In Figure 11.2, the solid line represents the expected pattern of prices over the coming year. The generator will want to capture the value represented by the dark shaded area, which represents the total annual value of the plant's output (at the market price), less the production cost (at its variable cost). However, this value is subject to risk and must be managed by the appropriate use of contracts.

PRICE RISK AND FORWARD CONTRACTS

Figure 11.3 shows another set of "market price duration curves". The dashed and dotted lines show two possible levels of market prices during the peak hours. The dashed line shows the effect of a price fall; the dark shaded area of the plant's net value is reduced accordingly. The dotted line shows the effect of a price rise; it would increase the plant's net value. The cost of electricity to consumers varies in the same way.

Suppose that both the generator and a consumer are reluctant to bear the risk of prices varying in the future. The generator wishes to fix the net value of the plant, to be sure that its revenues can cover its fixed costs. Similarly, the consumer wants to fix the price paid for electricity, rather than bear the risk of a sharp escalation in prices. The generator and the consumer can *share* these risks, by signing a *forward contract*, which locks in the expected market prices shown in the solid market price duration curve. This protects both the generator

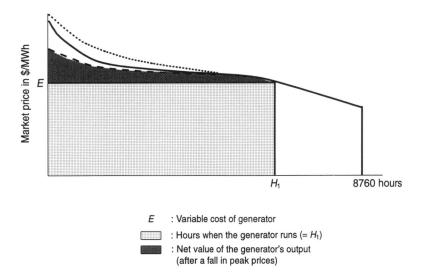

Figure 11.3 Effect of market price risk

and the customer against variations in the market price during the hours when the contract is valid.[3]

QUANTITY RISK AND FORWARD CONTRACTS

Forward contracts do not provide any protection against quantity risks, as illustrated by the "market price duration curves" in Figure 11.4. In this case, mid-merit market prices may vary in future, between the upper (dotted) line and the lower (dashed) line, in which case the generator's plant will run for a greater or lesser number of hours. If market prices rise generally, the generator can expect to make extra net revenue, by running in additional periods when the market price is above the plant's variable costs. The plant's total running time increases to H_2. If market prices fall generally, the plant will run for only H_0 hours. If the generator has signed a forward contract for the plant's output, variations in the quantity produced by the plant will affect the generator's profits. However, the variation will be all one way: apparently, quantity risk always increases the seller's profits at the expense of buyers!

1. If the market price falls and the plant does not run as expected (in hours H_0 to H_1), electricity can be bought from the market to fulfil the contract at a lower cost than the cost of running the plant.

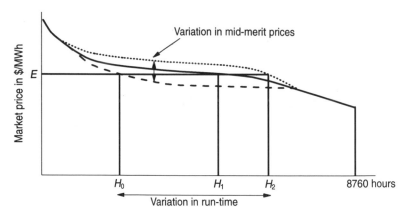

E : Variable cost of generator

Figure 11.4   Effect of quantity risk

---

[3] For a cogent analysis of the reasons why traders hedge market risks, see Froot, K. A. *et al.* (1994). *A Framework for Risk Management*, Harvard Business Review, November/December 1994 (Reprint 94604).

2. If the price rises and the plant runs unexpectedly (in hours H_1 to H_2), the plant makes a profit because the market price exceeds its variable cost.

Either way, the generator benefits and one might suspect that the generator would be willing to tolerate this residual risk. However, there are no free lunches in a competitive market.

In a competitive market, generators would anticipate the extra profits derived from quantity fluctuations when they decide to build generators, so the additional net revenue would encourage additional construction. This would drive down expected market prices to the point where generators had to *rely* on expected profits from spot transactions due to quantity risk, just to be reasonably sure of recovering their total costs, even if they signed forward contracts. The actual revenue from spot market transactions would be highly risky, and would encourage generators to investigate alternative forms of contract, which would provide better cover against variations in the quantity of output.

QUANTITY RISK AND OPTION CONTRACTS

Because it is difficult to match forward contracts to an unpredictable pattern of output, a more common form of wholesale electricity contract is the *option contract*. Although this may sound unfamiliar to many in the industry, it is really the wholesale equivalent of conventional power contracts with a "capacity" price per kW and an "energy" price per kWh. Figure 11.4 can be used to show how wholesale electricity option contracts work.

As explained in Chapter 9, an option contract for some asset has two prices: an "option fee" payable when the contract is signed; and an "exercise price" which is paid when the contract is called and the asset is delivered. The terms can be adapted to the needs of the electricity industry. The "option fee" is the equivalent of a kW charge; the "exercise price" is the equivalent of a kWh charge.

First, assume that the contract is a one-way call option. (See page 101.) The volume in the contract is Q kW in every hour, where Q is the capacity of the generator (and hence its output in any single hour when it runs).

Second, let the "exercise price" equal E, the unit variable costs (cost per kWh) of the generator. Suppose that the plant's actual variable cost does not vary and that availability is 100%. The generator's total variable costs will be QEH^*, where H^* is the actual number of hours in which the market price exceeds E and the plant runs. In these same hours, the contract will be called by the buyer, also because the market price is above E. The generator will receive contract revenues of QEH^* in total.

Third, suppose that the generator and the consumer agree an "option fee"

Table 11.1 Generator costs and revenues under different market price scenarios

Market price scenario	Low	Expected	High
Generator running time (hours)	H_0	H_1	H_2
Generator unit variable cost ($/MWh)	E	E	E
Generator availability (MW)	Q	Q	Q
Generator costs ($)	$F + QEH_0$	$F + QEH_1$	$F + QEH_2$
Generator contract revenues ($)	$R + QEH_0$	$R + QEH_1$	$R + QEH_2$
Generator profit ($)	$R - F$	$R - F$	$R - F$

at the start of the contract. The generator will demand (and the customer will be willing to pay) a fixed revenue (R) which exactly captures the expected value of the right to receive electricity at a price of E, i.e. the dark shaded area in Figure 11.2. The generator will use this revenue to cover the plant's fixed costs (F).

How does this contract structure affect the risk faced by the generator? The benefits of option contracts can be shown by considering variations in output due to changes in market conditions. Figure 11.4 shows alternative market price duration curves, both above and below the expected level. At the expected level of prices, the plant is expected to run for H_1 hours. If prices rise generally, the plant increases its running time to H_2 hours; if prices fall, running time drops to H_0 hours. The Table 11.1 shows the generator's revenues and costs in each case.

The generator's revenues from exercise of the contract always match the generator's variable costs. The generator's net profit depends on the gap between the plant's fixed costs and any other revenues. This gap may be positive or negative—there is no guarantee that the plant will cover its costs from one year to the next. However, an annual option contract enables the generator to fix the plant's net profit in the face of both price and quantity risk. This normally makes the project more attractive to investors.

GENERATOR RISKS AND INCENTIVES

The objective for generator risks may appear very similar to that for market risks: to eliminate profit variation. However, the owners of a generating plant are motivated by profit. If all profit variation is eliminated, they will lose all motivation to manage the plant efficiently. The result is bound to be higher costs for consumers. Many contracts are therefore intended to minimise the variations in profit due to exogenous factors, whilst ensuring that the plant's profits depend on the efficiency with which it is managed.

Fuel Price Risk

Fuel price risk was discussed in Chapter 10, in the context of PPAs. The managers of a generating plant are normally responsible for buying and arranging the delivery of the plant's fuel. If they carry out this task efficiently, they will minimise the price paid for fuel. However, it is difficult to tell whether the managers have bought fuel efficiently when world prices vary so widely over short periods.

As discussed above, the risk sharing properties of an option contract depend upon the accuracy with which the exercise price matches the plant's unit variable costs, E. However, it would be a mistake to link the exercise price to the actual price paid for the generator's fuel. The plant's managers would then have no incentive to minimise fuel purchase costs. As with PPAs, the solution is to tie the energy price—in this case the exercise price—to some independent, observable index of fuel prices.[4]

Indexation of prices gives the generator's managers an incentive to make profits by "beating the index". Figure 11.5 shows what happens when they succeed. The plant's unit variable cost has been cut from E to C, by an astute fuels purchasing policy. As would be the case with a PPA, this cost saving increases the generator's profits in the H_1 hours when it was expected to run. The size of this cost saving is indicated by the area which is lightly shaded.

Moreover, the availability of a spot market, and the generator's right to sell electricity to it, opens up an opportunity which was not available to a generator with a PPA. If the generator quotes a lower price per unit generated, to reflect the lower fuel cost, the plant will be dispatched in more hours. (A generator with a PPA cannot normally revise the energy price in this way, without renegotiating the contract.) At the lower price, $E_2 = C$, the generator will be dispatched for H_2 hours. By increasing the run-time of the generator (from H_1 to H_2), the generator earns an additional profit equal to:

● the market price of the additional output in the hours concerned;

less

● the additional variable cost of running.

The size of this profit is indicated by the dark shaded area in Figure 11.5.

Together, the two shaded areas sum to the profit incentive for managers to

---

[4] For some fuels, especially coal, it may be difficult to find such an index, because there is no well-established short-term market. In the negotiation over electricity contracts in England and Wales in 1990, it was necessary to use the retail price index (RPI), but the generators were protected from any risk by applying the RPI both to the coal purchase contracts and to their electricity sales contracts.

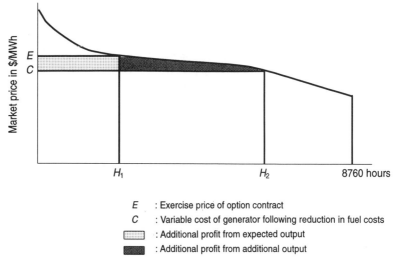

E   : Exercise price of option contract
C   : Variable cost of generator following reduction in fuel costs
▢   : Additional profit from expected output
■   : Additional profit from additional output

Figure 11.5   Incentive to reduce fuel costs

seek out the lowest-cost sources of fuel. However, the generator will only continue to earn the profit if market prices remain constant. Over time, of course, as every generator seeks out cheaper sources of fuel (or learns how to use fuel more efficiently), all the prices quoted by generators will slide downwards. Market prices will also fall generally, eliminating the generator's additional profit and transferring the benefits to customers. However, any generator with a relatively small market share will take the market prices as given, at any particular moment, and will have a constant incentive to reduce fuel costs, in order to "beat the market".

Availability Risk

All of the preceding discussion has assumed that generators are always available to generate when their variable costs are below the market price. In practice, of course, random failures and planned outages may cause any generator to be unavailable at a time when it is needed.

When this happens in a Model 3 or 4 system, the customer can still call the option. Being unable to fulfil the contract with his own plant, the generator must buy any deficiency from the spot market, or else the generator will be charged a market price for the resulting imbalance.[5] To the extent that the prices for spot market purchases or imbalances reflect the economic value of

---

[5] See Chapter 12 for a discussion of imbalances.

electricity at the time, the generator will face an efficient incentive to be available. For example, the generator will have no incentive to be available at times when the running cost of his plant exceeds the economic value of electricity. Market prices therefore replace the explicit availability bonuses or penalties found in PPAs when there is no wholesale market.

Generators are sometimes reluctant to accept the risk associated with unavailability. However, the incentive for availability clearly needs to lie with the company which possesses the means to respond, i.e. the generator. Generators commonly adopt three different techniques for managing their risks.

1. Generators may use additional option contracts to limit their risk, e.g. by taking out a further option with another generator to buy electricity when the price reaches extremely high levels. This strategy was described in Chapter 9 as the "fence" or "collar", which limits exposure to price risks (but does not eliminate them entirely).
2. "As-available" contracts contain provisions that allow the generator to restrict the volume sold in any hour to the level of availability of particular generating capacity. The problem with "as-available" contracts is the design of appropriate contract bonuses and penalties for availability, as with a PPA.
3. Generator companies can assemble a portfolio of generators so that responsibility for fulfilling one contract (and the associated risk) is spread over a number of different plants.

It is sometimes thought that generator companies have to be large to assemble a portfolio of generating plants, which raises the spectre of market power. However, small companies can develop a portfolio of generators by taking part in a large number of joint ventures, or even just by owning shares in a wide range of generator companies. In the electricity markets of the future, the diversification of shareholdings may allow private investors to spread their risks over several companies, which would greatly reduce the need for generator companies to manage their risks internally.

CONTRACTS AND THE CUSTOMER

The previous sections have discussed the sorts of contracts needed by generators to cover their risks and to provide the appropriate incentives. This section looks at the types of contract discussed so far from the buyer's point of view.

"Horizontal and Vertical Slices"

The conventional approach to design of advanced customer tariffs is to designate "time of use" prices, as illustrated in Figure 11.6, which charts the

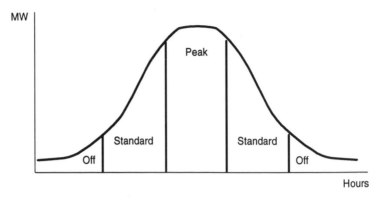

Figure 11.6 Prices averaged in vertical slices of the load curve

rise and fall in demand (MW) over a certain period. The period is divided into a number of sub-periods ("off-peak", "standard" and "peak") and the customer is offered a "time-of-day" tariff equal to an estimate of the average price in each of these sub-periods. Generators could indeed offer option contracts on this basis, by dividing their expected output into the "vertical slices" shown in the figure.

However, the amount taken by the customer in each sub-period depends upon the kWh price for the sub-period, which reflects average market prices. The amount generated by any plant depends on its own variable costs. There is no reason why these two amounts should be the same and, in any sub-period, the generator may generate an imbalance, i.e. a surplus or a deficit compared with the customer's demand. Surpluses and deficits must be made good via transactions in the spot market, which exposes the generator to some risk.

The alternative approach set out in the previous section divides demand instead into "horizontal slices", as shown in Figure 11.7, which charts the rise

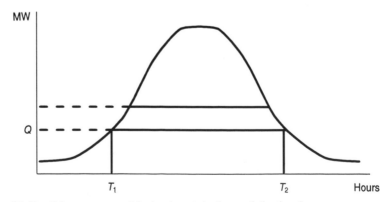

Figure 11.7 Prices averaged in horizontal slices of the load curve

and fall in demand (MW) over the same period. At time T_1, demand reaches the level at which the market price rises above the exercise price of the contract and triggers its calling. Given a specific exercise price, the contract provides cover for the period from T_1 to T_2 for Q units. In practice this volume may be divided among several customers, but they will all call the contracts at the same time, when the market price rises above the exercise price. Customers may have other contracts at other exercise prices, which cover other parts of the load curve: the higher the exercise price, the higher the market price must rise before the contract is called, and the shorter the period between T_1 and T_2.

Customer Risks and Incentives

We have explained how option contracts or CfDs can be used to hedge price risk. This need not mean that contracts obscure altogether the signals provided by spot markets. When contracts specify a fixed volume, the customer's incentive to buy more or less still depends on the spot price.[6]

For example, suppose that a customer has a contract for 100 units. As long as the customer buys only 100 units in total, the price is determined by the contract. However, if the customer buys 101 units, the extra one unit must be bought from the spot market at the spot market price. If the customer only wants 99 units, the unwanted unit can be sold in the spot market at the spot market price.

In each case, the bulk of the customer's purchases are covered by the contract. Customers are only exposed to the spot market price to the extent that they vary their purchases around the contract volume.

Option Contracts and the Spot Market

The situation is slightly more complicated for option contracts, which are used to hedge both price and quantity risks. However, customers call their options by reference to the spot market price, not their own consumption. Consumption incentives still depend on the spot market price.

To illustrate how customers with option contracts react to the spot price, suppose a customer has four option contracts with the following characteristics:

Contract number   = 1   2   3   4
Contract volumes = $Q1$, $Q2$, $Q3$, $Q4$ (Total volume = Q)
Exercise prices   = $P1$, $P2$, $P3$, $P4$

---

[6] We made a similar point on generator incentives earlier.

Now suppose that the market price rises to P^*, half-way between $P3$ and $P4$. The customer calls contracts 1, 2 and 3 (whose exercise prices are below P^*) and so buys by contract Q^* units of electricity ($Q^* = Q1 + Q2 + Q3$). Suppose the customer's total purchases are B^*.

- if B^* is larger than Q^*, the customer must buy the excess from the spot market, at the spot market price which varies from hour to hour;
- if the customer cuts back purchases so that B^* is less than Q^*, the customer will have to sell the excess electricity back to the spot market.[7]

Excess purchases above the contract volume Q^* cost the spot market price. Cut-backs in the amount purchased below the contract volume Q^* earn the spot market price. Consequently, the incentive for any small change in consumption is the spot market price. A portfolio of option contracts therefore gives customers a time-of-day price for marginal consumption decisions which signals the economic value of electricity as accurately as the market pricing mechanism allows.

Of course, wholesale markets and wholesale contracts only give price signals to wholesale customers. It may be some time before small retail consumers can appreciate the benefits of time-of-day pricing, principally because it is too expensive to fit hourly meters and controls on equipment that can react to price variation. Such consumers are likely to continue to prefer a stable tariff, with a constant energy price. However, large retail consumers can already afford to fit time-of-day metering. Where a wholesale market exists, many large consumers prefer to operate through a combination of option contracts and spot purchases, rather than through a specific time-of-day tariff.

CONCLUSION

This chapter has looked in detail at the structure and application of wholesale contracts, that is, electricity contracts which can be fulfilled by supplying electricity bought from the spot market, as well as electricity produced by specific generating plant.

The purpose of any contract is to provide cover against risk and to improve or maintain incentives for efficiency. We have tried to show how option contracts look very like a PPA, with a kW payment (option fee) and a kWh price (exercise price), and how they provide cover against market price and

---

[7] In practice, this is often handled through the cash settlement system applied to Contracts for Differences, as discussed in Chapter 9.

quantity risks. Fuel price risk can be handled by indexing the kWh price, just as with a PPA.

A contract like this provides strong incentives for efficiency. The use of a fuel price index gives the generator an incentive to minimise fuel costs, in wholesale contracts just as in PPAs. The existence of a spot market provides an outlet for additional generation (and a source of additional profits) which is not available under a PPA (at least, not without renegotiating the contract).

Furthermore, if the contract is "firm" (i.e. if its volume is not tied to the availability of individual plant), the spot market price of electricity determines the incentive for availability. If the spot market price rises above the plant's variable costs and the contract's exercise price, generators will produce electricity from their own plant to fulfil the contract. If a plant is not available, the generator must purchase electricity from the market to fulfil the contract. The cost of these purchases, which the plant's output would otherwise displace, is the spot market price. The incentive ("bonus" or "penalty") for availability is therefore provided by the spot market price of electricity (i.e. its "economic value"), even if the contract contains no detailed provisions on the availability of individual generators. This avoids the need for detailed clauses on availability targets and penalties. It makes wholesale contracts much simpler to design and operate than PPAs.

Wholesale forward and option contracts therefore offer many advantages over PPAs. Where a spot market for electricity exists, they will often become the main form of contract used by generators and large consumers. The next chapter looks at the requirement for establishing a spot market in electricity and for organising the trade in electricity.

12

SPOT MARKETS AND THE ORGANISATION OF TRADE

INTRODUCTION

In the electricity systems characterised by Models 1 and 2, electricity is already traded i.e. bought and sold. Utilities trade with customers and (in Model 2) with generators connected to their own network. They also trade electricity with the utilities that own neighbouring networks.

The introduction of customer choice in Models 3 and 4 opens up a new dimension. Under wholesale or retail competition, customers[1] are allowed to buy from distant generators (or from distant utilities). To deliver electricity from a generator to the customer's door whenever someone switches on a light, it must be possible to trade electricity over networks. Wholesale competition (Model 3) requires sales of electricity from generators to distribution companies, over the high-voltage transmission networks. Retail competition (Model 4) requires sales of electricity to final consumers, over the low-voltage distribution networks. This is the Big Idea which motivates the need for this book: that electricity can be produced and transported like any other product, and can be sold in a competitive market.

The creation of trade over networks (in addition to trade at the entry and exit points) requires a number of new institutions and contracts. This chapter sets out to identify what institutions are required in a competitive electricity market, and how they should operate.[2]

An example may help to explain the additional problems created by allowing customer choice.

- Suppose Generator A has a contract to sell electricity to Customer X (contract AX), while Generator B has a contract to sell electricity to Customer Y (contract BY). If the contracts were for something other than electricity, their operation would be relatively simple. Suppose we were

---

[1] We use the term "customer" to denote any individual or corporate person who buys electricity in a spot market or by contract. In Model 3, for example, this term includes the retailers. The final user of any power is a "consumer".

[2] Throughout this chapter, we ignore the costs of transmission, including transmission losses. These problems are addressed in subsequent chapters.

talking about carpets. When Customer X wants to take delivery, he asks A to supply the carpet. Carpet seller A makes the delivery and invoices Customer X, who pays for the carpet. There is no question about who sold what to whom and the deal can be made and settled entirely bilaterally.

● With electricity, the situation is different. When Customer Y switches on a heater, he gets electricity, even if Generator B is not actually generating at that particular time. However, Customer Y has a contract with Generator B and dutifully pays Generator B for the power received. In practice, the power may have come from Generator A, who was generating enough to supply both Customer X (under contract AX) and also Customer Y. Given that Customer Y will pay Generator B (under contract BY), some means has to be found for Generator B to pay Generator A for actually supplying the power.

In advance, the two generators could agree an additional short term or spot contract (AB) to cover the sale from one generator to another. However, many of these imbalances between contract amounts and actual flows are only identified after the fact, when meters have been read. In these cases, the solution lies in a "market for imbalances", which records trades and sets the price for any outstanding imbalances between contracts and actual flows in each period (hour or half hour). In this section, we take a look at this mechanism, which is needed to support the operation of any electricity spot market. We begin by considering the way in which the volume of imbalances is measured and then examine the procedures for setting the price of imbalances.

SETTLING ENERGY TRADES

It has sometimes been suggested that each generator should be required to generate exactly the amount needed to supply a customer's demand, to avoid any discrepancy between the two. This would supposedly avoid the need to set up any formal system for settling imbalances (or, indeed, a spot market). However, the instantaneous nature of electricity use makes it either impossible or, at least, highly inefficient to operate power plants on this basis. Suppose an electricity system were to try to keep generation in line with contracts, through sophisticated on-line metering of the customer's use, and immediate instructions to the generator. Several obvious problems arise.

1. What happens if Generator A is available to run to supply Customer X, but Generator B is cheaper and is standing idle? Generator B should supply instead. This is the concept behind merit order dispatch, which has

(rightly) been a cornerstone of cost-minimisation in the integrated utilities and in Model 1 pools. The purpose of competitive markets in other sectors is to allow customers to find and exploit the lowest-cost sources of supply. It would be unthinkable to abandon merit order dispatch in order to institute competition.

2. What happens if the customer's demand rises or falls faster than the generator is able to alter its output? Should the rate of change of the customer's demand be restricted and, if so, how? Should the generator be constrained to sell only to customers whose demand alters slowly? If so, how would this be policed?

3. What happens if a generator breaks down? The customer's supplier must find a substitute immediately, within a split-second. In fact, it will take some time to find a suitable replacement generator and, in the meantime, the customer will be supplied from the reserve capacity of other generators.

Hence, for any of the above reasons, there will *at all times and in all circumstances* be a smaller or larger mismatch between contract amounts and the production of individual generators or the consumption of individual consumers. It is essential that a mechanism be set up to deal with these mismatches, or "imbalances".

The imbalances must be settled as if they were *instantaneous spot transactions*, i.e. sales of electricity arranged at (infinitesimally) short notice, for immediate delivery. Each trader who is deficient in generation has to make up the contract sales volume with a purchase from some other generator. Each trader who has surplus generation has to be able to sell the surplus to someone else. It is physically impossible for these trades to be arranged at the time, one by one. Traders cannot therefore be made responsible for arranging their own purchases and sales beyond a certain deadline (e.g. an hour in advance). Instead, last-minute (or, rather, last-second) transactions are normally arranged by the dispatcher and accounts are settled after delivery has taken place, by a "Market Operator" (MO) acting in accordance with some joint agreement among the players.

In this respect, electricity markets differ from most other spot and contract markets (although comparable restrictions apply to gas markets which use pipeline networks). The establishment of an electricity market requires joint agreement of settlement methods, so that all sellers pay to fulfil their contracts (if the seller does not deliver enough) and all buyers pay for uncontracted offtake (if their consumption exceeds their contracts).

Any imbalance between trades arranged in advance and actual flows on the day must be treated as an energy trade arranged at short notice. These trades must be settled afterwards by a single trader (the MO) identified as the buyer and seller of last resort. One MO must be identified for each network, or for each part of an interconnected network. The MO enforces payment for these trades by making all traders who have access to the network open a "settlement account". Although this concept may seem unfamiliar, it is in fact common to all electricity systems, in one form or another. The operation of settlement accounts is explained below.

TRADING OVER A NETWORK

Figure 12.1 shows in schematic form how electricity contracts and other trades are arranged and settled for a single network. It features a simple contract to send 100 MWh over the network from A to B, in conditions where the seller actually generates 110 MWh at A and the buyer actually consumes 120 MWh at B.[3] The seller has an imbalance discrepancy between actual and contract flows which amounts to a surplus (or sale) of 10 MWh. The buyer has a similar, deficit imbalance of 20 MWh, which must be paid for. The net imbalance of 10 MWh is made up of supplies from other traders.

This simple example can be used to illustrate the role of markets and other institutions needed to facilitate competition in electricity. The process by which this set of trades is arranged and settled pin-points the roles that need to be performed for each network. The four stages of the process are: gaining access to the network; arranging the energy contract; scheduling and dispatching actual flows; and settling the imbalance between contracts and actual flows. Only some of these stages involve the MO, as explained in the following sections.

Network Access

First, either the seller or the buyer (or both) needs *to pay for the right to use the network* for their transactions. The seller must have the right to deliver 110 MWh onto the network, and the buyer must have the right to take 120 MWh from the network. Between them, they must also possess the rights which allow the seller to transmit 100 MWh over the network to the buyer. Network users buy these rights from network owners, or from a Transmission System Operator (TSO) appointed to run several networks jointly. The definition of these rights and the associated pricing principles are discussed in Chapter 14.

---

[3] The example works just as well for any *net* inputs and offtakes, e.g. flows over interconnectors, load management, cut-backs in generation, etc. The following example is set out in terms of generation and consumption for the sake of clarity. Physical losses on the network are also ignored for simplicity.

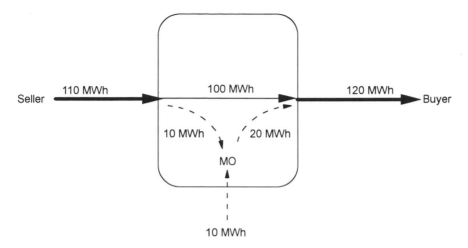

Figure 12.1   Settlement of imbalances

Arranging Contracts

Next, the seller and the buyer have *to negotiate and agree a contract* for the sale of 100 MWh. They may do this entirely bilaterally, or they may be put into contact with one another through a centralised market arrangement. Markets can themselves perform any of a number of functions.

- *Provision of information.* Many markets operate as simple "bulletin boards" on which sellers post offers and buyers post bids. Arrangement of contracts is left to the contracting parties.
- *Identification of trading opportunities.* If a seller offers a low price and a buyer bids a high price, there is potential for trade between them. Some market organisations expand into the role of broker, identifying the potential and helping the traders to reach agreement.
- *Price setting by market maker.* Some market organisations expand out of trading organisations. Instead of trading purely for their own purposes, market makers offer prices at which they will buy and sell any quantities, according to standard terms for the size of the delivery, delivery date and location, and so on. They raise and lower the prices to maintain a balance of supply and demand, so that their posted prices become acknowledged as a good indicator of "the" market price, i.e. the market price for a trade on the standard terms quoted by the market maker. Other traders can use this price as an indicator of the appropriate price for their own contracts.[4]

---

[4] In 1995, the proposals for "direct retail access" in California effectively awarded the role of market maker to incumbent utilities.

- *Price setting by auction.* In some markets, the price is identified in an auction. Many traders (and regulators) prefer public auctions, so that the price can be observed by all present. Unlike market makers, auctioneers do not participate in any trades.[5]

Usually, as long as there is plenty of time to agree the terms before delivery is required, electricity traders prefer to arrange contracts bilaterally. Centralised markets for electricity run by the Market Operator are more important for shorter-term contracts, i.e. for electricity to be delivered in the immediate future, such as a week, a day or an hour later. The reason for this dichotomy is the conflict between transactions costs and the convenience of standard terms. Negotiating specific terms to suit the conditions of each party is expensive and is often only worthwhile if the contract covers a large volume and is expected to last for many months or even years. For smaller transactions, on a shorter time-scale, it makes sense for traders to adopt the standard terms of the market in order to save the cost of protracted negotiations, even if the terms do not exactly suit the requirements of either trader.

Scheduling and Dispatch

A further reason for the involvement of the MO in short term transactions is the role of the dispatcher. The operator of the network often requires traders to submit information about their contracts as the basis for planning the real pattern of energy flows. This is known as "scheduling contracts". However, in any electricity system, conditions change very rapidly, sometimes from second to second. Traders are not expected to revise their contracts as fast as conditions change, so the system operator or dispatcher is given the task of adjusting output in the short term.

To carry out this function, the dispatcher needs to be able to command flexible power plants to increase or decrease their output as fast as load varies. Some commands demand an instant response (dispatch instructions), whilst some commands give the power plant time to start-up or ramp-up slowly (scheduling instructions).[6] These commands must be treated as electricity purchases and sales: the generator sells more electricity when asked to increase output and buys back electricity when asked to decrease output. In Figure 12.1, for example, additional input of 10 MWh is bought at short notice from "other generators".

---

[5] This approach applies in England and Wales and in Norway.
[6] "Scheduling" is sometimes called "commitment".

The centralised nature of the dispatcher's role requires a centralised market to log, price and settle the transactions associated with scheduling and dispatch. This role falls to the MO who is responsible for settling imbalances. Often, the MO uses on the price of short-term transactions in scheduling and dispatch to set the price for imbalances.

In some cases (notably the Electricity Pool in England and Wales), the dispatcher attaches such high importance to system security that traders' contracts play no role in deciding who produces. All physical flows over the network are decided by a central dispatcher and are settled by the MO. Contracts between traders have to be settled entirely outside the Pool. A later section shows the different methods of scheduling and settling contracts and how they produce equivalent results. For the remainder of this explanation, we assume that (at least some) contracts are scheduled and are notified to the MO.

Settlement of Imbalances

Because no trader can guarantee to fulfil exactly any contract with other traders or with the dispatcher, discrepancies are bound to arise between trades arranged in advance and actual flows over the network. Traders must agree to pay for any electricity they take off the network in the form of imbalances— and they will want to be paid for any electricity they accidentally supply to the network. Before they begin trading, therefore, both the seller and the buyer approach the MO responsible for settling imbalances on the network concerned. They sign the MO's settlement agreement and open a settlement account. They may then begin trading.

The MO's settlement procedure for the quantities in Figure 12.1 is described in Table 12.1 and explained overleaf:

Table 12.1   Settlement accounts for a fixed volume contract

	MO	Seller	Buyer	Others
Contracts		−100	+100	
Generation		+110		+10
Consumption			−120	
Imbalances	+10	−10		
	−20		+20	
	+10			−10

+ = Generation or Purchase
− = Consumption or Sale

- both the seller and the buyer inform the MO of the quantity (in this case 100 MWh) to be sold under their contract in the current period; the MO checks that the figures reported by both sides agree and enters the contract volume as a debit against the seller and a credit for the buyer;
- the MO then records the output of every generator as a credit, in this case 110 MWh for the seller and 10 MWh for other sources;
- the MO records consumption as a debit of 120 MWh against the buyer;
- the MO then identifies imbalances as the net purchases and net sales which balance the accounts for each party;
- the MO sets a price for each imbalance and settles each outstanding imbalance as a purchase or sale at the appropriate price.

In the settlement account shown in Table 12.1 for the trades in Figure 12.1, the MO buys 10 MWh from the seller and sells 20 MWh to the buyer. The balance of 10 MWh is made up by the MO, as purchases from other sources. The agreed basis for settling trades at the margin allows any contract to stand, regardless of actual flows.

On any single network, the MO occupies the position of a monopoly, since no-one else is able to settle imbalances. If the MO is part of an integrated utility which is competing with the seller to supply the buyer, the prices charged by the MO for buying and selling imbalances may have to be regulated. Alternatively, the MO might be established as a club or "pool", in which traders agree an administrative or competitive process for setting the price of imbalances. Such processes are discussed below in the section on price setting. If the pool uses a competitive process to set the price of imbalances, the extent of the MO's market power is rather limited. The only area which might require regulatory oversight is the charge for pool membership because each MO enjoys a monopoly over the roles it performs for the network.

Full Requirements Contracts

Figure 12.2 shows an alternative form of contract, usually called a full requirements contract, in which the contract volume is defined by the buyer's actual consumption of 120 MWh. This means that the contracting parties cannot tell the MO in advance what volume will be sold by contract, but can only provide volume information after the buyer's meter has been read. Such contracts slow up the process of settlement, but can be settled in the same way as other types of contract.

Table 12.2 shows how settlement proceeds, now that the contract volume is 120 MWh. The seller is responsible for the full difference between his own generation of 100 MWh and the buyer's consumption of 120 MWh. The buyer has no imbalance, because the contract covers all his requirements.

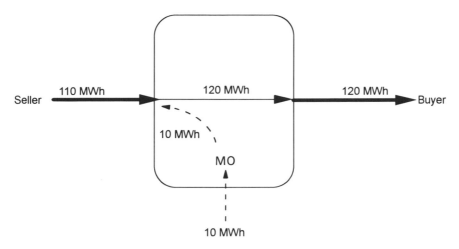

Figure 12.2   Full requirements contract on a single network

Table 12.2   Settlement accounts for a full requirements contract

	MO	Seller	Buyer	Others
Contracts		−120	+120	
Generation		+110		+10
Consumption			−120	
Imbalances	+10	−10		
	0		0	
	+10			−10

+ = Generation or Purchase
− = Consumption or Sale

The MO still makes up the seller's imbalance, by buying 10 MWh from other sources.

In each case, the MO is merely a conduit for imbalances; its sales equal its purchases. If the MO uses the same price to settle all imbalances in any period, the MO will be left with no profit or loss after clearing all the settlement accounts. The only effect of changing the size of the contract is to shift liabilities for imbalances between the buyer and the seller.

Roles Performed by a Market Operator

The clearest example of a MO operating in the way described above is found in Norway, in the operations of Statnett Marked (SM), the state grid electricity market. SM receives information on hundreds of contracts every day, both before and after delivery has taken place. The information covers contract volumes, but not prices. SM enters the contract volumes into the settlement accounts of all generators, wholesalers, retailers and customers who choose to trade over the most important networks in Norway.[7] The settlement process follows the procedure set out above very closely:

- SM credits members for contract purchases and debits them for contract sales;
- SM also operates some short-term markets, and pool members are credited for purchases and debited for sales in these markets;
- the difference between total net credits and actual net consumption is recorded as a net sale (or purchase) of "regulerkraft" ("regulation power");
- SM sends out invoices for sales and purchases of "regulerkraft", and for the other transactions arranged in pool markets, but not for the contracts themselves;
- payment of money due under the contracts is arranged by the seller and buyer involved.

This example shows a pool which has extended its functions beyond the simple settlement of net imbalances, into operation of short-term markets. However, the Norwegian electricity pool could change its functions in two specific ways. First, it could reduce the number of short-term markets it operates. (Currently, it operates a long-term weekly market and a daily market, as well as the market for "regulerkraft".) Secondly, it could abandon the attempt to record contract volumes, especially if the number of customers trading through the pool continues to grow as a result of liberalisation. The abandonment of these functions would leave only imbalances to be handled by SM, with contracts being settled entirely outside the pool. This is in fact how the Electricity Pool for England and Wales operates, as explained below.

The MO's Role in Scheduling Contracts

The examples in Figures 12.1 and 12.2 assume that traders inform the MO of their contracts. This is the normal starting point for most discussions of competitive trading arrangements, which begin when customers are allowed to sign contracts with distant generators. However, it is perfectly possible for contracts to be settled bilaterally between the seller and the buyer, without

---

[7] Some distribution companies remain outside the pool and effectively operate their own settlement accounts for traders using their networks.

Table 12.3   Settlement accounts without contracts

	MO	Seller	Buyer	Others
Contracts		0	0	
Generation		+110		+10
Consumption			−120	
Imbalances	+110	−110		
	−120		+120	
	+10			−10

+ = Generation or Purchase
− = Consumption or Sale

involving the MO at all. Using the same data as in Figure 12.2, the settlement table for the MO would then be as shown in Table 12.3.

In Table 12.3, contract volumes are set to zero. Imbalances simply equal the actual inputs and offtakes of each trader with a settlement account. Under the rules of this type of MO, the seller's output is paid for in full as an imbalance and the buyer has to pay for total consumption as an imbalance. However, the seller and the buyer can restore the position reached in Table 12.2, by agreeing *between themselves* to settle a financial contract for 120 MWh. The settlement of this account is shown in Table 12.4, using an equivalent format.

This bilateral account omits any reference to generation or consumption, but it contains the missing contract for the sale of 120 MWh from the seller to the buyer. This implies a corresponding "imbalance", which would normally be settled by delivering electricity. However, the buyer has already taken delivery from the network, at the price quoted by the MO. To settle the contract, therefore, the seller agrees to give the buyer the cash value of 120 MWh of electricity bought from the MO (in lieu of delivered electricity). This method of settling energy contracts was discussed in Chapter 9, under Contracts for Differences.

Table 12.4   Bilateral account for contract settlement

	Seller	Buyer
Contracts	−120	+120
Imbalances	+120	−120

+ = Generation or Purchase
− = Consumption or Sale

Contracts for Differences, payments and dispatch

When the Market Operator no longer schedules physical contracts, the pattern of dispatch and payments will not change. Net payments are identical in both cases, which means that traders have no reason to change their behaviour. If this is difficult to believe, the following example may help.

Supposing the contract price is $10/MWh, whilst the price of imbalances is $15/MWh. In Table 12.2, the seller's receipts consist of $1200 (120 MWh at $10/MWh) under the contract, less $150 paid to the MO for an imbalance of 10 MWh at $15/MWh. The seller's net receipts are therefore $1050.

In Table 12.3, the seller and the buyer sign a Contract for Differences (CfD) which is settled bilaterally, as explained in Chapter 9. Since the MO ignores such contracts, the seller earns $1650 from the MO for a total (positive) imbalance of 110 MWh at $15/MWh. The seller also earns $1200 from the buyer, for a contract sale of 120 MWh at $10/MWh, making $2850 in total. However, under the CfD, the seller must return to the buyer the cash value of the contract volume at the spot market price, i.e. the value of 120 MWh at $15/MWh, or $1800. The seller's net earnings are therefore $2850 minus $1800, or $1050, just as in the previous example! A similar calculation will show that the same property holds for the buyer.

If scheduled contracts are notified to the MO, the volume of imbalances is equal to the variations around scheduled flows. If the MO ignores contracts, all physical generation and consumption is treated as an imbalance by the MO, although the bulk of sales through the MO's markets are offset by bilateral settlement of contracts. The choice of settlement method does not affect the marginal cost of each generator, nor the least cost pattern of generation, nor (under efficient pricing rules) the spot market price.

This example also provides an oppotunity to consider the implications of such contracts for operational efficiency. Whether the contract is physically scheduled or a financial CfD, reducing the seller's output reduces the seller's imbalance, but leaves the contract volume unchanged. Reducing output by 1 MWh therefore reduces the seller's earnings by the spot price of $15.

Now, the seller can fulfil the contract in a number of ways, either by using own-production, or by buying imbalances from the MO at the spot market price, or by buying from others (at a price similar to that offered by the MO). A rational seller will choose the lowest cost source. The seller will therefore decide to generate only if the costs of own production are less than the MO's spot price of $15/MWh, *regardless of the contract price*.

This is a remarkable result. If the price of imbalances quoted by the MO reflects market conditions (as we discuss later in this chapter), decisions about dispatch and maintenance will be taken by comparing costs with the spot market price (current or expected), which means that generating plant will only be used when it is efficient. In contrast, PPAs lock in the incentives for operations and maintenance at the time of signature; if these incentives are not based on market prices, they may distort operating decisions. The combination of bulk power contracts and market pricing of imbalancing therefore offers the prospect of much greater efficiency than PPAs.

Bulk power contracts in practice

The Electricity Pool for England and Wales was set up from scratch in 1990. At that time, it was decided that central collation and assembly of information about electricity contracts would be costly and inefficient. The National Grid Company also wished to retain control over scheduling and dispatch, to maintain the security of the system during a very difficult transitional period. The dispatchers therefore pay no attention to generators' contracts with their customers. Instead, they schedule and dispatch all generation in the least-cost manner consistent with system requirements. The Electricity Pool provides the market for all physical output of the generating companies and for all real consumption. Both generation and consumption are treated as a form of imbalance, to be settled at the pool price.

Electricity contracts still exist within England and Wales; in fact, at any time, they apply to 80% or more of all sales of electricity. They are negotiated and settled entirely by the contracting parties, but they are settled bilaterally, with reference to the price quoted by the pool. The pool is therefore able to avoid any involvement in the thousands of contracts between generators and their customers.

A full explanation of the workings of the Electricity Pool for England and Wales is given in Appendix B.

Imbalances and Metering Requirements

In Figure 12.2, the imbalances covered by the MO's settlement accounts depend on metered flows and on any contract sales data provided by traders. The imbalances in settlement accounts are calculated by subtracting contract sales data from the seller's actual deliveries into the network, and from the buyer's actual consumption. The accuracy with which deliveries and consumption are measured depends upon the quality of the metering.

If imbalances are settled at a constant price all year round, the MO need only meter total integrated demands once a year (or every few months, for convenience of billing). The imbalance of any consumer simply equals total metered consumption minus total contract purchases. All such imbalances are charged at the same price during the year concerned and it does not matter when the imbalances arise.

In fact, many networks have cost conditions and prices which change by the hour, in which case the MO will want to measure consumption (and contract purchases) every hour.[8] If the meter is read less frequently, it will be impossible to tell whether an imbalance occurred during a high-price period or a low-price period. The MO might charge the average price over all periods between meter readings, but there is a risk that the consumer actually consumed more than average in high-price periods and less than average in low-price periods, in which case the MO will be out of pocket (or, more likely, will recover the loss from other users of the network). In principle, each MO will want to measure deliveries and consumption at least as frequently as the price of imbalances changes. *Hourly trading therefore requires hourly metering.*

Traders who refuse to fit hourly metering are not trading with the market, because they do not pay the true hourly cost of their purchases, but are instead pushing the MO into the role of a retailer, quoting average price tariffs. This role may be unacceptable to the MO, or to other traders. If the MO is to limit its role to settling imbalances at the appropriate price, the MO must be allowed to specify appropriate metering standards as a condition of trading over the network.[9]

Summary of Settlement Requirements

This section has explained how discrepancies, both small and large, can arise between contract sales and actual flows over any single network. We refer to these discrepancies as "imbalances". Each network (or the traders using the network) must therefore appoint a Market Operator who accounts for and charges for these imbalances. The MO must operate a *settlement system* which at the very least carries out the following roles:

- measuring the difference or "imbalance" between actual net output (or consumption) and net contract sales (if notified to the MO);
- deciding who is a *net buyer* and who is a *net seller* of imbalances;
- putting a *price* on the net purchases and sales of imbalances; and
- arranging for *settlement* of imbalances in a way that does not lead to disputes or high transactions costs.

---

[8] The Electricity Pool of England and Wales has adopted a half-hour settlement period.

[9] The pools in both Norway, and England and Wales have decided to opt for the use of "consumer load profiles" as a way to allocate integrated demands to hourly or half-hourly settlement periods. This approach avoids the need for many consumers to install expensive time-of-day meters. However, in both cases, the pool has established a protocol for sharing any errors in allocating total generation to individual consumers or to physical losses. Consumers without time-of-day meters therefore participate in a joint cost-sharing scheme, instead of trading exclusively on their own behalf. Furthermore, implementation of load profiles has proven extremely difficult. In 1994, the pool auditor for England and Wales was forced to qualify the pool's accounts because he could not be certain whether every customer had been charged the right amount.

In order to carry out these roles, the MO will normally need:

● to specify the standard of *metering* to be installed by each generator and customer (or their appointed agents).

An example of this procedure is found in Norway, where the electricity market receives information on the volume of sales by contract, and organises a number of short-term markets (e.g. a week ahead of the delivery time). However, its main function is to calculate and settle instantaneous imbalances recorded as "regulerkraft" ("regulation power").

Settlement of imbalances is the only role for which an MO is an absolute requirement. The MO may also settle other forms of transaction as a service to traders if, for example, it is more efficient to handle short-term trades centrally. However, the MO does not need to receive any information about wholesale contracts, as they can be settled by other parties (including the seller and buyer themselves). If traders do not notify their energy contracts to the MO, all physical generation and consumption will appear as imbalances. The Electricity Pool for England and Wales runs a day-ahead market for generators, but measures both output and consumption as an imbalance. It plays no role in the settlement of contracts.

In order to carry out its basic functions, the MO must be able to measure actual deliveries into and out of the network as often as the price of imbalances changes. This means that the MO may have to lay down conditions for the standard of metering to be installed by any trader who wishes to buy or sell electricity over the network.

However, measuring imbalances is only the first step in operating a settlement system. A price must also be attached to any imbalances, before the MO can send out an invoice. This price is very important because it provides the incentive for efficient operation and trading. We will therefore turn next to the thorny question of how prices should be set for spot trades and imbalances.

SETTING THE PRICES

If the spot market could be organised as a set of bilateral deals, negotiation over the price could effectively be left to the trading parties. However, there must be some kind of pricing rule for imbalances. As we shall see, these pricing rules become central to the character of the whole electricity market.

Why are pricing rules needed at all? Because they make it easier for traders to agree a price in conditions where a trade must be agreed quickly. In electricity spot markets, both the buyer and the seller have something to gain from trade, but there may be a long drawn out period of haggling during which they argue about the allocation of the gains from trade. It is even more difficult to reach agreement if buyer and seller are negotiating the price for an imbalance which has already been delivered. The seller would no longer have any bargaining power and the buyer could refuse to pay anything. Ultimately, this might lead to the collapse of the trading system, or to inefficient methods of dispatch which fail to exploit economic opportunities for trade.

Unnecessary delays in reaching agreement over both spot trades and imbalances can be avoided, if all potential buyers and sellers agree in advance on a formula which allocates the gains from trade fairly. The price rule also has to meet certain efficiency criteria but, usually, a price which is efficient will also be accepted as a basis for sharing the gains for trade (which suggests that the allocative question may be secondary). However, the efficiency criteria are complicated. When establishing a price setting rule, the division of gains will sometimes seem more important than the efficient identification of trading opportunities.

Efficiency Criteria

The chief criterion for selecting a price setting rule is that it should achieve the same results as efficient central dispatch based on marginal costs. This may be interpreted in one of two ways:

- in a bilateral trading system, it should permit all cost-saving energy trades; and
- in a centrally dispatched system, it should make generators willing to accept dispatch instructions issued by the central dispatcher.

This criterion can be translated into a number of subsidiary conditions.

At the very least, the price must be set high enough for the generator to be prepared to supply, i.e. the price must be higher than the marginal costs of the supplier. Ideally, the price should also be below the marginal costs of any more expensive generators which are not required. The generator told to run will then be prepared to do so; generators not told to run will not want to.

Similar conditions should apply to buyers. The price must be lower than the marginal value placed on electricity by the buyer and no potential buyer should be prevented from obtaining energy at that price if prepared to do so. In Model 1 pools, where buyers and sellers are other utilities, the buyer's valuation is the cost of the generator displaced. Pool members are required to reveal their costs as a condition of membership, so this value is well known and the conditions are usually met. In other types of pool, the provision of price signals from customers is somewhat under-developed.

A pricing rule which achieves all of these aims will set prices at which traders are always willing to accept central dispatch. This is important for more than just the settlement of imbalances. Even if a trader signs a contract, the trader retains the option of leaning more or less heavily on the suppy of imbalances. For example, a seller will decide whether or not to generate the amount in a contract, depending upon whether the price for imbalances is higher or lower than the cost of running his or her own plant. A buyer will decide whether to consume electricity from the network, or whether to run a generator instead (if one is available) using the same criterion. The market for imbalances always provides an alternative to using one's own generation. The price for imbalances is therefore a major determinant of the willingness (or otherwise) of generators to follow dispatch instructions.

In addition, the market for imbalances competes with longer-term transactions as a means for trading electricity. Generators need not sell their output at a price lower than the price they expect to be offered for imbalances. Similarly, customers need not agree to buy electricity at any price higher than the price they expect to pay for imbalances. Consequently, the price for imbalances plays a major role in setting the price for other contracts and underpins the revenue of the sector as a whole. In Models 3 and 4, where competitive markets provide the only means for recovering the costs of generation, the pricing rule for imbalances underpins the efficiency of investment decisions. The following sections therefore consider different pricing rules, before returning to the question of cost recovery.

Market or "Opportunity Cost" Pricing Rules

In recent years, the development of pricing rules has been devoted to eliminating the scope for "gaming", in other words, to removing any incentive for traders to lie about their costs. This is particularly important in a competitive market, where producers will not generally allow their costs to be scrutinised by others. In general, the solution is to ensure that the price for any single trade is set at the level dictated by general market conditions, without regard to the costs of the buyer and seller concerned. This prevents traders from gaining a higher (or lower) price by manipulating their cost information. By implication, traders can be expected to quote their costs correctly.

This does not mean that the price can be set arbitrarily. The incentive to declare cost information accurately will actually be greater if the market price is set according to the "opportunity cost" of the commodity being traded.

The opportunity cost is the value of the commodity in alternative uses. In most cases, the alternative opportunity is defined by cutting back supply from the current level, and saving the inputs for alternative opportunities (i.e. production of another commodity, or of the same commodity at another time). At such times, the opportunity cost is the additional cost of supplying the marginal unit of the commodity. Occasionally, however, supply and demand can only be balanced by rationing demand, in which case the opportunity cost

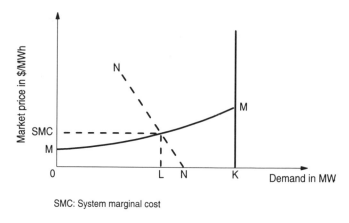

SMC: System marginal cost

Figure 12.3 Opportunity cost = system marginal cost of generation

is the value of the commodity in its marginal use.[10] These general concepts can be applied to electricity, as explained below.

The marginal cost of additional output

In the electricity industry, the marginal cost of extra output ("system marginal cost" or SMC[11]) is defined as the *offer price of the highest cost generator which is currently running*. This cost can be inferred from data on system configuration.

Figure 12.3 sets out the calculation in graphical terms. The horizontal axis measures demand on the system in MW. The upward sloping line MM shows the marginal cost of all power plant on the system, arranged in ascending order. For a least-cost dispatch, the cheapest plant is dispatched first and more expensive plant is only used as demand rises. Total capacity on the system is shown at the point K.

In normal circumstances, demand for electricity can be represented by the dashed line NN.[12] The market is in balance at the demand of L. The SMC

---

[10] These concepts and arguments are part of conventional economic theory and it is not our intention to explain them in detail here. Interested readers will find an adequate discussion in most economics textbooks.

[11] In England and Wales, although there is a presumption that generators offer a price related to costs, there is no rule requiring them to do so. For this reason, the same variable is called the "System Marginal Price" (SMP) in England and Wales..

[12] The gradient on the line shows how much consumers interrupt or reduce their demand as the price rises.

is defined as the marginal cost of the last plant dispatched to meet demand, i.e. the marginal cost of the most expensive generator running. The SMC is the economic value of electricity at times when demand can be met with available capacity.

Identification of the SMC begins with an analysis of the marginal costs of generating electricity. For thermal generators (i.e. steam and combustion turbines), the cost information used for dispatch usually comprises three major elements:

- "start-up cost" for starting up the generator;
- "no-load cost" per hour for remaining connected to the system (even if "idling" with "no load"); and
- one or more "incremental costs" per MWh for actual generation at different levels of output.[13]

There is some question as to which costs should be attributed to production of any particular MWh of output. Some definitions of the SMC include just the incremental costs of generation, whilst some also include a share of the start-up and no-load costs.[14] In addition, the costs of running any generator are dependent upon non price characteristics, such as "ramp-rates" (maximum rates of change in output) and "minimum stable generation" (at the lowest setting for burners).

The correct approach depends upon the timing of the transaction, because more costs are "marginal" (i.e. can be avoided) with longer advance warning. Instantaneously, the SMC may well be represented by the incremental cost of generating an additional MWh from a generator which has already started up and is "on-line". A day in advance, however, generators will be reluctant to obey scheduling instructions unless they can be sure that the price for producing energy will allow them to recover the additional start-up and no-load costs. The pricing rule may also have to allow for non-price characteristics, e.g. by identifying inflexible plant which is unable to meet incremental demand, and excluding it from the calculation of the SMC.

---

[13] This structure of offer prices is found even in the competitive spot market for England and Wales. It was adopted because generators could not be sure how long their plant would run each day, nor what price it would earn at the time. This disaggregated price structure allows the dispatcher to examine running costs in many different conditions and the Electricity Pool constructs the total offer price per MWh, as appropriate for each plant's actual pattern of generation. The Norwegian hydro system presents generators and dispatchers alike with fewer problems. Running costs depend solely on the value of water behind a dam and, typically, not on plant run times. Generators therefore calculate a single price per MWh which is relayed directly to the dispatcher and to the pool.

[14] The Electricity Pool for England and Wales uses just the incremental cost to identify SMC in off-peak periods, but attributes all start-up and no-load costs to the marginal cost of generation during peak periods.

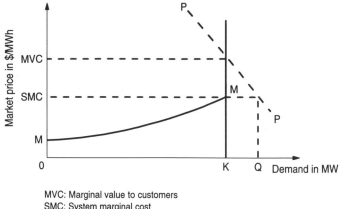

MVC: Marginal value to customers
SMC: System marginal cost

Figure 12.4 Opportunity cost — marginal value to consumers

The marginal value to consumers

The principal behind the marginal value to consumers (MVC) is shown in Figure 12.4. At peak times, the demand for electricity is represented by the line PP. If the market price were to be set at the marginal cost of the most expensive generator (SMC), demand at Q would exceed supply at K. Demand and supply will only balance if the price rises to the level indicated by MVC. Enough consumers will then interrupt (or merely reduce) their demand to bring it in line with available capacity. The MVC is the economic value of electricity when demand is being rationed.

There is less agreement over the value of electricity to the customer than over the measurement of marginal costs. Three main methods seem to be emerging.

1. In the US, wholesalers can usually buy in the spot market at a price based on SMC, but only if they have already bought a "capacity ticket". Traders can only sell capacity tickets if they can show to the pool that they own capacity (i.e. either real plants or contracts or tickets). Capacity tickets are traded in a separate market, for "capacity". The value of "capacity" (i.e. of the option to buy energy at SMC) depends upon the penalty charged by the Pool to any traders who buy more energy than their capacity entitlement.[15] This penalty therefore underpins electricity prices.

---

[15] This system has also been adopted in Argentina, where the capacity charge is set at a fixed level in peak hours. In Chile, wholesale customers buy an annual capacity ticket at the price needed to cover the generators' total costs in each year. These two systems are notable for the degree of competition they allow in energy trading, alongside the organised procedure for checking capacity entitlements.

2. The Norwegian Pool requires customers to bid directly for electricity they wish to purchase (or else it debits them with purchases of "regulerkraft").
3. The system in England and Wales allows a few customers to offer load management, i.e. to quote a price at which they are willing to be cut off, but for most customers the pool simply uses a regulated value, the "Value of Lost Load" (VOLL). In the UK, VOLL is currently set as £2 per kWh, plus an annual adjustment for retail price inflation since April 1990.

This additional element in the price of electricity is vitally important for the ability of generators to recover their total costs through the market and is considered further below.

The pros and cons of market pricing rules

If the market price is derived from information about the costs of the marginal (i.e. most expensive) plant generating at any time, there is little scope for generators to manipulate the market price. Individual generators cannot increase the market price by raising their own offer prices unless they know that their plant is actually at the margin (i.e. setting SMC) or unless there is insufficient competition.[16] Provided that neither of these conditions holds, generators have an incentive to offer a price which is equal to their costs for two reasons:

- if they offer a price which is too high, they may not be dispatched at times when the spot market price is above their real costs;
- if they offer a price which is too low, they may be dispatched at times when the spot market price is below their real costs.

The incentive properties of these rules are important for the efficiency of dispatch. They give generators an incentive to declare cost information accurately. Furthermore, when the generator's plant is dispatched, he will accept the instruction, knowing that the price is bound to exceed his marginal costs. The market pricing rule therefore encourages efficient selection of plant by the dispatcher.

In addition, if the price is "exogenous" to (i.e. not influenced by) a generator's costs, the generator has an incentive to increase efficiency and lower costs. In the short term, any reduction in costs is captured by the generator as increased

---

[16] If any single generator company supplies a large share of the electricity market, it may be able to increase its profits by raising the offer prices of some plant. The output of this particular plant may fall and be replaced by output from other generating companies. However, the net increase in the market price earned for the company's remaining output (from this plant and from its other plants) can more than compensate for any reduction in total sales.

profits. In the longer term, the accumulation of such cost reductions will reduce all the generators' offer prices and hence the SMC. As a result efficiency savings are passed through gradually to customers as lower prices. The market pricing rule therefore encourages efficient operation of generators by their owners.

Hence, market pricing rules not only produce a price at which traders are willing to trade, but also encourage efficient dispatch and operation of generating plant.

Unfortunately, although market pricing rules have all these desirable incentive properties, they tend to be very difficult to implement in practice.

1. The marginal costs of any plant can be difficult to identify, especially if some costs (e.g. start-up costs) are not directly related to any particular unit of output, or if the cost of running plant depends on non-cost information (like ramp-rates). The MO will normally need to liaise closely with the dispatcher in order to capture and process all the necessary information about generator costs.
2. Some dispatch systems allow generators to decide their output regardless of overall system efficiency. The calculation of the SMC must then ignore any costs incurred voluntarily by the generator, for example, in the case of "must-run" plant dispatched at the request of the generator.
3. An electricity network will have different opportunity costs at different points on the system, because the electricity market is segmented by transmission constraints on the grid. (See Chapter 14 on the costs of transmission.)
4. Opportunity costs can also vary from minute to minute, as demand rises and falls. Pricing rules usually operate on a slower basis, with trading periods which last for a half-hour, an hour, or even longer. Some reconciliation between prices for trading periods and the costs in real-time dispatch will be required.
5. There may be insufficient competition between generators (especially in isolated locations), so that the desirable incentive properties of a spot market do not operate.
6. Calculating the marginal cost of hydro plant is particularly difficult since it depends on the expected value of water. Individual generators may not be aware of system conditions which affect this value. On the other hand, the dispatcher may not fully appreciate the cost structure of an individual generator. The calculation often has to combine information from both sources.

Because of these difficulties, electricity markets cannot implement market pricing rules, unless traders are prepared for the price to depend on a large and complex set of calculations. In practice, market pricing rules always include some approximations. Traders must learn how to adjust their offers and bids to compensate for minor distortions. Whether these adjustments affect the efficiency of dispatch depends on how well the generators understand the market pricing rule and the dispatcher's decision process.

The system in England and Wales is an attempt to carry out the necessary calculations for a fully competitive electricity system, albeit with approximations in some places. A number of the problems mentioned above are still unsolved, but the major generators have learned to live with the system and know how to construct their offers in order to achieve their commercial objectives. Sometimes, the generators are accused of quoting offer data which do not match their operating costs. Often, the "distortion" in offer prices is intended to offset an equivalent distortion in the pricing rule. It would be wrong to conclude that the resulting pattern of dispatch is inefficient.

"Pay-as-Bid" Pricing Rules

Even after the inception of a spot market for England and Wales, many traders continue to ask why sellers should not simply be paid the price they ask, which is what happens in any supermarket, after all.[17] Very few (if any) electricity markets practice this rule generally, owing to factors specific to the electricity industry. These factors need to be understood, because they determine what trading procedures are feasible.

To illustrate the problem, consider a hypothetical electricity trading system in which generators are in fact paid the prices that they quote. We call this rule "pay-as-bid". We will consider how this pricing rule would work, first in a market where traders are free to adjust their prices as often as they like, and then in a market where there is some constraint on price flexibility.

Pay-as-bid markets with flexible bidding

Most producers will not quote a price equal to their costs, but a price equal to "what the market will bear". Where customers can choose their supplier from competing sources, they need not bear any price higher than the cost of production of the most expensive producer needed to meet their demand. Any attempt to charge prices above this level will be undercut by other potential competitors. In a competitive electricity market, therefore, all offers and bids would tend to cluster around the economic value of electricity—usually the SMC, but occasionally the MVC. We will assume for the sake of this example that capacity exceeds demand and the economic value depends on the SMC. Only plants with costs higher than SMC would quote higher prices, in each case equal to their own marginal costs.

In these circumstances, the dispatcher would run all those generators quoting prices which are at or below SMC and none of the more expensive generators.

---

[17] The Office of Electricity Regulation was provoked into examining this question in 1994, four years after the start of operations by the pool.

The pattern of dispatch would be the same as it would be with full knowledge of each generator's cost conditions, and the price would equal (system) marginal cost, as required for economic efficiency. So far, the pay-as-bid system seems to work. However, consider the response required when conditions change.

If demand rises, an additional, more expensive generator will be dispatched. The generator chosen will be the next most expensive, since the dispatcher has price quotes reflecting the cost of all generators which were not running before. Generators who were running already will now revise their prices up to the new, higher SMC, because they know that is what the customers are prepared to pay. The "cluster" of prices around SMC will therefore move upwards to the new economic value.

Similarly, if load falls, the dispatcher will have to remove some plant, because the customers' marginal valuation of electricity will fall below the current price. If all generators continue to offer the previous SMC, the dispatcher will pick one at random to dispatch to a lower load. However, most generators will want to continue running. Only the marginal generator will continue to offer a price equal to its own marginal costs. All the other generators will revise their prices downwards, to the new economic value, so that they continue to run. The dispatcher will know which plant should be told to run down, since it will be offering a higher price than all the rest.

Hence, in a system where generators are paid the price they offer, they need to revise their offer prices as frequently and as fast as conditions change in the market. If they do not, they will lose income when demand rises, and may be dispatched inefficiently when demand falls. It is not feasible or efficient to pay producers the price they offer, unless they can revise their offers as frequently and as fast as market conditions change.

If there is any constraint on the rate of change of offer prices, the dispatcher will be presented with out of date information, which may result in "wrong trades", i.e. the inefficient selection of producers.

Pay-as-bid markets in electricity

As far as electricity markets are concerned, the freedom to revise prices depends upon the level at which trading takes place.

If the sellers in the electricity markets are *individual generator plants*, it is *extremely* unlikely that they will be able to change their offer prices every time system conditions change.

Normally, the dispatcher requires generators' offer prices to be constant and valid over several hours or even days. This allows the dispatcher to optimise the dispatch over a longer period, taking into account any time constraints such as ramp-rates. If generators' offer prices changed every time system conditions changed, the job of the dispatcher would probably be impossible.

On the other hand, if trading is carried out on a *utility-to-utility* basis (e.g. with each utility providing one set of offers to supply), each utility may be able to appoint a trader who changes the quoted prices every minute. This trader can revise prices to keep them in line with efficient market prices on the wider system, without upsetting dispatch on the local system.

Even if trade is conducted on a utility-to-utility basis, it may be difficult to update prices as frequently as is required, since not all traders will have detailed knowledge of the cost conditions on other systems (and hence they will not know the efficient market price on the wider system).

Whether the spot market is established as a market for individual generators or for system traders, it is unlikely that offer prices will be able to vary as quickly as system conditions. Traders are usually required to quote the same price information for longer periods. As a result, it is difficult to ensure that price information accurately reflects current market conditions. Some kind of price setting rule is normally required to convert static information from traders into fluctuating market prices.

These price setting rules must encourage both sellers and customers to quote stable prices (offers and bids) that are consistent with efficient dispatch. Experience suggests that opportunity cost pricing works best.

Other Price Setting Rules for Electricity Markets

Several other formulae have been proposed and implemented to allow generators and customers to quote fairly stable prices which:

● divide the gains of trade "fairly" (as closely as possible to the result that would be achieved in a competitive market); and
● encourage generators and customers to quote information which permits efficient dispatch, i.e. their marginal costs.

The record of pricing rules which ignore opportunity costs is not one of success and markets which use them tend to collapse. The following sections examine two rules which are commonly found in electricity pools: "penalty rates" and the "split-savings rule". Our discussion is intended to show what problems they cause.

Penalty rates

A common starting point for discussion of prices for imbalances is the suggestion that traders should be penalised for failing to abide by the scheduled inputs and offtakes they have notified to the dispatcher. Imbalances are penalised if traders are charged a high price for deficits and are also paid a low price for surpluses. For example, suppose the penalty were ten times the market price for deficits, and one-tenth the market price for surpluses. In an electric sector where the market price of energy was commonly $10/MWh, the price for a deficit would be $100/MWh, and the price for a surplus $1/MWh.

The purpose of such penalties is to encourage traders to abide by scheduled flows, or to encourage them to rearrange their schedules if they foresee an imbalance. For some time now, this method of pricing imbalances has been used successfully in the US gas industry. Traders are encouraged to "balance" their inputs and offtakes by the imposition of penalty rates for any outstanding imbalances. For the most part, this encourages traders to avoid imbalances. However, several factors suggest that this system is not appropriate to the electric sector.

Traders can avoid penalty rates if they arrange to trade their surpluses and deficits amongst themselves, instead of letting them accrue as imbalances. Such trading takes time—time which is available within the relatively slow moving, daily or monthly gas markets. Electricity is commonly traded on an hourly basis, or even a half-hourly basis, with very different prices for different periods. Conditions can change even within these short periods, if only because of a sudden forced outage at a generator or at a consumer's premises. Traders would find it extremely difficult to match their inputs (generation and net purchases from other networks) to offtakes (sales to customers) in time to avoid hourly or half-hourly imbalances.

What is more, the dispatcher would find it very difficult to operate the system, if traders were continually making minor adjustments to their inputs, in anticipation of possible imbalances. Such adjustments might undermine the least-cost nature of dispatch. Instead, dispatchers usually prefer to arrange any last minute rebalancing, by controlling generator outputs on a least-cost basis.

Submitting a power plant to central dispatch is a risky business for the owner. It is much easier to run a generator at some constant level than to try to abide by ever-changing instructions. Centrally dispatched power plants are therefore more likely to run up temporary imbalances. If these imbalances are priced at a punitive rate, generators may be reluctant to offer any flexibility of output to the dispatcher. The task of maintaining system security would then be rendered difficult, if not impossible.

Electricity markets are therefore unlikely to flourish within a framework of penalty rates for imbalances, at least until the mechanisms for control and trade can operate much faster and more accurately than at present. For the immediate future, imbalance prices will have to be more market-based.

"Split-saving" pricing rules

These rules are usually found in power pools which coordinate the dispatch of multiple Model 1 vertically integrated utilities. They can also be applied in spot markets which rely mainly on bilateral trades, such as are used by US utilities for economy energy trades, where low-cost sellers are brought together with high-cost buyers, and where both buyer and seller quote prices related to their costs.

A quick example will show how split savings rules work. Suppose a generator offers to sell electricity at a cost of \$10/MWh (which is his own marginal cost) and that a buyer offers to buy at a price of \$15/MWh (which is actually the cost of a generator on her own system). A broker can help to close the trade at a price of \$12.50/MWh (= average of \$10/MWh and \$15/MWh). If the broker follows a rule of always uniting the lowest-price seller with the highest-price buyer, further trades can be organised until the offers of the remaining sellers are higher than any remaining buyer's bid and there is no potential for any further trade. The price set in this way meets the two criteria:

- it divides the gains of trade ("splits the savings") in approximately the same proportions as the market price would (especially if the market maker always links the highest-priced buyers with the lowest-priced sellers); and
- it guarantees that sellers will be willing to supply and buyers will be willing to take, which is the essence of efficient central dispatch.

However, the split-savings pricing rule can give some buyers and sellers a price at which other, more expensive generators would also have been willing to supply. For example, it is not inconceivable that a generator with costs of \$12/MWh stands idle whilst others trade at \$12.50/MWh. This can lead to criticism of the broker who arranges the trades. Furthermore, even the desirable outcomes listed above are not guaranteed, as the rule used by the broker to link buyers and sellers gives both parties an incentive to lie about their costs. If the seller increases the posted price to \$12/MWh, the closing price of the transaction rises to \$13.50 (= average of \$12 and \$15). If the buyer reduces the bid to \$14, the closing price falls to \$13. Hence, split-savings rules give sellers an incentive to over-state costs, and buyers an incentive to understate their valuation of electricity.

The offers and bids in a split-savings regime therefore tend towards pay-as-bid prices which, as explained above, work efficiently if offers and bids are completely flexible. If prices are not completely flexible, these offers and bids may cause the pattern of generation to become distorted and less efficient.

Power pools operating a split-savings rule try to prevent generators from quoting inaccurate information, usually by auditing each generator's costs at least once a year. Although such audits are supported by the cost-of-service regulation practised in many parts of the world, it can represent a major additional burden on the pool administration. Annual audits of costs tend also to be inconsistent with the free play of competition, since such audits rarely allow the flexibility required in a truly competitive market.

A split-savings rule works if generators always quote prices which reflect their costs and customers always bid their true valuations. However, split-savings rules give everyone an incentive to adjust their prices towards the expected market price, and this may undermine the efficiency of dispatch.

Spot markets applying the split-savings rule must adopt further rules, under which the prices quoted by traders are audited. In principle, most spot markets prefer to avoid the need for auditing, by adopting an opportunity cost pricing rule.

Cost Recovery Pricing Rules and Access to the Market

In an earlier section, we stressed that the price for imbalances becomes the definitive standard for other contract prices in any competitive market. The pricing rule will therefore undermine contract prices if it is distorted by technical dispatch rules.

Many power pools were established by Model 1 vertically integrated utilities not only as a protocol for optimising dispatch, but also as a joint agreement to build and to schedule enough generator capacity to meet demand on their own networks. In these pools, the only "marginal" costs are the incremental costs of each generator. Pool members have to incur the fixed, start-up and no-load costs of generation as a condition of pool membership.

If the price for imbalances is based solely on the incremental costs of the marginal generator, market prices will not cover that generator's no-load or start-up costs, nor will the revenues from sales at market prices cover all the fixed costs of building and maintaining the plant. Customers of the pool would pay only a fraction of the total costs of generation. Such a system is only sustainable if pool members are allowed and able to recover the additional costs from a captive customer base. Effectively, this means that access to the market can only be granted to monopoly utilities which are willing and able to abide by the pool's rules on construction and scheduling.

Even power pools which pay for generator commitment face similar problems. A market price based on start-up, no-load and incremental costs of generation will reward generators for obeying scheduling instructions, but will only cover a small proportion of their fixed costs of construction and maintenance. Hence, if customers were allowed to buy at this price, generators would be unable to recover all their fixed costs. Access to such pools must also be restricted.

The only way to allow open access to electricity markets or power pools is to ensure that the price for imbalances reflects the full costs of generation, i.e. fixed and variable costs alike. This means that the spot market price must occasionally reflect both generators' non-incremental cost and the marginal value to consumers (by whatever means) and must not be tied to generators' incremental costs. If generators are required to incur some costs under a general obligation, and if the spot market price is tied rigidly to the remaining marginal costs of generation, competitive generators will be unable to recover all their costs. Many will go bankrupt *even if their investment and operating decisions are efficient.*

Conclusion on Setting Prices

In any market where traders have different cost conditions, and value the product differently, there must be a process for agreeing the price for each transaction. Even in schemes based on bilateral negotiation, there is scope for delay if there is a large difference between the seller's cost and the buyer's valuation. This suggests why it is normal to use an agreed price setting rule.

1. *Penalty rates* can interfere with the efficiency of trading and dispatch, because of the short term nature of dispatch optimisation in the electric sector.
2. Conventional approaches, such as *"splitting the savings"*, tend to work best in a non-competitive environment. Competition and/or the profit motive will introduce incentives which undermine the efficiency of such arrangements.
3. The best alternative is to base prices on *"opportunity costs"*. Such market pricing rules give good incentives, but can be complicated to implement fully. The main requirement is that generators should be prepared to accept central dispatch, safe in the knowledge that the price will always cover their marginal costs, and that they will not miss profitable opportunities.

The rule for setting prices is often the main topic of debate in any move towards more competitive electricity markets. The method of dispatch and the range of generator cost structures will all be important in deciding which pricing rule can be adopted under which conditions. A crucial decision is how much central direction of the price setting process will be allowed, i.e. which markets the MO will organise centrally.

If there is central dispatch, the dispatcher receives information on costs from generators (or from operators of regional sub-systems). This cost information must be converted into a spot market price for use by the MO in settling imbalances. Under Model 1 (and Model 2), pool members all have a degree of retail monopoly; pool prices need only contain information on the marginal costs of generation, since other costs will be recovered from captive customers. Under Models 3 and 4, however, the potential for competition means that the spot market price must cover generators' total costs. If information on some cost items (e.g. fixed costs) is not provided for the purposes of central dispatch, a proxy for the missing cost items must be drawn from another source. For example, in England and Wales the administered VOLL substitutes in pool prices for the cost of generating capacity.

Finally, it is important to remember that prices—and pricing rules—should encourage not just efficient dispatch and the efficient use of energy but also efficient energy trading. These objectives may dictate a very complicated price setting formula, especially if it is necessary to estimate some generator costs not indicated in dispatch information. However, any rules adopted by electricity markets must balance the need for efficient dispatch and use against the need to limit transactions costs. In many cases, it will be cheaper and more efficient to let individual traders adapt to rough-and-ready pricing rules than to try to capture every piece of market information in a central system.

MAKING ELECTRICITY MARKETS WORK

The creation of competitive markets is a major challenge for any electricity system, but experience from around the world indicates what key elements must be put in place. We are now in a position to summarise the main requirements.

Someone has to be given responsibility for recording and settling imbalances between contracts and actual flows. The role of MO must be performed by a single body for any network, or part of a network, over which traders are allowed to buy and sell electricity.

The MO may or may not record the (scheduled) contracts between traders. However, the MO will coordinate and record short-term trades, including instructions issued by the dispatcher. The MO will meter actual inflows and outflows, for comparison with recorded trades, and will define what standard of metering is acceptable. The MO will calculate what imbalances have occurred due to uncontracted flows and will set a price for each imbalance. The pricing rule should reflect market principles whenever possible. Finally, the MO will issue invoices (and pursue defaulters).

The MO's role is already performed for most electricity networks, at least in a rudimentary fashion. However, the broadening of customer choice and competitive generation to embrace more traders increases the number of imbalances. Settlement methods which rely on "honesty" and "cooperation" may break down. If imbalances are not recorded and settled according to market principles, traders may be able to lean on the network for free supplies of electricity. The role of MO is therefore crucial to contract performance and efficient operation.

The main tool available to the MO to encourage efficiency is the price charged or paid for imbalances between contract and actual flows. The MO can choose which way to measure and to price imbalances, but there are only three main contenders, as described in Table 12.5.

The main choices facing any MO are (a) whether to ask traders to provide information on their contracts (i.e. scheduled flows) and (b) whether to price imbalances at a market rate, or at a penalty rate. If traders notify their contracts, only net imbalances are traded by the MO. This approach has been adopted in the Norwegian electricity pool and is also common in gas markets, especially in the US.

Table 12.5 Conventional types of market operator

Imbalance Pricing Rule	Notification of Scheduled Flows?	
	Yes	No
Market price	Electricity pool in Norway	Electricity pool of England and Wales
Penalty rate	Gas market in the US	n.a.

n.a.: not applicable

The Electricity Pool of England and Wales requires traders to settle their contracts outside the pool; all flows over the network are treated as some form of imbalance. However, as was demonstrated in the discussion of contract settlement, traders are able to achieve the same financial result as if contracts were notified to the pool. The only difference lies in the relative convenience of central and bilateral settlement methods.

The other major dimension of any MO's activities is the rule for pricing imbalances. The US gas market operates efficiently with a penalty rate for imbalances (net of contract nominations), because conditions on a gas system change relatively slowly. Traders have time to react to changes and to avoid building up imbalances. In electricity markets, however, conditions change faster than traders can react. Continual imbalances are a fact of life and have to be priced on a market basis to avoid upsetting the incentives for least-cost dispatch. The pools in Norway and in England and Wales both price imbalances on the basis of an economic valuation of electricity in each period.[18]

The economic value of electricity can normally be derived from the (marginal or incremental) costs of generation, but must also take into account the value to customers. Identifying this economic value can prove troublesome—but has been achieved in some electricity markets around the world, specifically in Norway and in the UK. Many pools in the US take a different, but comparable approach which maintains the distinction between energy costs and the value of capacity to consumers. When applied to competitive markets in Chile, the value of capacity has been regulated to guarantee that generators recover their costs.

This experience suggests that electricity can be bought and sold in competitive spot markets, without upsetting system operations, and without undermining the incentives for investment in generation. However, few industries rely entirely

---

[18] The bottom right-hand corner of Table 12.5 is empty for good reason. A pool which insisted on handling all physical deliveries at penalty prices would be completely unsustainable.

on spot markets. For a variety of reasons, traders prefer to balance their portfolios and to secure their cash flows, by signing long term contracts. The role of electricity spot markets is to provide a degree of flexibility at the margin. Spot markets may also define the price for uncontracted electricity flows, or "imbalances". When used this way, spot market prices underpin all other contract prices. Hence, even if they only handle trade at the margin, electricity spot markets ultimately determine the viability of competitive generation.

APPENDIX B:
THE UK ELECTRICITY POOL

Sir, I can't get William Midwinter's fleeces at under £3 3s 4d the hundred, and I shall go up to that price... I have bought options on 7000 reasonably good fleeces at three pounds.
  Richard Cely to his brother George, a wool merchant, 13 May 1482.

The Electricity Pool of England and Wales can be seen as a set of parallel markets: forward, option and spot. This appendix develops the conceptual framework of the pool, and identifies areas where it might be strengthened.

In England and Wales, electricity is sold through the Electricity Pool, which is often described as a spot market with a different price for each half-hour. Pool prices are published and can be read in several daily newspapers.

Anyone who looks up these prices will notice that they appear in the morning papers for the day on which they apply. In other words, Monday's prices are available in Monday's papers, Tuesday's prices in Tuesday's papers, and so on. Those familiar with the operation of markets may wonder how the pool can function as a spot market when the price is apparently announced in advance.

The key to understanding the pool is to know that the generators' side of the pool has actually been constructed as a set of parallel markets, in which most energy is traded in day-ahead forward markets at the so-called pool price, some is traded via day-ahead option markets, and only a small amount really passes through spot markets.

The purpose of this appendix is:

● to set out the structure of these parallel markets in the pool;
● to show how some of these markets might be developed in future.

THE ENGLAND AND WALES POOL

The Electricity Pool is an unincorporated association of its members:

● The members include all licensed wholesale buyers and sellers of electricity, including such diverse organisations as Electricité de France and fairly small industrial customers.

- The Pool Executive Committee has 10 members: one seat for each of the three major UK generators; two seats for representatives of the smaller generators; one seat for independent retailers ("suppliers"); and four seats for representatives of the 12 regional electricity companies (RECs).
- A Chief Executive administers the pool on a day-to-day basis.

The "pool rules" are set out in Schedule 9 of the Pooling and Settlement Agreement (PSA):

- The pool rules define a set of trading arrangements between pool members.
- The pool cannot trade in its own right, but acts as a holding account for energy purchased from a variety of sources *on behalf of* the customers.

The National Grid Company (NGC), which owns the transmission wires, has several roles in the pool:

- It performs the dispatch of energy as grid operator.
- It supplies operational information (such as demand forecasts) to the pool.
- It administers the pool's settlement system on behalf of the pool members, under the Pooling and Settlement Agreement.
- It computes and publishes the pool prices, in its role as settlement system administrator.
- It buys ancillary services on behalf of pool members.

THE POOL'S TRADING RULES

The pool rules, which dictate how trading takes place, stretch over 300 pages of the PSA.

The pool rules are expressed as a complex series of equations, with a minimum of explanatory text. To the new reader, they are almost impenetrable, but a number of "guides" have been written which explain the settlement process in terms of the following steps.

1. A day in advance of trading, generators submit data on the forecast availability of generating sets ("gensets") and the offer price at which they are prepared to generate. NGC prepares a detailed demand forecast for each half-hour of the coming day.
2. A computer program is used to produce an "Unconstrained Schedule", or "U-Schedule". This is a plan of generation which meets forecast demand at least cost (in terms of offer prices), ignoring any transmission constraints.

3. For any half-hour, the offer price of the marginal (most expensive) genset operating in the U-Schedule determines the "System Marginal Price" (SMP). The Pool Purchase Price (PPP) is equal to the SMP augmented by an element related to the expected degree of capacity surplus on the system.
4. Any genset capacity offered but not needed in the U-Schedule is awarded an availability bonus, which is also related to the expected degree of capacity surplus on the system.
5. On the day, NGC issues instructions to gensets as to when and how much to generate.
6. Where NGC instructs a generator to deviate from the level of U-Schedule output, the change in output is bought or sold by the pool at each genset's own offer price. Failure to meet instructions, or to be available as declared the previous day, is penalised.
7. After all of these transactions have been completed, the price to consumers (Pool Selling Price or PSP) is calculated as the sum of net payments to generators divided by the total amount actually generated.

This type of description does not really explain how the pool works. Apart from the inherent difficulty of following the equations in the pool rules, it is not at all clear what incentives are faced by generators, consumers and the NGC at each stage of the procedure. A better approach is to revert to the *market structure* that lay behind the original design of the pool. Such analysis not only shows what incentives are faced by each player, but also why problems have arisen and will continue to do so.

TAXONOMY OF MARKETS IN THE POOL

The reader may already be familiar with the Contracts for Differences (CfDs) which are written against the PPP, to hedge pool transactions, and which have the economic effect of long-term contracts for power. This aspect of the markets was covered extensively in Chapter 9. The present appendix is concerned only with the shorter-term markets in the pool itself.

Three types of energy transaction are implicit in the pool rules: forward, option and spot. The transactions in the markets follow closely the decision process of the grid operator, NGC, as set out in Figure B.1.

Rather than looking at the pool as a set of equations or as a series of rules, Figure B.1 shows the market processes: there is a day-ahead market in which the generators make *forward sales* to the pool at the PPP. There is an option market in which reserve is sold day-ahead as an *option* to buy energy; if the option is called on the day, output is paid for at its strike price. On the day there is also a *spot market* which reconciles differences. Sales to customers are then made by the pool at the average price of all these markets, PSP.

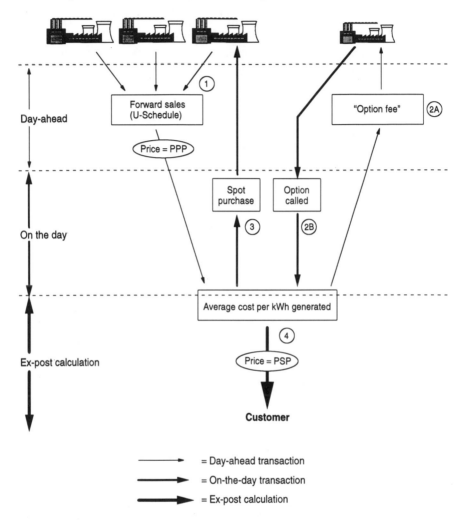

Figure B.1 Poll transactions in every half-hour

We now look in more detail at each of these types of market, and their counterpart in the pool.

Forward Markets

A forward sale in any product is a contract *arranged in advance* between a buyer and a seller which commits the seller to deliver to the buyer a specified quantity of the product at *a later time, at a specified price* and *in a specified place*. In any such contract, the price reflects the expected value of the product at the time of delivery.

In the pool, the U-Schedule can be seen as a record of contracts arranged in advance. The outputs in each half-hour of this generation plan are treated as the acceptance of offers to generate, or as *forward contracts* to deliver energy in the respective half-hour, a day later. The price paid for these planned outputs by the pool is the respective Pool Purchase Price (PPP) for the half-hour (transaction 1 in Figure B.1). PPP is the forward market price, one for each half-hour of the coming day.

PPP is the expected value of energy, looking one day ahead. It is derived by complicated equations from the offer prices of those generators whose bids are accepted, after allowing for the value of lost load (VOLL) and the loss of load probability (LOLP). The market concepts behind the PPP are explained more fully below.[1]

Option Markets

An option contract in any product is also *arranged in advance*, but whereas a forward sale is a commitment to deliver and to take delivery, an option contract gives the holder the right to buy (or sell) an item from (or to) a trader, *only if the holder wishes*. The terms of the sale include the time and place of delivery, and the price, the *strike price*, to be paid on delivery. A trader only offers ("writes") such a contract in return for a fixed fee, the "option fee". This fee reflects the expected value to the holder of being able to obtain (or offload) an item at the *strike price*, given that the spot market price may be higher or lower at the time of delivery.

For any capacity which is declared available a day in advance but which is not committed in the U-Schedule (referred to here as "reserve capacity"), the pool pays the generator an *option fee* (Transaction 2A in Figure B.1). If such capacity is instructed to generate, the output is paid for at the *strike price*, defined as the generator's own offer price (Transaction 2B in Figure B.1).

Reserve capacity may be called under an option contract because of generator errors, demand forecasting errors or transmission constraints. We will return to the costs imposed by these factors below.

An *option fee* normally reflects the expected value of the *option to buy at the strike price*. In a commodity market, traders would relate the option fee to the expected spot price. However, the next section explains that there is no unique spot price within the pool, so the option fee is set by formula, instead of by competitive bidding. The formula is similar to the capacity (LOLP × VOLL) element of the day-ahead PPP.

---

[1] For detailed discussion of the pool price formula, the technical reader is referred to Crew and Kleindorfer (1) or Green (2). The less technical reader may prefer Hunt (3).

Table B.1 Description of the pool's quasi-spot transactions in energy

Transaction type	Reason	Pricing rule
Retirements (on instruction from grid operator):	Transmission constraint or demand overestimate	Genset's own offer price
Generator errors*	Gensets in the U-Schedule:	
	—declared unavailable	PPP
	—under-generation	Genset's own offer price
	—over-generation	Genset's own offer price
	Gensets not in the U-Schedule:	
	—declared unavailable	Cost of option fee
	—under-generation	Genset's own offer price
	—over-generation	Genset's own offer price
Urgent supplies		Maxgen price

* Persistent generator errors may be subject to a one-off penalty enforced jointly by NGC and the pool.

Spot Markets

A spot market is characterised by *immediate* delivery of the product, with the price varying to equalise supply and demand. Many spot transactions are actually made to undo previous contracts, and to remove the obligation to deliver by making an offsetting deal.

The pool is only a substitute for a true spot market, in that some decisions made *at short notice* are recorded as transactions priced according to special rules (Transaction 3 in Figure B.1). Many of these transactions are made to offset previous commitments, such as forward and option contracts, so that no energy need actually be delivered. Table B.1 sets out the various short notice decisions ("quasi-spot transactions in energy") which cause generators to sell to or buy from the pool. The wide variety of pricing rules shows that there is no unique spot price.

CALCULATION OF PPP—THE FORWARD MARKET PRICE

The value of the PPP is intended to reflect the expected value of the spot market price. In practice, because there is no unique spot market price, the expected value must be calculated by a formula.

In those cases where demand is less than total available generating capacity, the marginal cost of extra supplies would be given in a spot market by the highest offer price of any generator on the system. This price is estimated from the U-Schedule, a day-ahead forecast of generation, and is designated the "System Marginal Price", or SMP. (The derivation of this price was discussed above.)

In cases where demand would exceed total available generating capacity, supply and demand could only be balanced by raising the price to the level where some customers would prefer to reduce their demand. In the absence of active bidding by customers, the regulator has to set this price, which is designated the "Value of Lost Load", or VOLL.

The probability that demand will exceed capacity ("Loss of Load Probability", or LOLP) is calculated by comparing expected demand with the capacity expected to be available, and allowing for each variable to differ from the expected level. The probability of meeting load from available generation is then $(1 - \text{LOLP})$. PPP is then set at the probability-weighted average of the prices in the *two* possible cases:

$$\text{PPP} = [(1 - \text{LOLP}) \times \text{SMP}] + [\text{LOLP} \times \text{VOLL}]$$

MARKET LOCATION AND TRANSMISSION

The pool's design assumes a unified market covering England and Wales, without any separate allowance for location. This allows the pool to operate without having to specify different prices for each location on the grid.

Reconciliation with dispatch

If a generator is unable to fulfil a forward energy sale because the plant is kept off the system by a transmission constraint, the forward sale is cancelled by an offsetting spot transaction on the day, but the generator is compensated by the pool for the lack of transmission. This works as follows.

● *Constrained off.* Generators who have sold output forward at the PPP, but who cannot generate owing to transmission constraints, are allowed to buy back the energy at their own offer price. This is the kind of spot transaction which cancels a previous contract. The net result is to leave the genset with a purely financial surplus equal to PPP less the offer price. Since the offer prices of such generators are usually lower than the PPP, the pool makes a loss on the net deal. This loss is carried forward into "uplift", which is discussed in the next section.

● *Constrained on.* Some generators are called upon to generate, to replace others who are constrained off. In addition, NGC sometimes requires a generator to provide services such as reactive power in particular areas; such plant may also be regarded as "constrained on". These generators, who have not committed plant to a forward sale, have already been paid an option fee; when asked to generate under the option contract, they are paid their offer price, which is usually higher than the PPP. The extra cost above the PPP is carried forward into "uplift".

Implied transmission contracts

The pool's treatment of generators "constrained off" assumes that every trader has a "firm" transmission contract.

Implicit in the design of the pool is an assumption that all traders have access to the transmission facilities they need to complete any trades arranged via the pool. This assumption is not stated in transmission contracts offered by the NGC: it is simply implicit in the fact that the pool compensates generators whenever they are unable to use the transmission network. Paying compensation on this basis is equivalent to reimbursing the generator's lost profit on the forward sale. The compensation is also equal to the short-run (or spot) value of the transmission right being denied.

The result of these transactions is that the full difference in cost between the generators constrained off and those constrained on is carried through into "uplift".

COST SHARING BY CUSTOMERS

The customers' side of the market is simpler: all energy is purchased at the PSP.

The previous sections have shown how generator incomes depend upon a number of different market transactions, each conducted at a variety of prices, of which the PPP is merely the most common. The customers' side of the market (Transaction 4 in Figure B.l) is much simpler. Most customers do not put in bids: NGC estimates the amount of energy that they will require. All of the extra costs of energy above the PPP, including those made necessary by transmission constraints on the National Grid, are simply lumped together in "uplift"[2]

---

[2] The other components of uplift need not concern us in this paper.

and spread over all kWh taken by customers through the calculation of a single half-hourly consumers' price, the PSP.

$$PSP = PPP + uplift$$

Some customers have recently been allowed to start bidding for their demand on an experimental basis. This feature was introduced in 1994, as a result of pressure from the customers concerned. The operation of "demand side bidding" is discussed below.

The extra costs of the balancing transactions in the option and spot markets are initially borne by the pool, but are then carried forward and appear as the energy components of uplift. The costs of the option and spot markets thus appear as part of uplift. They are set out below.

Transmission Constraints

Constraining generators off, and replacing the output by constraining on other generators, incurs additional costs above PPP. All transmission constraints therefore contribute towards uplift.

Demand Forecast Errors

Even in the absence of transmission constraints, the pattern of dispatch will differ from forward sales in the U-Schedule. The volume of forward sales is derived from the NGC's forecast of demand, which will inevitably turn out to be either an overestimate or an underestimate. Supply is then matched to demand, either through exercising some of the option contracts to obtain additional output, or through the quasi-spot transactions required to retire generation, or to call forth urgent supplies.

The costs associated with these transactions also increase uplift.

Generator Errors

When generators deviate from the outputs to which they have been instructed by the NGC, the differences are dealt with as market transactions. In principle, the price charged for under- or over-generation should reflect the cost of the energy that has to be bought (or sold) by the pool, but it is still difficult to identify all generator errors and the definition of the spot price is not well-developed. Attempts have been made, without much success, to remedy this shortcoming but even under the current system generators contribute towards the cost of generator errors.

PROBLEMS WITH COST SHARING

The cost of all energy transactions is shared by all customers

Once the settlement of payments to generators has been determined, the pool can calculate the value of uplift and compute PSP, which is published about 28 days after energy is taken by customers. Spot market elements are therefore missing entirely on the customers' side, their aggregate energy use being forecast by the NGC, rather than individually declared or negotiated. Customers share the costs of operating the system and do not bear only those costs which they impose themselves.

New entrants want to opt out of some of the cost sharing

Already, customers who supply most of their own needs from on-site generators, and customers in transmission-constrained areas with a surplus of generation, have expressed concern over the costs of accommodating transmission constraints (and, for that matter, transmission losses, which are treated in a similar fashion). This issue has grown in importance as a result of the projected increase in the number of co-generators; if they wish to sell surplus energy to the pool, they find themselves liable, as pool members, for a share of the costs caused by others. The pool has therefore been required to make concessions for on-site generators, which reduce their contribution towards uplift.

Even the sharing of reserve costs causes problems

The costs of reserves are the option fee for providing reserve capacity plus the extra costs above the PPP of calling an option if the energy is needed. At first sight it might seem fair to allocate these costs to all customers. However, there are bound to be customers with particularly stable (or even just predictable) demand, who would rather pay for unforeseen energy consumption as and when it arises, instead of contributing to the costs of reserve capacity incurred to meet the unpredictable demands of other customers. The pool has therefore had to consider new ways for customers to buy and sell energy in the pool.

LOOKING AHEAD: DEVELOPING THE MARKETS

The pool rules as they currently stand have a coherent basic structure

The pool rules have already been changed to reflect perceived problems with the way in which costs are shared by generators and customers. Further changes will follow.

Experience of other power pools suggests that even apparently minor rule changes can have a major impact on the underlying incentives. Incremental changes will lead the pool in one of two directions:

- development and rationalisation of market arrangements; or
- widening the scope of cost-sharing arrangements.

Sharing costs can undermine the market structure

Cost sharing in a competitive market distorts incentives and creates discord. Any system where members do not pay the full costs of their own actions provides opportunities for some pool members to free-ride on others. Experience in the pool to date confirms this: uplift is the primary focus of complaints so far.

Strengthening the market arrangements will place the pool on a firmer footing. The key areas are: transmission; simplifying the markets; and attention to the demand side of the market.

The treatment of transmission constraints will change

There is no logical reason why members of the pool should pay for the costs of transmission constraints through uplift. Responsibility for causing or alleviating transmission constraints lies ultimately with NGC, which builds and operates all high-voltage transmission. The regulatory revenue formula for transmission use of system (TUOS) charges gives NGC an incentive to minimise investment and maintenance, even if the result is more constraints and a higher uplift. Pool members have frequently complained that the NGC is doing too little to reduce uplift and OFFER (the UK "Office of Electricity Regulation") has expressed similar views in a number of pool price enquiries.

Beginning in 1994, NGC agreed to share the cost of uplift with the pool for one year, in return for a fixed fee.[3] If the relevant portion of uplift rose above £587 million, NGC would pay 20% of the excess (up to £15 million); if it fell below £570 million, NGC would keep 30% of the savings (up to £25 million). The fixed fee (plus the pool's share of uplift) was still recovered as a surcharge on the price of energy sold by the pool, just like uplift.

This agreement gave NGC a *partial* incentive to reduce the cost of uplift. In future, NGC may be given an incentive to *optimise* the balance between transmission investments and transmission constraints, by being made liable

---

[3] The agreement covers most of the elements of uplift, including the cost of transmission constraints and demand forecast errors, but excludes the option fee paid to reserve capacity.

for the full cost of uplift (or at least the cost of constraints) over a period longer than a year. Such arrangements will become possible, once NGC understands better how to manage the commercial and regulatory risks. NGC should eventually recover the cost of constraints in TUOS charges, rather than from uplift. In time, NGC may even offer lower TUOS charges to generators who give up the right to compensation for constraints.

The forward market could be simplified

The PPP is derived from the U-Schedule, by a mass of equations which actually perform the following tasks:

● amalgamate the three-part bid for each generating unit and turn it into a simple £/MWh bid for each half-hour;
● stack up the bids in ascending price order, ignoring plant deemed to be "inflexible" (i.e. not able to supply output at the margin);
● identify the highest price generating set which has been called in the U-Schedule: the $/MWh bid price of this set defines the SMP component of the PPP.

An alternative would be to allow *more frequent bidding*, i.e. forward markets for hours ahead rather than simply a day ahead. Such a system would offer at least as much flexibility, even if the bids were placed in the form of *simple $/MWh prices*. Such bids could avoid the need to redesign settlement systems to cope with new technologies (e.g. combined cycle gas turbines), whose cost structure over a day as a whole does not fit easily into the current three-part pattern of start-up, no-load and incremental costs.

Longer-term forward markets could also be developed

This would permit the pool to "contract" for plant a week or even six months in advance. These markets would set their own prices, which would show how tight the market was expected to be. This might allow NGC to plan the system with a greater degree of certainty, and reduce the difficulty of coordinating maintenance of generating plant with maintenance of transmission. (Alternatively, NGC could use transmission contracts with generators as a way to provide equivalent incentives, by withdrawing transmission rights during a maintenance outage.)

The spot market is not as well developed as the forward and option markets.

Currently, spot market trades make up only a small share of total trades conducted through the pool. They occur at a variety of prices bearing more or less resemblance to the instantaneous short-run value of electricity.

The current arrangements do not allow the pool (or NGC) to shop around for revised energy bids on the moment, nor to find the most profitable outlet for energy which is surplus to requirements. In situations of sudden shortage, the courses of action available to the grid operator are limited by the lack of real spot markets. A simpler spot price formula, more closely related to effective prices, would increase the scope for spot market deals.

Discontent over uplift has already led the pool to allow "demand-side bidding"

Because the demand of some customers can be interrupted at short notice, they believe it provides as much flexibility as a generator. Hence, instead of paying for reserve capacity through uplift, they have been allowed to buy and sell energy as follows:

- selected customers buy energy in the day-ahead market at the PPP, by declaring an anticipated demand; but
- if the actual demand of such customers deviates from their declared demand, they face penalties for increasing or reducing their kWh take.

The "penalties" for increasing or decreasing demand are similar to those for generator errors, but should really be based on a better estimate of the short-run or spot market price of energy.

The role of customers should be expanded

The demand-side bidding proposal is equivalent to extending the scope for forward and spot market transactions into the customers' side of the market. There is enormous scope for devising such schemes, once the underlying market arrangements are understood. However, as the scheme expands, the Pool will need to ensure that customers who opt out of cost-sharing arrangements still make an appropriate contribution to the costs of providing reserve capacity and a stable frequency. Some components of the cost-sharing arrangements are therefore likely to persist.

CONCLUSION

The new power pool in England and Wales is a major feat of negotiation, comprising as it does a complex set of day-ahead and spot markets. However, the pool runs mainly on day-ahead arrangements and the spot market elements are relatively undeveloped: the loose characterisation of the pool as a spot market is inaccurate.

Placing more emphasis on the market arrangements leads to the conclusion that the areas for future development are:

● the separate identification of costs associated with transmission;
● consolidation of the spot market and extension of forward markets; and
● opening up more of the Pool's markets to customers of the Pool.

REFERENCES

(1) Crew, M.A. and Kleindorfer, P.R. (1986) *The Economics of Public Utility Regulation*, MIT Press, Cambridge, MA.
(2) Green, R. (1990) *Reshaping the CEGB: Electricity Privatisation in the UK*, Cambridge University Department of Applied Economics.
(3) Hunt, S. (1991) Competition in the Electricity Market: the England and Wales Privatisation, *NERA Topics*, Issue 2.

13 THE COST OF TRANSMISSION SERVICES

The aim of this chapter is to explain briefly what it means to provide transmission services, and what incremental costs are incurred in doing so. We also consider how common costs should be allocated to system users, when there are economies of scale. To begin with, we need to recap the role of transmission prices within the different structural models set out in Part 1 of this book.

THE ROLE OF TRANSMISSION PRICING UNDER DIFFERENT MODELS

As long as transmission is vertically integrated with generation, as in Model 1, the separate pricing of transmission is not an enormous problem, since there is no need to unbundle costs. Transmission costs are part of the total costs to be minimised by any efficient utility. The concepts on which we base this chapter, investment cost, transmission constraints and marginal losses, are familiar to system planners and system operators as cost elements which must be taken into account in overall cost minimisation. But in most integrated systems, the knowledge of costs is used to minimise the total cost of building and operating generation and transmission, not to set prices. Frequently there is no geographic differentiation between prices charged to customers and no attempt is made to influence customers' decisions about location by signalling the cost of transporting power to different areas.

However, as we move to competition, transmission prices become more and more important. For Model 2 systems, with competition in generation, the evaluation of bids must include the cost of transport. The contract for purchasing power should specify where the power is bought (at the plant "bus bar" or at a central market place), who is responsible for the transportation of the power, and who takes the risk that the transmission system is constrained so that the plant cannot run. The monopoly over wholesale and retail customers is often retained in order to allow limited geographic variation in end-user tariffs.

In Model 3 systems (wholesale competition), where customers can buy electricity over the high-voltage network, the transport price becomes central to the model. Model 4 (retail competition) extends the importance of transmission pricing into the low-voltage networks. In both Model 3 and Model 4, the transmission system is usually unbundled from generation, and will usually be operated by a company called, in this book, the transmission system operator (TSO).[1] We concentrate in this chapter on the requirements of unbundled open access systems, since all the reasoning can be applied where appropriate to Models 1 and 2. Chapter 14 on transmission prices also provides a short discussion of approaches which have been developed for open access regimes on networks owned by "bundled" utilities.

We begin this chapter by examining the tasks of a TSO, to define the nature of the service offered by a TSO and to investigate the costs incurred in providing this service. We then analyse how these costs affect decisions to invest in the network. In the next chapter, we will look at how these cost concepts are handled in different contractual and regulatory systems.

TRANSMISSION SERVICE

A business must define its products and services, know how much each costs to provide and set prices which at least cover these costs.

The Nature of the Service

We will therefore approach the task of identifying the costs of transmission by first defining the product or service the TSO (a transmission company) is selling. We can then identify the inputs and costs involved in providing this service, after which we will be in a position to suggest how they might be charged as prices. We will approach the identification of costs by discussing the operating methods of a TSO. The implicit subtitle of this section is "maintaining system security"; besides being a major concern of system operators, a stable and secure transmission system is an important part of the product the TSO is selling. Most of the other roles of the TSO stem from this responsibility for ensuring system security.

The product or output provided by a transmission system is a transport service: the movement of electricity, from one named point on the network to another, at the request of a system user. Chapter 12 explained how open access

---

[1] In terms of the transmission functions described in Chapter 6, the TSO acts as both the Transmission Provider and the dispatcher, i.e. the TSO owns, maintains and dispatches the transmission system. A Transmission System Operator (TSO) should not be confused with the Independent System Operator (ISO) found in many of the California restructuring proposals. In those proposals, the ISO acts solely as dispatcher, while another entity owns and maintains the transmission wires.

systems allow a generator at point A to sell electricity over the network to a customer at point B. Before completing any such transaction, the generator and/ or the customer must secure the right to transmit electricity from A to B. The service can be provided for single units, at short notice. However, most networks do not let traders start trading without first securing a right to use some of the network's capacity for a day, a month, a year or longer. The right to use capacity as and when desired has all the risk-sharing properties of an option contract, which we described with reference to energy contracts in Chapter 11.

This right can be offered with more or less "firmness", i.e. with a stronger or weaker guarantee that the service will be provided when needed. Rights can be combined, to allow transmission to and from a number of points. Any right will have to be accompanied by an assurance of quality, in terms of frequency control and reactive power control and the reliability of the service (i.e. the probability that electricity will be transmitted as requested).

The next section explains, in very general terms, how a transmission utility might be expected to accommodate demands for transmission from independent electricity traders. The TSO may use a variety of inputs to supply transmission service at least cost, not just lines, towers, cables and other hardware, but also a range of "ancillary services" such as reactive power (voltage control) and reserve generation (frequency control). The description of operations will lead to a description of inputs and the cost of those inputs. This general model provides the basis for exploring the costs of transmission services and the principles of transmission pricing.

The Basic Commercial Framework

The trading process set out in Chapter 12 assumes a decentralised method of arranging trades, but it can also be applied under central dispatch, where the TSO decides which generators run in order to meet actual customer load. The nature of the traders varies from system to system, as will the degree of integration between the TSO and the generation business. However, this disaggregated model allows us to identify the key elements of any commercial system which allows third parties to gain access to the network:

1. The TSO must define and allocate transmission rights to system users.
2. System users must notify the TSO in advance of *scheduled energy transfers* consistent with their transmission rights.
3. The dispatcher may have to reschedule *actual energy transfers* over the network to make them consistent with available transmission capacity;
4. The dispatcher must arrange for electricity to be supplied to make good transmission losses, and must dispatch reserve generation (or manage load) for frequency control;

5. Someone must measure flows of active (and reactive) energy into and out of the network and then liaise with the market operator (MO) (see Chapter 12) to arrange payment for imbalances (and ancillary services).

These five elements of a commercial framework appear to be essential to the operation of any open access system, if it is to meet the physical, operational and commercial concerns of the network users and operators.[2]

Of these elements, only the third may require further clarification at this stage. Consider a situation in which the TSO sells a trader annual transmission capacity from A to B of 100 MW. In any one particular hour, the trader may notify the TSO of a scheduled flow of 100 MW, as allowed by the terms of access. Suppose the TSO discovers that a short-term constraint prevents the flow from A to B exceeding 95 MW. The TSO must arrange for flows to be "rebalanced", by reducing generation at A and increasing generation at B, in both cases by 5 MW, so that the net flow from A to B is reduced by 5 MW to 95 MW. Commercially, this rebalancing can be accounted for in a number of different ways. As we shall show below, the cost of rebalancing is immensely important for investment decisions.

Some commentators have suggested that these elements of system operation should be unbundled to the point where reserves, frequency control, reactive power and other system support services are bought in a competitive market by, or on behalf of, individual consumers. This seems impracticable. The role of the TSO is to maintain the quality of transmission service to all system users. Many aspects of transmission are common to all system users in a given area, for example the frequency and the voltage. The commonality of service makes it impossible to charge individual system users on the basis of metered consumption.[3] Each system user has an incentive to free-ride on the quality of service provided by others. In the end, the quality of service would fall below the desired level.

The standard solution which avoids free-riding is to negotiate a joint agreement, whereby all beneficiaries appoint an agent to provide the service and agree how to share the costs among themselves. Only those who sign the agreement are allowed to receive the service. In other words, if a monopoly TSO did not exist to provide system support, system users would have to invent one.

---

[2] For a fuller exposition of the role of a TSO, see Hunt, S. and Shuttleworth, G. (1993) Operating a Transmission Company under Open Access: The Basic Requirements *The Electricity Journal*, Vol. 6, No. 3.

[3] When the amount of reserve energy or reactive power consumed or supplied by an individual can be metered, it is sometimes possible to charge them for it. However, short-term variations in output and consumption are not normally metered, so it is impossible to charge for the use of short-term reserves or frequency control. Similarly, most reactive power is consumed within the transmission system and does not flow over any consumer's meter.

THE COSTS OF TRANSMISSION SERVICE

As the previous section emphasised, transmission moves energy from one point to another. Each individual user of the system requires a slightly different service, since they specify different points of entry and exit, different time periods when service is needed, and different quantities of energy to be moved in each period. The costing methodology must therefore define as far as possible the service offered to each electricity trader who uses the system and identify the costs imposed by that trader's use of the service. As a means of identifying the costs of providing a transmission service, this chapter begins by discussing the *marginal costs* imposed by each user. The *common costs*, which cannot be directly assigned to individual users, are considered in later sections.

Identifying the Marginal Costs

Marginal costs are all costs present and future imposed on the system by an increment of use, given the demands placed on the system by all other users. The following distinction is sometimes made:

- *Short-run marginal cost* (SRMC) is the cost of increasing (or decreasing) output to meet an increment (or decrement) in demand when capacity is fixed; or, if demand would exceed the level of capacity, it is the price necessary to ration demand so that it remains within existing capacity. In a transmission system the short-run marginal costs are the energy costs of losses and constraints.
- *Long-run marginal cost* (LRMC) is the cost of producing an increment in output when capacity can be altered. In transmission, the long run marginal costs include the cost of building new capacity (the "cost of expansion"), *plus* any remaining losses.
- *Incremental cost* is sometimes used instead of marginal cost, when referring to the cost of an increment of use sustained over a long period. It is the difference between total system costs with and without the increment in use. (A similar concept applies to decrements in use.)
  In a real world system, a "transmission request" may cover transport over various parts of the network, some of which can be met by increasing losses and constraints, and some of which require expansion of the facilities. The cost of any particular request may include both short-run and long-run costs. *It is often preferable simply to refer to "the" marginal cost or "the" incremental cost of the request.*

We will now demonstrate how these cost concepts relate to each other in the case of a single line, or on a simple network.

The SRMC of Transmission and Nodal Spot Prices of Electricity

In the short-run, the costs of transmission consists of energy costs. Additional energy flows over a network change total physical losses. The cost of the incremental losses is a short-run cost of transmission. The additional flow may also tighten constraints on the system. When a constraint binds, some generation has to be "backed off" on the input side of a constraint, whilst more expensive generation is dispatched on the output side. The net cost of these adjustments to dispatch is another short-run cost of transmission.

If transmission were costless, the dispatcher would minimise total costs of generation by equalising the economic value of electricity at each node (bus) on the system. The economic value of electricity is given by the marginal cost of energy in dispatch, or by the price in a market.[4] Since transmission is not costless, a central dispatcher minimises the total cost of energy production on the system when the *difference* between the economic value of electricity at any two nodes equals the *marginal* cost of energy production caused by additional flows between the nodes. It follows that the SRMC of transmission cannot be calculated and minimised separately from the cost of generation.

Transmission costs and optimal dispatch

For example, if a "high" cost generator is being dispatched at node B (e.g. at $30/MWh) while "low" cost generators have spare capacity at node A (e.g. at $20/MWh), we can *deduce* that the cost of moving energy from A to B is equal to the difference between the marginal costs of generation at A and B (i.e. $10/MWh):

- if the marginal cost of transmission were *less than* the difference in the cost of generation, the TSO could reduce total costs by increasing generation at A and transmitting it to B to replace the output of the more expensive generator; and
- if the marginal cost of transmission were *more than* the difference in the cost of generation, the TSO could reduce total costs by transmitting less electricity from A to B.

This implies the following general rule:

- *Axiom* 1: in an optimally dispatched system, the SRMC of transmission from A to B is equal to the difference between the marginal cost of generation at B and the marginal cost of generation at A.

---

[4] See Chapters 10–12 for a discussion of the economic value of electricity and associated market pricing rules. We assume here that the economic value equals the marginal cost of generation.

Hence, if the marginal cost of generation is $20/MWh at A and $30/MWh at B, the marginal cost of transmission from A to B must be $10/MWh, *or else something will change.*

This general rule lies behind the use of complicated power flow models to yield transmission prices as a by-product of optimising generation. Transmission costs are derived from the model's estimate of the marginal cost of generation at all points on the network. However, any dispatch which is believed to be optimal, or close to optimal, will allow the same rule to be applied.

Transmission costs and nodal spot prices

The close link between energy costs and transmission costs was first explored by a team at the Massachusetts Institute of Technology, largely under the guidance of Fred Schweppe. The explanation of transmission costs set out in this chapter is a simplified, two-node version of the multi node engineering model for which the MIT team developed a general solution.[5]

The MIT approach was picked up and adopted by others, who noted that explicit pricing of transmission would become redundant, if the MO could signal the economic value of electricity at *every* node on the network ("nodal spot pricing").[6] At the time of writing, there is no fully operative example of nodal spot pricing. The Norwegian electricity market uses a similar approach, but with prices for only four or five zones, not a price for each node.

Nodal spot pricing has some merit for pricing transmission *between* major markets, as in Norway. However, nodal spot pricing may never be applied universally to the point where transmission pricing becomes unnecessary. The balance of argument may tip in favour of nodal spot pricing, as computers become more powerful. Until then, we suspect that spot prices will only be calculated for those nodes where they serve a particular commercial need. Transmission to and from other nodes will require explicit transmission prices. Furthermore, nodal spot prices may not recover the total costs of transmission where there are economies of scale.

We have therefore drafted this chapter and the following one on the assumption that some form of transmission pricing will emerge out of current pricing arrangements, and will not be obviated by a radical reform of electricity spot pricing.

In any case, the complex algebraic models used to describe nodal spot pricing are easiest to understand in terms of the short-run costs of electricity

---

[5] See, for example, Bohn, R.E., Caramanis, M.C. and Schweppe, F.C. (1984) Optimal Pricing in Electrical Networks over Space and Time, *Rand Journal of Economics*, Vol. 13, No. 3.

[6] For a recent exposition of this approach, see Hogan, W.W. (1995) *Electricity Transmission and Emerging Competition*, J.F.K. School of Government, Harvard University, MA (prepared for the Public Utility Research Center Annual Conference, April 27, 1995).

transmission caused by real operational factors: transmission losses and constraints. We consider each in turn, to show exactly how transmission costs are related to the economic value of electricity.

Transmission Losses

Transmission losses (and hence transmission costs) increase exponentially to the flow (or current) over any line. Marginal losses increase more or less proportionately to the flow.[7] The SRMC of any particular request for transmission therefore depends on the existing flow of electricity due to other system users. To identify marginal costs, we assume that these other flows remain constant. We then consider the effect of additional flows. The following discussion applies this theory to a simple line which runs between two nodes ("West" and "East") and which has no transmission constraints.

Suppose first that energy is flowing from West to East. If an increase in demand in the East is met by increasing generation in the West, there will be a net increase in the line flow from West to East. This line flow will have a measurable effect on transmission losses. The increase or decrease in total losses on the system is the marginal loss associated with transmission from West to East. If the marginal loss is positive, the generator in the West must supply more than the increase in demand in the East.

For example, any generator supplying an additional 100 MWh in the West may find that customers in the East can only draw off an additional 95 MWh. In this case marginal physical losses would be 5 MWh (or 5% of generation). This situation is illustrated in Figure 13.1, where the arrow represents the whole network linking East and West.

The marginal cost of moving electricity from West to East is easily defined in terms of physical losses. In order to calculate the value of these losses, and hence the SRMC of transmission, we need to look at the equilibrium price difference between West and East. If the marginal cost of generation in the West is $10/MWh, the total cost of the additional 100 MWh will be $1000. Customers only receive an additional 95 MWh, but they will still need to pay a total of $1000 to cover the generator's incremental costs. This implies a price of $10.53/MWh in the East (that is, $1000 divided by 95 MWh). Hence, moving energy from West to East has increased its price by 53 cents/MWh; this price increase defines the SRMC of transmitting electricity from West to East.

---

[7] For the technically minded, losses are a quadratic or "square" function of current ("I", which is proportional to MW line flow at a constant voltage) and a linear function of resistance (R, which depends on the line's length and material characteristics). Total losses are often represented by the following expression: losses $= I^2 R$. *Marginal* losses due to an *increase* in line flow (i.e. additional current) are given by the first derivative, $2IR$.

100 MWh
@$ 10.00/MWh

95 MWh
@$ 10.53/MWh

WEST

EAST

Transmission Cost = 53 cents/MWh

Figure 13.1 Transmission losses

- *Axiom* 2: in an unconstrained system, the SRMC of transmission is derived from the marginal physical losses.

Generally speaking, losses increase with distance. To supply nodes which are further away, the generator must charge a higher price to recover the original costs of generation. However, additional line flow only raises total losses if it moves in the same direction as the existing net flow. If additional line flow moves in the opposite direction, losses will fall and the SRMC of transmission will be *negative*.

For example, if system users request an incremental flow from East to West, against the existing net flow, total system losses will fall. Only 95 MWh in the East is needed to meet additional demand of 100 MWh in the West; the marginal effect on losses is to save 5 MWh. In this case, if the marginal cost of generation in the East were $10.53/MWh, generation costs would be $1000 in total, and the generator would only need to charge $10.00/MWh in the West. In other words, the effect of moving electricity from East to West, against the current net flow, would be to *reduce* the price of electricity. Thus the SRMC of transmission from East to West would be *minus* 53 cents/MWh, or the exact negative of the West–East cost.

The notion of the "back-haul" cost being negative is sometimes dismissed as irrelevant, since few generators wish to schedule sales from an expensive region to a cheap region. However, if costs of transport are measured to and from a central node for convenience, as we will later suggest, the concept of a negative cost becomes important. The cost of transmission from A to B is divided into two stages: from A to the central node; and from the central node to B. Either of these stages may have a negative cost, even if the total cost is positive or zero overall. For example, if a generator and a customer are in the same location, the cost of transmission from one to the other is zero. However, it can conveniently be described as two transactions: delivery to the central node at a cost of (say) 53 cents/MWh, and a delivery from the central node to the customer at a cost of minus 53 cents/MWh, giving a total of zero as desired. Ignoring negative costs (at least, negative short-run costs) can lead to an inefficient dispatch.

Constraints

Not all requests for transmission can actually be accommodated just by increasing flows and losses. An electricity transmission system suffers from three major types of constraint: thermal limits, voltage limits and stability limits. Whatever the cause, they usually force the TSO to restrict the maximum flow over some lines. Some generators, who might have been dispatched to minimise the total cost of generation, will be replaced by others in a more advantageous location. This drives a wedge between the marginal cost of generation on either side of the constraint, and the cost difference between either side exceeds the value of marginal line losses. However, the SRMC of transmission is still given by the difference in marginal costs of generation:

● *Axiom* 3: where there are constraints on line flow, the SRMC of transmission equals the difference between the marginal costs of generation (i.e. economic values of electricity) on either side of the constraint.

The impact of constraints can be illustrated by considering a transmission system which consists of two zones, A and B, with demand equal to X and Y respectively. The "supply curves" for each zone are shown in Figures 13.2 and 13.3. In each zone the marginal cost of generation increases as more expensive generators are dispatched: that is, the supply curves are upward sloping. If the two zones were unconnected, the marginal costs of generation would define economic values of $12/MWh in zone A and $20/MWh in zone B: these are the prices at which the supply curves intersect with the level of demand in the market in each zone.

Now turn the graph for zone B through 180 degrees and superimpose it on the graph for zone A. Figure 13.4 shows total demand for both zones as $X + Y$, to be met by generation in one zone or the other. In the absence of constraints,

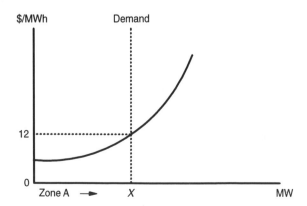

Figure 13.2   Zone A generation costs

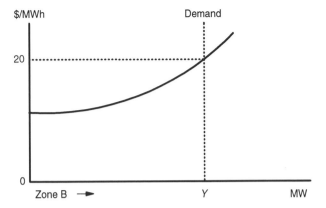

Figure 13.3 Zone B generation costs

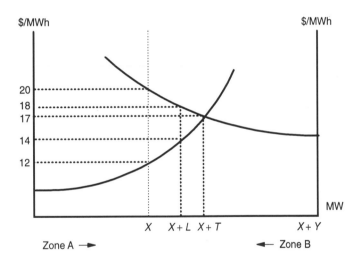

Figure 13.4 Joint generation

transmission would be costless (if we assume no losses) and the least-cost solution would require marginal costs to be equal in both zones. This happens at the intersection of the two supply curves, where generation is $X + T$ in zone A and $Y - T$ in zone B. Line flow from A to B, in MW, would be T and the marginal cost of generation would be \$17/MWh in each zone.

However, if there is a constraint on transmission between the two zones it is not possible to reach this position. For example, if the capacity of the link between A and B (L) is less than the unconstrained level of transmission between them (T), the level of generation in zone A will need to be pulled back to $X + L$. Figure 13.4 shows that this would reduce the price of generation in zone A from \$17/MWh to \$14/MWh. Generation in zone A would need to be replaced by more expensive generators on the other side of the constraint. The marginal cost of generation in zone B would increase to \$18/MWh, and the total cost of generation for the two zones together would be higher.

In this example, the short run marginal cost of transmission from A to B is \$4/MWh. It is calculated as the difference between the marginal costs of generation in the two zones (that is, \$18/MWh minus \$14/MWh). Similarly, the SRMC of transmission from B to A will be *minus* \$4/MWh.

The SRMC of transmission can be understood in three alternative ways:

1. *Generation costs*: demand for an incremental MWh of transmission across the constraint causes an addition to total short-run generation costs of \$4. This might occur, for instance, if another network connected to zone A tried to wheel energy to a third network connected to zone B. The only way in which the local dispatcher could accommodate the additional input into zone A would be to back off local generation, thereby saving \$14/MWh; however, any additional demand out of zone B would have to come from local generation costing \$18/MWh. Even before accounting for transmission losses, the demand for wheeling over the constraint raises generation costs by the net figure of \$4/MWh.

2. *The opportunity cost of the transmission right*: the right to transmit over the constraint is a right of way, with a value like any other property right. In this case, any generator or customer who has the right to use the link is able to buy energy in zone A at the price of \$14/MWh and to sell it in zone B at the price of \$18/MWh, making a profit of \$4/MWh on the deal. The profit foregone by existing owners of an asset (in this case, a transmission right) is usually referred to as the "opportunity cost"; it is determined by the user who is prepared to place the highest value on the asset and to outbid all others for the use of it. Any other seller who wishes to buy a transmission right over the constraint will therefore have to pay the existing users at least this much for it, to compensate them for the profit foregone.

3. *Reinforcement or expansion cost*: the final sense in which the transmission price of \$4/MWh relates to marginal costs is in regard to the cost of reinforcing the link. If some users are prepared to pay \$4/MWh to transmit energy from A to B, it would be worth building additional capacity, if it could be built for less than \$4/MWh. If a constraint is allowed to persist, it should be possible to infer (though only in a fully competitive transmission sector) that the cost of reinforcing the link lies above \$4/MWh.

This last comparison points to a relation between the SRMC of transmission and the incentives to invest in system expansion. This issue is examined in detail in the following section.

System Expansion Costs

A transmission request may be accommodated in the first instance by increased losses. As flows increase beyond a certain level, security standards dictate that generation be backed off in the export-constrained zone, incurring costs of constraints.[8] When more requests for transmission are received, there comes a point where the discounted present value of all losses and constraints on the system as presently configured, integrated over all hours of system use, and projected into the future, rises above the minimum cost of an alternative system with new lines added. The marginal cost of transmission at this point must include the cost of system expansion.[9]

The economic rules for system expansion are as follows:

- *Axiom* 4: only build additional capacity if total savings in the cost of generation (and load management) exceed the total construction costs.
- *Axiom* 5: add capacity until the marginal generation savings equal the marginal cost of building additional capacity.

If these rules are followed, the value of any project exceeds its cost and the sum of future short-run costs equals the long-run marginal cost of further expansion.

In the example shown in Figure 13.4 above, if the LRMC of transmission were $4/MWh, building a transmission capacity greater than L would cost more than it would save. Building less capacity would forgo opportunities to make economic transactions. The transmission capacity of L would be optimal.

When transmission capacity is L units, the cost of the remaining losses and constraints (the new SRMC) is just equal to the cost of the last unit of incremental capacity. Therefore, if things turn out as expected, "spot" sales of L units of transmission at prices based on SRMC would cost the same as a long-term contract for L units of transmission capacity priced at LRMC.

However, there are several reasons why TSOs do not rely on spot pricing of transmission. First, if there are economies of scale the spot price will not yield sufficient revenues. Second, if the TSO has a monopoly in the transmission market, the TSO can raise the price (by reducing capacity). Third, things do not often turn out as planned, and it is risky to rely on spot prices to recover the cost of long-term investment in transmission. The difficulty of estimating future

---

[8] When this happens, the line or network is not necessarily loaded to its physical capacity. Conventional operating procedures may require many lines to be only partly loaded, in order to provide a minimum reserve capacity to cope with adverse events. We do not intend to discuss whether in practice these constraints are optimally determined.

[9] In fact, if there were no indivisibilities or scale economies, the system could always be configured so that it just accommodated existing users, and would require immediate expansion to accommodate new users. Capacity is only added at infrequent intervals because of the complications of indivisibilities and scale economies.

use suggests that TSOs may prefer to secure their revenues in contracts before building capacity, rather than relying on spot prices after capacity has been built.

The remainder of this chapter explains how economies of scale are related to cost recovery and how TSOs (or any other invester) should deal with the problem. In Chapter 14, we discuss how transmission contracts are used to manage a TSO's monopoly power, investment incentives and risks.

Simple Comparison of Short- and Long-Run Costs

Consider the situation in which there are no economies of scale. In Figure 13.5, we show the costs and benefits of investment in L units of transmission capacity. The vertical height of the arrows represents the LRMC of a unit of transmission capacity. In this example, the arrows are all the same length, so the cost of each additional unit of transmission is the same, and there are no scale economies. The total saving due to the first units transmitted ($=ST$) is much greater than the cost per unit of the transmission link. Each succeeding unit saves less, until the last unit saves just as much as it costs. There are two things to observe:

- it is certainly worth building a link since the total saving in generation costs exceeds the total cost of the link; and
- pricing transmission at short-run marginal cost will recover the total cost of the link.

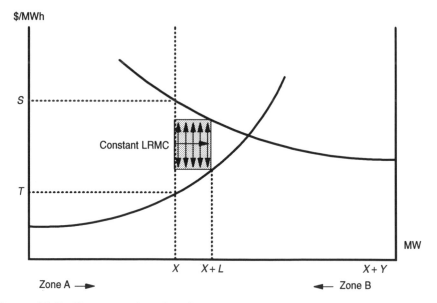

Figure 13.5   No economies of scale

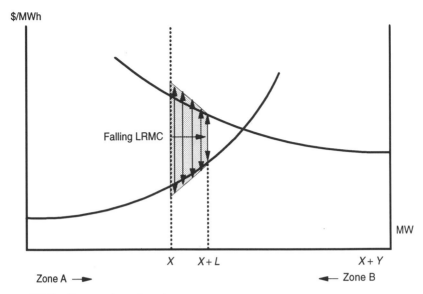

Figure 13.6 Economies of scale

Cost Comparison with Economies of Scale

If there are economies of scale, spot pricing of transmission will not recover the cost of the link, even if the world turns out exactly as planned. In Figure 13.6, for example, the first unit of transmission is represented by a long arrow, implying a high unit cost. Each successive unit of transmission is represented by a shorter arrow, to represent a falling LRMC, or incremental cost per unit of transmission capacity. The total cost of all the units of transmission capacity is represented by the shaded area. In this example, the total cost exceeds the total saving, so it is not worth building the link.

If the economies of scale were less sharp, the total cost of the transmission link might not exhaust the saving, in which case it would make sense to proceed with the project. However, even then, charges set equal to the short-run marginal cost of transmission would not cover the total cost of the project. To ensure that only efficient investments go ahead, the potential users of the expanded link must agree to pay the total cost before the project goes ahead. We consider how they might do this in the next section.

INVESTMENT RULES AND COST RECOVERY

The basic conceptual framework for determining marginal or incremental costs was described in the previous section. In this section we consider efficient

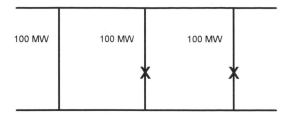

By N-2, three lines provide 100 MW of capacity.

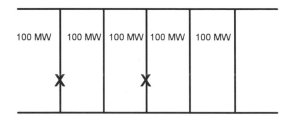

By N-2, five lines provide 300 MW of capacity.

Figure 13.7   Economies of scale in security standards

prices for incremental investment in the presence of economies of scale and scope. In transmission, much is made of scale economies. They are important in incremental projects (with which we are concerned here), but should not be confused with economies of scale in whole networks (which are less easy to identify). The analysis is also relevant to the recovery of sunk costs of investments already made.

Economic efficiency requires that every customer pays the marginal cost of providing a specific service. Unfortunately, where there are common costs caused by economies of scale or scope, the revenues from pricing all requests for service at marginal cost will not recover the total cost of providing the service. For example, under "$N-2$" or double contingency standards, the design of the network must tolerate the loss (planned or unplanned) of any two lines. A request for transmission capacity equal to the rated capacity of a single 100 MW line would actually require the TSO to build three 100 MW lines, in case two lines were ever unavailable at the same time. Transmission capacity could then be tripled to 300 MW, just by adding two more 100 MW lines, to give five lines in total. (By the $N-2$ criterion, five 100 MW lines give a capacity of 300 MW at any time, even if two lines are out of action (see Figure 13.7).) The marginal cost of adding each 100 MW of capacity is one extra line, or one third the cost of the first 100 MW. This is not simply a feature of rigid security standards: there are scale economies in reliability generally.[10]

Economies of scale raise questions concerning the timing of an investment (the need for advance construction) and the scale of any individual investment project (lumpiness). These issues are discussed below, but we begin with the treatment of economies of scale in a single period model, where the level of investment is infinitely flexible.

Dealing with Economies of Scale

The general rule for efficient investment is that total incremental revenues should be high enough to cover total incremental costs. This will discourage investments that customers jointly would not be willing to pay for. The associated pricing policy is: to set prices to individual customers no lower than the marginal cost of serving each customer and no higher than their willingness-to-pay; and to ensure that total revenues from all customers are no lower than total costs.

For example, the technology may have a cost function of the form:

$$\text{Total cost of expansion by } x \text{ units} = k + bx$$

The marginal cost of expansion is b, but it is not rational to make the investment, unless customers jointly are willing to pay the common cost, k, as well. Some investment rules, which require utilities to expand their systems to accommodate *all* requests for service, fail to obey this criterion.

Utilities often try to recover the total cost of investment by spreading it over all customers using the new facility. If k is large, spreading the costs *equally* over all users may raise the average price so high that some users are deterred from using the facility at all. This compounds the difficulty facing the utility, since some of these users would have been willing to pay at least the unit cost, b, and to make some contribution to common costs, k. The loss of these marginal users raises the share of total costs to be recovered from the remaining users— and increases the likelihood that they will be put off using the facility.

This problem has received a lot of attention from economists working on the problems of public utilities. Providing it is rational to make the investment, the general pricing solution is to ensure that the cost of k is allocated to customers in a way which does not distort the investment decision, by loading common costs onto the customers most willing to bear them, i.e. the customers whose demand is least sensitive to the price they have to pay (least *elastic*).

---

[10] There is also an economy of scope when requests are made for 10 year service but the equipment will last 20 years. The last 10 years of service are effectively provided at no extra cost.

Over the years, several practical methods have been developed for dealing with economies of scale, to ensure that common costs are efficiently allocated. Some of these methods have already been applied to investments in transmission and the most common are explained below.

Joint venture

The most obvious example of this practice is found in the allocation of common costs at the planning stage, which has long been used in transmission. While every user enters negotiations expressing disdain, and professes to be willing to pay only the marginal costs, some of the participants eventually agree to take on some of the common costs, for fear the project will not go ahead. The most "willing to pay" (or the worst negotiators) absorb the common costs.

Price discrimination

In unregulated markets, producers attempt to discriminate, and can succeed in doing so if they can prevent resale. Airlines have developed fine discriminatory procedures which rely for effectiveness not on monopoly, but on their ability to segment markets sufficiently to prevent customers with low-price tickets from selling them to customers in high-price segments of the market. However, discrimination is also the prerogative of monopolists. They are often accused of discriminating between customers at all points on the demand curve (by charging everyone according to their willingness to pay), and reaping all the economic rents. Discrimination by utilities is therefore usually prohibited, even though it has desirable efficiency properties in many cases.

Ramsey prices

An early solution to the pricing problems of economies of scale was proposed by Ramsey, whose name is associated with what is now referred to as "second best linear prices" or the "inverse elasticity rule". If the aim is to charge a single price per unit (a "linear price"), Ramsey proposed differentiating prices in inverse proportion to the elasticity of demand, and this proposal held sway for nearly 50 years. More sophisticated versions of Ramsey pricing require consideration of the elasticity of demand for complementary and substitute products. However, it proves quite difficult to ascertain the elasticity of demand by customer, or even by class of customer, so that implementation was always imperfect. Ramsey pricing also involves discrimination, which may be prohibited.

Non-linear prices

More recent work on the subject has shown that non-linear pricing solutions have better efficiency properties than linear solutions, in that they distort demand to a lesser degree. Non-linear pricing systems charge customers different prices for different blocks of demand. A common form of non-linear pricing is a lump sum (a share of k) to cover the common costs, with all increments in demand priced to all customers at marginal cost (b). Ideally, any lump sum or standing charge should be assigned according to each customer's willingness to pay. This can be hard to measure, but even a uniform standing charge is often preferable, on grounds of efficiency, to mark-ups on (linear) prices per unit. There are problems too, with two-part prices, in that "marginal costs" are frequently under-estimated (or even understated), so that too much is allocated to the category of common costs, and assigned to all customers as lump sum or standing charges. This will drive away some of the more price-sensitive customers, who might otherwise contribute to the common costs.

Simple average prices

Despite our criticism of this approach, there are many cases where a simple "linearisation" of the cost function will suffice. Linearisation attributes a share of the common costs to every increment in output, with the result that everyone pays the same average cost per unit. If the common costs are relatively small, the resulting increase in the price (above marginal costs) will not distort consumption greatly and the reduction in transactions costs (for computing complicated pricing schedules and assessing the characteristics of each customer) will more than compensate for a small loss of efficiency in consumption.

ADVANCE CONSTRUCTION AND FORWARD RIGHTS

There are times when economies of scale become particularly important. The managers of transmission companies are always particularly concerned about the need for advance construction ("to build ahead of demand"), and in-divisibilities ("lumpy" investments). Both advance construction and lumpiness are particular manifestations of economies of scale, and can be dealt with as such, as we will now explain.

If the $k + bx$ cost function applies to individual projects, a request for a service of x_1 units will cost $k + bx_1$, but x_2 units can be provided at the same time for an additional cost of only bx_2, making a total cost of $k + bx_1 + bx_2$. The total incremental cost of building capacity in advance must be compared with building the same amount later in a separate project, at a cost of

$k + bx_2$. If the time-lag between now and when the capacity is needed is t years, and the cost of capital (interest rate or discount rate) is $r\%$ per annum, the cost of advance construction and the cost of two separate projects can be compared as follows:

Total cost of increment built now $\qquad = k + bx_1 + bx_2$

Total NPV[11] to build now and again later $= k + bx_1 + (k + bx_2)/(1 + r)^t$

It is economic to build the extra capacity now, instead of in the future, if the former cost is lower than the latter, i.e. if

$$bx_2 < (k + bx_2)/(1 + r)^t$$

These cost conditions lead to the typical situation where a utility chooses to build in advance of needs to reduce overall costs, in the expectation that someone will want the extra units later.[12] Two problems then have to be solved jointly: how much to build ahead; and who should pay the common costs, k.

If system users reveal their demand preferences, it will be clear how much to build: capacity should be added so long as the builder can find system users who are willing to pay at least b per unit (now) for the construction (now) of a line which they might only use in the future. However, no-one is likely to offer this information freely, and some negotiation may be necessary. The outcome of negotiations (each system user's commitment to bear some of the costs, and their right to use the new capacity in future) would be set down in a contract for transmission capacity.

Efficiency in the development of the network requires that the project as a whole should only proceed if a group of system users is jointly willing to pay the common costs, k. The system users who are willing to pay more than b will eventually agree to pay a share of k, in order to ensure that the project goes ahead. Such negotiations will allocate the payment of k to the least price-elastic customers, as proposed above.

Whenever it is uncertain who will want the capacity in the future, some party must pay for the capacity initially, and then bear the risk that the future demand will not in fact materialise. Several practical schemes have been developed for dealing with this problem. The main contenders for a competitive or decentralised electricity system are described below.

---

[11] The NPV is the net present value of future expenditure, discounted to current values at the rate of interest, r.

[12] If there are no scale economies in construction projects, e.g. if $k = 0$, there is no need for advance construction, as everything can be built just as economically when required.

TSO builds in advance

If demand is expected to materialise in the future, the TSO may simply build in advance, hold the rights to future capacity, and sell them when the demand appears. The TSO will be holding "excess capacity" which might make the marginal costs look extremely low. If the TSO is required to offer prices based on incremental costs, it will be impossible to recover the cost of the advance construction. When estimating the incremental cost imposed by future users, therefore, the TSO must be allowed to include costs incurred in the past on their behalf. One estimation method is to exclude capacity built in advance from any baseline model of the system (or else to assign the spare capacity to "anticipated" commitments). Estimates of incremental cost made with this model will then include the cost of the capacity built in advance. Chapter 14 suggests alternative pricing methods which avoid this problem.

First user pays, but receives rebates from later users

In some jurisdictions, particularly for line extensions in distribution, the first system user who requests transmission capacity pays a substantial proportion of k, on the understanding that some share of these costs will be rebated, if and when other system users want to use the same installation. So long as the first system user and the TSO are willing (between them) to pay the full incremental costs of the project on this basis, this solution is efficient.

First user gets transferable rights to all capacity

A related scheme would permit the first system user to purchase transferable rights on the additional capacity, for sale to the subsequent users. The value of these transferable rights could never rise above the cost of constructing the same amount of capacity at a later date $(k + bx_2)$, or else any later users would arrange for additional facilities to be built. However, Chapter 14 explains how this type of pricing rule can nevertheless encourage efficient investment.

Builder takes bids for future capacity rights

A more complicated variant would allow other potential system users, or even brokers, to compete to buy rights to capacity which is built in advance of requirements. In the future, when a new system user requires transmission, the holders of these rights could offer them for sale. Rather than negotiating with potential system users, the TSO might auction these future transmission rights; if the TSO invited bids for a range of different project sizes, the bids might even help the TSO to identify how much to build.

Not all of these solutions can be guaranteed to limit the profit of the TSO to a specific rate of return. However, no matter who owns transmission capacity built in advance of requirements, it can never be sold for more than the cost of constructing a new facility with the same capacity, which is $k + bx_2$. This price may be much higher or lower than the cumulated cost of advance construction, including interest, $bx_2(1 + r)^t$. If the TSO keeps all the initial rights to capacity, but is expected to earn a regulated rate of return, it may be necessary to regulate two specific aspects of the transmission sector:

- to limit the TSO's transmission prices (in case the cost of building new capacity is higher than the accumulated cost of past construction); and
- to limit the right of others to build alternative capacity (in case it becomes cheaper for them to build alternative capacity than to pay the accumulated cost of the TSO's capacity).

The price charged by the TSO for transmission capacity constructed in advance depends upon the regulatory regime: some regimes favour prices based on the cost of new construction; some only allow the TSO to recover the cumulated cost; some regimes adopt a different rule according to circumstances (e.g. whichever cost is higher). Some regimes apply these rules to individual transmission prices, whilst others refer directly to the TSO's total revenue. The selection of the appropriate pricing policy depends on the attitude of public policy towards risk and incentives for regulated utilities.

If transmission rights are allocated initially to system users or brokers, the initial price charged by the TSO might have to be regulated (if the TSO is a monopoly provider of transmission), but there is rarely any need to restrict the price of resale.

"Lumpiness"

Lumpiness is a special type of economy of scale, where the quantity of capacity constructed by any one project cannot be exactly tailored to requirements. Instead, capacity must be created in discrete amounts and has a marginal cost (b) of zero over some ranges. Lumpiness is sometimes a function of economies of scale elsewhere in the production chain (e.g. if wires are only produced in certain sizes, to maximise production runs).

Where there is lumpiness, initial expenditure by the first user provides the capability for adding capacity at lower cost, to be used either at the same time or later. Lumpiness is therefore a special case of economies of scale and advance construction. As far as possible, the same principles should be applied as in the sections above.

The additional complication is the unavoidability, in some cases, of creating surplus transmission capacity which might never be used. If any costs associated with this capacity cannot be charged to individual system users, because of general regulatory constraints on the TSO's investment and pricing policies, they would have to be recognised in the process for agreeing the total revenues of the TSO.

CONCLUSION

In this chapter, we have shown how the costs of transmission can be divided into losses, constraints and system expansion. We have also shown how the incentive for system expansion is a reduction in the cost of losses and constraints. In general, it is worth investing if the long-run cost of *additional* capacity (including the losses incurred in using it) is less than the expected future level of short-run costs (losses plus constraints) incurred when using *existing* capacity. The incidence of short-run costs is therefore important as a spur to efficient investment.

Many transmission investment projects appear to be prone to economies of scale, in other words they incur common costs which cannot be directly allocated to system users on the basis of their use of the system. We have applied the basic theory of allocation of common costs to the case of an incremental investment with economies of scale and have devised two rules:

- *the investment rule*: invest only if users as a whole are willing to pay the total cost of the project.
- *the pricing rule*: make everyone pay at least the marginal cost and mark up prices to cover the common costs in ways which least distort decisions about usage.

How this is done depends upon the contractual terms for using a transmission network. We now turn to this question, in order to consider the "agency problems" which arise in relations between system users, transmission companies and their regulators.

14 TRANSMISSION CONTRACTS AND PRICES

This chapter explains the main design elements of contracts for use of a transmission system, and the basic methods of transmission pricing. Each method implies close links between prices for *transmission* and costs of *generation*. Attempts to set up transmission prices which ignore the relevant costs of generation will distort incentives for efficient use and development of the transmission system.

THE REGULATORY BACKGROUND

So far, regulatory authorities around the world have failed to settle on a single view of transmission access.[1] The most important questions to have arisen so far include: whether transmission access should be provided on a purely voluntary basis, or whether it should be mandatory; whether the terms of access are a matter of law, or of individual concessions, or of negotiation between those involved; and whether the company which owns the network should continue to own generation and/or trade in electricity.

These questions imply that the eventual structure of the electricity industry could take many forms. However, there is a clear trend in favour of more network access by third parties, that is, direct sales of electricity over a network, from independent producers to customers (either final consumers or other electricity traders).

The structure of the electricity industry will be a major determinant of the form of transmission prices. Two basic structures are likely to emerge:

- "transmission channels" through an integrated electric utility;
- "open access" over an independent network.

---

[1] Regulators and government agencies are known to be grappling with the issue in the US (at state and federal levels), in Europe (at national and Community levels), in Canada, Latin America, Australia and NewZealand.

Provision of network access may be voluntary or mandatory in either case and there are forms of transmission pricing which are common to both structures. However, where the Transmission System Operator (TSO) is part of an integrated company (which sells electricity as well as running a transmission network), it is possible to use "top-down pricing", where transmission prices are derived from customer tariffs. This method (which is also known as "efficient component pricing" or "netback pricing") has been applied in telecommunications and in other sectors. However, it cannot be applied when the network is owned by an independent network utility which does not sell electricity to wholesale or retail customers.

Independent networks are often established to remove concern over discrimination by the TSO against other system users. When the network is independent of electricity sales operations, transmission prices must be derived from a "bottom-up" analysis of the costs of transmission. However, congestion on the transmission system, which results in higher costs of generation, must still be reflected in the design and pricing of transmission contracts. This presents a major design problem for transmission contracts and tariffs.

OBJECTIVES FOR TRANSMISSION PRICES

Each of the different approaches to transmission pricing is intended to meet a common set of objectives. Each approach meets these objectives with different degrees of success, and which approach is therefore chosen depends on which objective is considered most important. No single approach is necessarily the "right" one. The most commonly quoted objectives are listed below.

Objective 1: economic efficiency

The main objective ought to be to derive a set of transmission prices which meets the criterion of economic efficiency. This requires prices that give the correct signals in four key areas: location of new generation and demand (and retirement of the old); use of the network by system users; operation of the network by the TSO; and development of the network.

The pricing system and contract terms must recognise the division of responsibilities between system users and the TSO. Both will need an economic incentive to carry out their responsibilities efficiently and these incentives depend upon the terms of access to the network. Finding an appropriate division of responsibilities has often proven to be one of the most difficult and important issues in the design of transmission contract terms.

The consequences of failing to set transmission prices which provide incentives for efficiency are spelled out in Appendix C, which examines "the case of the Yorkshire Pylons", a real-world example from the early years after the system was restructured in England and Wales.

Objective 2: revenue sufficiency

For any transmission company, this objective is paramount. Transmission companies must be able to earn sufficient revenue to achieve their target rate of return. Given the low rates of return allowed by most regulators, transmission companies have little or no interest in taking on risk, which means that they are concerned simply with recovering all the costs incurred in building and operating the network.

Objective 3: efficient regulation

Since most TSOs are natural monopolies, they need to be regulated. Efficient regulation should encourage minimum-cost operations by means which keep intervention by the regulator to a minimum.

These three objectives are the most common to arise in discussions of transmission pricing, but other objectives also have to be recognised. These include a desire for *stable* prices, a commitment to provide *equitable* terms for access, and other *social* objectives which affect prices.

The following sections explain how these objectives might be met, first by vertically integrated utilities offering "bundled" transmission, and second by "unbundled" independent transmission companies.

TOP-DOWN PRICING FOR BUNDLED TRANSMISSION

In several vertically integrated network industries, "top-down pricing" (also known as "efficient component pricing" or "netback pricing") has emerged as the preferred basis for charges for use of the network. Proponents claim that it avoids giving system users any incentive to choose an uneconomic source of the competitive service using the network (e.g. generation or international telephone calls).

A major concern of integrated utilities is the potential for "cherry picking", i.e. the tendency for competing producers to attract customers who are profitable to serve, whilst leaving the incumbent serving only unprofitable customers. The loss of profitable customers would prevent a utility from recovering the cost of stranded assets, or from implementing any government policy which requires profitable customers to cross-subsidise unprofitable ones.

Incumbent utilities and their regulators have therefore sought to set transmission prices which encourage a customer to select an independent producer only if the change of supplier would be economically efficient, not just where it would lower the price to the customer concerned. The method of top-down pricing has been developed in telecommunications and applied in several other sectors with this aim in mind.

Calculation of top-down transmission prices begins with the bundled tariff currently being paid by the customer who wishes to select a different supplier of electricity. In the electricity sector, tariffs normally comprise the following components:

- the avoidable costs of generation to meet the customer's demand;
- a contribution towards the sunk costs of generation;
- the avoidable costs of transmitting energy from existing generators to the customer;
- a contribution towards the sunk costs of transmission;
- a contribution towards the corporate overheads of the utility; and
- profit.

The top-down tariff for transmission, to be paid by any other generator willing to supply the same customer, is simply the sum of all these items except the first one, i.e.

Top-down transmission price = customer tariff

minus

avoidable costs of generation required to meet customer's demand.

Its main advantage is that it encourages customers to select the least-cost source of generation available at any time. Customers must continue to pay the *sunk* cost of all investments that were incurred on their behalf in the past, including investment in generation. They therefore choose between existing and alternative sources of electricity by comparing only their *avoidable* costs, as required for economic efficiency. This may help the incumbent utility to accept competition from new entrants more readily. Also, administration may appear simple, because it requires information only about the customer's current tariff, and the avoidable costs of generation needed to serve the customer. The efficiency properties of this tariff are shown in Appendix D.

Top-down pricing has, however, run into opposition on many fronts. Firstly, the static efficiency gains are offset by giving the incumbent a head-start, since the new entrant's full costs are compared with only the incumbent's avoidable costs. Some regulatory regimes feel that this approach is inherently discriminatory. It has been argued that this discrimination limits the scope for true competition, and any longer-term *dynamic* benefits which competition can bring. Furthermore, the method is open to manipulation by the incumbent utility, which has an incentive to understate the avoidable costs of generation. The utility may even invest in capital intensive production methods in order to push down avoidable costs and to make competition more difficult for others in the future.

Top-down pricing is impossible to apply in cases where the incumbent utility is not already selling to the customer, or is not selling on a regulated tariff. For example, sales off the system from independent sources connected to the utility's network ("wheeling out") and sales over the utility's network ("wheeling through") are both cases where there is no customer tariff to use in the calculation. In these cases, utilities wishing to charge for transmission must fall back on "opportunity cost" concepts relating to the value of transmission in a competitive market. Such cost concepts are easier to apply when a competitive market exists and are explored in the discussion of "bottom-up" pricing below.

For these reasons, some regulatory regimes have pushed the industry towards the open access model, in which networks are run by separate companies, or are at least organised as separate businesses (with separate management and separate accounts), distinct from any interest in generation or wholesale and retail sales.

Once an independent network has been established, top-down pricing is no longer relevant. A transmission company no longer has any bundled customer tariffs, nor does it incur any avoidable cost of generation to meet demand. Instead, transmission prices must be built up from the bottom, by estimating the individual components of the costs of transmission discussed in Chapter 13.

CONTRACT DESIGN FOR UNBUNDLED TRANSMISSION

When an independent network is set up, transmission prices must serve a number of functions. "Cherry-picking" ceases to be a major concern for monopoly TSOs, but transmission prices need to encourage efficiency in location of generation and demand, and in use, operation and development of the network. This is a tough set of conditions to fulfil and requires transmission prices which accurately reflect the incremental cost of providing transmission services to any system user. These costs can only be identified if the services have been adequately described in the terms of the contract for use of the network.

Transmission services mean moving energy from A to B. In transmitting energy, the transmission company may also be responsible for improving the quality of the energy supplied to a customer, by operating the system within certain standards for voltage, power factor and frequency. The transmission company may also be involved in "network settlement", i.e. in accounting for imbalances on its network, which is the function of the Market Operator. However, quality and settlement issues will not be discussed in detail in this chapter, which concentrates instead on the provision of transmission capacity for moving bulk energy.

The costs of providing transmission depend on the standard of service promised in the agreement or contract between the transmission company and its users. One way to understand these standards is to answer a number of straightforward questions about the terms of this agreement.

From Where, To Where?

Viewing transmission as a transportation system naturally raises questions about the location of the source and destination of the energy to be transported. The source and destination can be defined as the points of connection of a generator and a customer, but these points will be specific to each energy contract. In a trading system with multiple, short-term energy contracts, it is advisable to develop a "hub-and-spoke" system, so that transmission capacity can be used more flexibly.

Electricity is generated at a number of locations; consumers are highly dispersed. In order to create a liquid market, both generators and consumers will want to trade through a few key market locations. Generators will want to deliver their output to a central market, and customers will want to buy energy from it. Each generator must then pay a charge for sending energy to this common point of sale, and each customer must pay a charge for delivering energy from this point of sale to their own points of connection. The combination of routes from generators to the market and from the market to consumers will look like a central hub with radiating spokes.

In large systems, it may be sensible to extend the system, by identifying multiple trading hubs linked by "trunk routes", so that the standards of service on different parts of the system can be varied. In an integrated electricity system, each interconnector between utilities may be regarded as an individual section of a trunk route, separate from the hubs and spokes within each utility's own network. (Large utilities might also specify "trunk routes" within their own networks.) Service on trunk routes might be subject to availability, whilst connections to generators and consumers are more or less guaranteed. We consider the availability of service in greater detail below.

How Much, For How Long?

Transmission contracts must specify a quantity of energy and the period over which the quantity is to be delivered. In practice, system users may not want to schedule fixed energy flows at the start of the contract. Instead they will probably want to retain the *option* to transmit energy, up to a certain capacity limit in MW, in any hour over some extended period (a year or longer). Such arrangements would be consistent with the uncertainty inherent in normal methods of dispatch.[2] However, in some cases, the TSO may want the contract to specify particular MWh quantities in particular hours, in order to make the pattern of usage (and the associated costs) more predictable.

Whatever degree of choice system users have over their use of transmission capacity, transmission prices should distinguish carefully between the sunk costs of creating transmission capacity and the avoidable costs of using it. Treatment of the avoidable costs of losses and constraints has wider ramifications and is discussed later in this chapter.

Transferable to Other System Users?

If a transmission contract is valid for a long period, it may become superfluous to the needs of the person who holds it. In such circumstances, it would be efficient for a system user to transfer some or all of a transmission contract (e.g. capacity on certain common spokes) to other users. In a system of annual tariffs, such transfers can be encouraged by raising tariffs. System users who occupy scarce capacity that they don't need will then vacate it, allowing others to take it up. However, most system users would prefer transmission prices to be stable, i.e. to be known in advance for relatively long periods. The objectives of efficiency and stable prices can both be achieved if the transmission company offers transmission contracts which are both long-term and transferable.

For example, a generator may become uneconomic and therefore a candidate for closure, before the expiry of its transmission contract. At the same time, new generators may be waiting to connect at a nearby location. Different contract terms allow different pricing policies and will result in different outcomes.

1. If the contract is *short-term* (as in the case of annual tariffs), the transmission company may have trouble signalling the costs of long term investments in transmission. The first problem is that system users can avoid paying off the sunk cost of past investment, just by closing down their facility (e.g. a generator or a factory). This could encourage the premature closure of existing generators or consumers. On the other hand, when there is excess demand for some transmission routes, the transmission company can only ration the available capacity by raising short-term tariffs for *all* those using this part of the system. In the long-term, the tariff need never rise higher than

---

[2] See Chapter 11 for a discussion of option contracts and their advantages in the face of uncertainty over quantities.

the cost of building new capacity. If excess demand for transmission remained at this price, it would then be economic to expand capacity. However, in the short-term, tariffs might have to rise to extremely high levels. Variation in short-term tariffs often leads to complaints from existing users, who prefer to be protected from increases in transmission tariffs caused by variation in demand from other users. It is therefore difficult for a regulator to sanction short-term tariffs which rise and fall in line with actual costs.

2. If the contract is *long-term, but non-transferable,* the owner of a transmission right would be protected from future tariff increases. Furthermore, generators and consumers could not save all their transmission charges by closing down plant, as only some items on the bill would be avoidable. This would remove the incentive for premature closure and would also allow the transmission company to recover sunk costs. However, it could encourage inefficient generators to remain connected to the system for too long. New generators would then have to request duplicate facilities, even when existing generators would be prepared to sell them existing capacity at a lower price.

3. If the contract is *long-term and transferable,* the transmission company remains assured that sunk costs will be recovered, whilst every system user will seek out better alternative uses for the capacity, particularly when a generator becomes uneconomic. If a new generator wishes to use a congested part of the network, the transmission company might offer to build additional capacity if the generator will pay the full cost of the expansion. However, existing generators will also sell their current transmission contracts if anyone is prepared to pay more than they earn from continuing to generate. A new generator will select the cheapest of these alternatives, thereby ensuring that capacity is allocated to the users who place the highest value on it, and that new capacity is constructed only when the market value of capacity exceeds the cost of construction. This approach avoids the need to raise transmission tariffs to existing generators who already hold transmission capacity, and protects them against the risk of cost escalation.

Hence, transmission contracts are useful for providing long-term security against changing prices, but they should also be made transferable so that they are allocated to the most valuable uses at all times. In comparison, non-transferable contracts may lead to unnecessary duplication of facilities, whilst short-term contracts can lead to disruptive price changes for existing users, and inappropriate incentives to avoid sunk costs.

In practice, few electricity systems rely exclusively on short-term tariffs. Even where there are no long-term contracts, transmission companies usually operate a connections policy which controls access and imposes long-term commitments on each new generator and customer. Usually, demands for connection are only granted if the new system user agrees to pay some long-term costs of transmission (i.e. for the local connection and/or any reinforcement of the general network required to accommodate the new system user).

This long-term contractual framework reduces the need for annual tariffs to give economic cost signals about efficient location of new users.

Guaranteed or Conditional Availability?

When a transmission company sells transmission capacity, it is rarely possible to guarantee that a specific level of capacity will always be available. Random fluctuations in the pattern of flows over the network and occasional forced outages of generation and transmission can all affect the amount of capacity available on any part of the network. One of the most important determinants of the cost of any transmission contract is the method used to reconcile contract commitments with the actual availability of transmission capacity. Several methods have been developed already.

1. *"As-available" or "curtailable" capacity.*[3] Some contracts allow the transmission company to curtail capacity rights, so that system users may not schedule flows in excess of available capacity. This method is common in the United States and is often applied to interconnectors between utilities. The conditions in which capacity may be curtailed (weather, relative costs, net load flow patterns) and the form of curtailment (cancellation, proportional reduction, fixed reduction, prioritisation of contracts, etc) can both become extremely complicated if capacity on a spoke is held by many different users. This method makes system users responsible for finding alternative ways to cope with the physical effects of a constraint.
2. *"Bottleneck fees"*. Where capacity is constrained, it can be rationed by quantity (through curtailment) or by price. The transmission company responsible for the constrained piece of network can allocate capacity to users by charging explicit tariffs for crossing the constraint. The charge would ideally be based on the difference in value between electricity on either side of the constraint, which must be derived from knowledge of the dispatch. This method is practised in Norway. It imposes the cost of constraints directly on system users, as an avoidable out-of-pocket expense.
3. *"Limited interruptibility and compensation"*. Some contracts provide a guaranteed level of capacity, which may only be withdrawn for a certain number of hours in any year. Any transmission company which offers such contracts must fulfil them, first by curtailing transmission and second by redispatching (or "rebalancing") generation, so that system users can schedule flows in accordance with their contract rights. If these measures are insufficient to guarantee the service levels in the contract, or are simply not available to the

---

[3] This type of arrangement is sometimes called "interruptible capacity". However, we have tried to avoid using this term, because it is often associated with many other terms and conditions.

transmission company, the service must be curtailed or "interrupted" more than is allowed by the contract. When this happens, the transmission company must compensate the holder of the transmission contract, by refunding the opportunity cost (or value) of transmission during the interruption (see page 192). The transmission company has an incentive to make sure transmission is available, if the costs of rebalancing are charged to the transmission company, as well as any compensation. A related system is practised in England and Wales, where transmission capacity is guaranteed to generators all year round.[4]

This aspect of transmission contracts is immensely important for the future development of the network. The main purpose of investment in transmission capacity is to reduce the cost of rebalancing generation to cope with constraints. The incentive to carry out network investments (and to undertake network maintenance) lies with whichever party bears the cost of constraints. We return to this theme when discussing contract prices and the role of the transmission company.

CONTRACT PRICING FOR UNBUNDLED TRANSMISSION

Given the range of contract terms set out in the previous sections, it is possible to identify each of the costs involved in providing transmission service to the specified standard. "Bottom-up pricing" refers to the process of building up transmission prices from each of the cost elements. The following sections discuss how transmission contracts might reflect the costs of:

● building capacity (including the problem of recovering sunk costs);
● marginal losses; and
● congestion.

Past Costs or Incremental Costs of Building Capacity?

As in Chapter 13, we will divide the cost of building new capacity into two elements, to reflect the economies of scale which seem to be present in most investment projects. First, there is an initial or common cost, k, which includes the cost of establishing planning permission and rights of way, hiring contractors,

---

[4] In 1994, the National Grid Company became responsible for a share of the costs of rebalancing. See Appendix B.

and laying down the basic foundations for providing a transmission link. Second, there is the marginal cost of providing x MW of transmission capacity over a particular route, which may be characterised as b per unit. It represents the cost of steel, aluminium and other materials required to carry 1 MW over the route concerned. The total incremental cost of a new investment in transmission capacity is therefore the sum of common and marginal costs, $k + bx$.[5]

Alternatively, the transmission company may have some available capacity which was created t years ago by expanding the capacity of a past investment project at the incremental cost of only bx. The accumulated cost of this capacity is $bx(1 + r)^t$, i.e. the original cost plus interest at an annual rate of r. Should this capacity be priced at its accumulated cost ($bx(1 + r)^t$), or at the cost of a standalone facility ($k + bx$)?

To limit profits to the cost of capital, transmission companies should set prices equal to the costs they actually incur, i.e. $bx(1 + r)^t$. However, in a deregulated environment where anyone could build transmission, the transmission company could charge anything up to $k + bx$. At prices in excess of this level, someone else could build a standalone facility at lower cost. The transmission company would have to bear this cap in mind at the time of undertaking the investment. It would only be economic to undertake the investment if the expected future value of $k + bx$ in year t was higher than the accumulated cost of $bx(1 + r)^t$. Comparison with Chapter 13 will show that this is an efficient investment rule for advance construction. Pricing transmission at the cost of a stand-alone alternative is therefore consistent with efficient, decentralised investment decisions.[6]

However, few transmission companies would be prepared to take the risk associated with speculative investment in a competitive environment. After all, it is possible that demand for some transmission capacity never reaches the expected level. In a risky enviroment, the price might fall as low as the short-run marginal cost of using the capacity (i.e. physical losses), at which level they would fail to recoup the accumulated cost of construction. Most regulators also prefer to impose a pricing system (or at least a total revenue allowance) which is closely linked to actual costs incurred, rather than the short-run value in the market value. In many systems, therefore, regulators and regulated alike prefer to set prices equal to the accumulated sunk cost,

---

[5] Nothing is lost in this analysis by adopting a more complex, non-linear cost function. Indeed, most economies of scale follow a non-linear pattern. We have chosen this simple formulation in order to keep a close association between the algebraic terms and the economic concepts of common costs (k), marginal costs (b) and output (x).

[6] The prospect of deregulation in the electricity transmission sector may seem rather far-fetched. However, the high pressure gas pipeline system is moving rapidly in this direction in the US. Control of gas pipelines is easier to decentralise than control of electricity transmission, because conditions change more slowly and so there are fewer of the difficulties caused by loop flow, but network control mechanisms are improving in the electric sector as well.

$bx(1 + r)^t$, rather than short-run marginal costs, or the cost of a standalone facility.

Given the vagaries of actual demand, this raises a number of questions as to how such prices can be maintained, since they may bear no relation to competitive market prices. The following section examines how regulated utilities can achieve the aim of cost recovery in an uncertain environment.

Method for Recovering Sunk Costs?

Regulators tend to allow transmission companies a rate of return which is consistent only with a minimum risk strategy. Transmission companies therefore need to ensure that they are able to recover all the costs of long-term investments, even though future demand for transmission capacity remains highly uncertain. The following methods remain the most popular:

1. *Regulated monopoly network.* Given a legal or natural monopoly, transmission companies can recover their sunk costs via annual tariffs, by spreading them over a captive market. A monopoly avoids most problems of cost recovery, even though individual system users are still not committed to paying off the sunk cost of assets built for their benefit. The transmission company remains subject to the risk that the regulator will disallow some costs at a later date or introduce some form of competition.
2. *Long-term capacity contracts.* Every system user could agree to pay the full cost of investment carried out on their behalf, and in return they would receive a long-term right to use any capacity created by their investment. If this right can be made transferable, it would improve the ease of reallocating capacity to other users whenever the original user no longer needs the capacity.
3. *Termination payments.* Charges paid when quitting a connection (as levied by the National Grid Company in England and Wales for dedicated connection facilities) are another way of ensuring that system users pay off the full cost of facilities built for their benefit. They amount to more or less the same as a long-term contract for capacity (although the contract may be lacking many other terms).

The terms of long-term contracts differ according to the date on which they are agreed, because cost conditions vary over time. If terms differ for transmission contracts of different dates, the transmission company may be accused of discrimination. Regulators and system users must accept that it is nondiscriminatory to vary the terms offered to different system users at different dates, if conditions have changed.

Actual or Expected Losses?

Transmission losses are one of the main avoidable costs of moving energy over a network. Efficient dispatch requires an accurate assessment of the marginal losses imposed by each source of generation. There are two ways to incorporate such cost signals in transmission pricing:

● charge users the actual, real-time marginal losses imposed by their usage; or
● charge users a fixed kWh price for transmitting energy over the network.

Real-time pricing of losses will encourage efficient use of the network, but is difficult to implement on a transparent and non-discriminatory basis. A fixed price may or may not reflect the actual cost of losses very accurately. In a competitive electricity market, load flows depend on relative fuel costs and the location of demand. Obviously, the price will be more accurate for more of the time, if the pattern of load flows over the network is predictable. However, it should not be difficult to specify different prices for each of the main sets of conditions, e.g. winter/summer, day/night, etc. Such prices would provide reasonably accurate signals to encourage efficient use of the network in dispatch.[7]

Who Pays for Constraints?

The final element of cost which must be reflected in transmission prices is the cost of congestion, i.e. the costs imposed by transmission constraints. If these costs are not reflected in the terms of transmission, there will be excess demand for transmission services over congested parts of the network. Unless all the network's capacity is assigned to system users through long-term contracts, the transmission company (or the regulator) will have to ration the available capacity. Whoever receives capacity will benefit from being able to trade over a constraint, from a low-price area to a high-price area. An arbitrary allocation system is bound to lead to allegations of discrimination and inefficiencies in the allocation and use of transmission capacity.

As discussed above, the cost of constraints can be reflected in transmission contracts in three different ways:

● by withdrawing transmission capacity according to some agreed protocol when a constraint occurs, so that system users must adjust their trades in energy;

---

[7] In England and Wales, incidentally, marginal losses are not included in transmission prices, but are spread over all customers of the pool. This removes any incentive for dispatch to take losses into account.

- by charging an explicit "bottleneck fee" for each kWh that crosses a constraint, so that system users pay more for scarce capacity;
- by including an allowance for the costs of redispatch in the kW payment for transmission capacity.

In each case, system users are ultimately responsible for paying the costs of constraints, but in the last case, they pay the expected cost, not the actual cost; the transmission company pays the actual costs as they arise. It is only in the last case that the cost of constraints gives the transmission company a financial incentive to invest in the network. In the other two cases, the cost of constraints and the incentive to invest both fall on system users. The form of transmission contract and pricing used to recover the cost of constraints therefore plays a major part in deciding the respective roles of transmission companies and system users in the future development of the transmission system.

Financial Contracts for Transmission

The charges levied for transmission losses and for crossing transmission constraints both affect the willingness of generators and consumers to use the transmission system. The pattern of usage will be most efficient if system users are always charged the short-run marginal costs of losses and constraints. However, these marginal costs vary considerably from hour to hour, day to day and year to year. Few system users are prepared to tolerate such wide variation in their costs and most would prefer to fix transmission charges in a long-term contract. On the other hand, fixed price contracts conceal up-to-date information about real costs and can cause grossly inefficient patterns of dispatch. Fixed price contracts therefore help to manage risk but are difficult to reconcile with short-term efficiency in network usage.

This problem is directly comparable to the trade-off between risks and incentives in electricity pricing, which was investigated in Chapter 11 on wholesale contracts. The solution in electricity markets is to establish fixed price wholesale contracts for a specific volume; trades at the margin are then conducted at the spot price. A similar solution has been proposed for transmission.

Chapter 13 explained how the instantaneous cost of transmission is defined by the difference between the economic values of electricity at either end of a transmission line. The spot price of *transmission* therefore emerges from any system of "nodal spot pricing" for electricity as the difference between two *electricity* prices.

Given a spot price for any product or service, it is possible to construct fixed price, fixed volume contracts as financial instruments, such as "Contracts for

Differences" or CfDs (see Chapter 9). CfDs can be used to hedge the risk of variation in spot prices for transmission, just as for any other product or service. The contract denotes an "exercise price" for a given volume of transmission between A and B. The spot price of transmission between A and B is defined as the difference between the nodal spot prices for electricity at A and B. If the spot price of transmission rises above the exercise price, the seller of the contract gives the holder financial compensation equal to the difference between the spot price of transmission and the exercise price, multiplied by the contract volume.

An example may help to illustrate how a CfD for transmission works.[8] Suppose someone holds a call option (in the form of a CfD) for 50 MWh of transmission from A to B at \$1/MWh. Suppose also that nodal spot prices for electricity are \$10/MWh at A and \$15/MWh at B; the spot price of transmission is \$5/MWh. The holder will call the option to buy 50 MWh of transmission at the exercise price:

- the buyer owes the seller \$50 (i.e. the value of 50 units at the exercise price of \$1);
- the seller owes the buyer \$250 (i.e. the value of 50 units at the spot price of \$5);
- to settle the contract, the seller transfers \$200 to the buyer (i.e. the difference between \$50 and \$250).

If the buyer is paying \$5/MWh for transmission from A to B, the cost of moving 50 MWh is \$250. The compensation of \$200 paid under the CfD reduces the overall cost to \$50, or \$1/MWh, as per the contract.

The advantage of using CfDs for transmission is that they do not affect the pattern of dispatch (in which respect they are just like CfDs for electricity). They therefore provide a means of fixing transmission prices which allow efficient dispatch to be determined purely by real-time cost conditions. They are economically equivalent to a tradable contract for physical transmission rights, but do not have to be traded to achieve the correct dispatch.

CfDs can only develop when there is a well-defined spot price for electricity at both ends of the transmission link covered by the contract. The applicability of financial contracts for transmission will therefore depend entirely on the number and sophistication of electricity spot prices quoted for individual nodes on the network. The prospects for nodal spot pricing are discussed in Chapter 12.

---

[8] The example is adapted from the discussion in Chapter 9, where the design and settlement of CfDs is explained in full.

Investment Incentives and the Role of the Transmission Company

Chapter 13 explained how investment decisions are made by comparing the short-run costs of using the existing network with the long-run costs of expanding it. The form of transmission contracts determines who pays the short-run costs, and therefore who has an incentive to invest in the network. The allocation of this incentive will determine the range of functions carried out by transmission companies, as explained below.

System users decide investments

If transmission contracts are "curtailable" or subject to "bottleneck fees", the short-run marginal costs of transmission are clearly borne by system users, either in the form of lost transmission opportunities, or as explicit charges. One would therefore expect system users to play a large role in deciding what investments take place and how the network is maintained.

In principle, system users would decide when short run costs had risen high enough to justify further investment. They would then instruct the transmission company (or some other contractor) to build new transmission capacity.[9] This pattern of incentives gives the transmission company a relatively limited role. Effectively, any transmission company which passes the short-run costs of transmission over to users should only be required to carry out the following functions:

● build transmission capacity according to instructions from system users (or from the regulator);
● award contracts for the new transmission capacity to the system users who commissioned it (if appropriate); and
● operate the network as required to allow system users to trade electricity.

A transmission company which performs only these functions is responsible only for the hardware of the transmission network itself. Some other body, such as a club of system users, would be responsible for operating the network.

Transmission company decides investments

If the costs of constraints are borne by the transmission company, it has the same investment incentives as an integrated utility. When a constraint bites,

---

[9] Alternatively, the regulator might have to authorise investments on behalf of system users, but this approach exposes the transmission company to a higher degree of regulatory intervention and also to the risk that the regulator will disallow investments later.

the transmission company pays the additional cost of rebalancing generation to accommodate the flows scheduled by system users. The transmission company therefore has an incentive to invest in transmission capacity whenever the cost of capacity is less than the (generation) cost of constraints. In this case, the transmission company:

- sells a particular standard of "transmission service" (by contract or tariff); and
- bears all of the costs incurred in providing that standard of service (including the cost of constraints).

A transmission company which performs all these functions is responsible not only for the hardware of the transmission network, but also for the support services needed to provide secure and reliable transmission of electricity over the network, such as redispatch around constraints, voltage support, frequency control, maintenance of transmission hardware, etc. Giving the transmission company responsibility for decisions about these components of a transmission can be more efficient. For example, it would be very difficult for system users to make decisions over the supply of voltage support or maintenance contracts for the transmission network. On the other hand, system users may be just as well placed as the transmission company to decide where new transmission capacity is required.

If the transmission company bears the short run costs, incentives for efficient operation lie with the transmission company itself, but the transmission company must expect to recover these additional costs in the prices of transmission contracts. Ideally, each system user should have a specially negotiated contract, whose price includes the expected cost of redispatching generation when transmission capacity is not available to meet the user's needs.

Unfortunately, the range of possible variation in the costs of rebalancing may impose an unacceptable degree of financial risk on the transmission company (e.g. if there are large and unpredictable loop flows on an integrated system). The risk can be shared with system users, if transmission contracts allow for short-run costs to be passed through, but this would undermine the incentive for the transmission company to minimise total costs by operating the network efficiently. Some other mechanism must therefore be found to share the risk.

One option is to allow the transmission company to interrupt the transmission contract for a certain number of hours in each year. The transmission company would have an incentive to concentrate these limited interruptions into hours when the cost of rebalancing flows around constraints was highest. The transmission company could provide a warning of these interruptions in transmission access, to tell generators when would be a good time to carry out their own maintenance.

Implications for contract negotiations

The appropriate contract design for each transmission company and system user will depend on a number of considerations:

- the cost of constraints should be borne by whoever is best able to bear the risk of the variation in these costs; but
- whoever bears the costs should be able to decide network investments, because the cost of constraints provides economic signals and incentives for expansion of transmission capacity.

In some cases, both these considerations will point towards the transmission company and, in some cases, both considerations will point towards system users. Problems will arise if the cost of constraints is allocated to one party (for reasons of risk allocation), whilst another party remains responsible for deciding investments (without any economic incentives).

It is often thought that the main issue in negotiation of transmission prices is the fair allocation of total costs among the system users. However, after the initial allocation of costs has been decided, it is at least as important to negotiate an appropriate allocation of risks and incentives, or the resulting set of transmission prices will not be sustainable.

CONCLUSION

This chapter has examined in some detail the way in which the costs of transmission should be reflected in transmission prices. Throughout the chapter, it has become apparent that different types of contract are appropriate for different types of transmission company.

"Top-down pricing" obviously holds many attractions for vertically integrated utilities which offer transmission channels over their networks. It allows recovery of sunk costs and promises static economic efficiency. However, it is easy for practitioners of top-down pricing to be accused of distortion and discrimination against competitors. It may therefore be a useful transitional stage, before moving towards an open access regime.

Top-down pricing is impossible to apply to unbundled transmission companies and the price of their transmission services must be based on constituent costs, or "bottom-up pricing". Bottom-up pricing of transmission services needs to take into account the three main types of cost:

- the cost of building capacity (including sunk costs);
- the cost of marginal losses; and
- the cost of constraints.

In developing the terms of any transmission tariffs or contracts, two important objectives of contract design must be borne in mind.

First, the *duration* of any user's rights and the degree to which they can be *transferred* from one user to another are both important for the efficiency with which transmission capacity is used. Long-term transferable contracts can be sold and resold, to ensure that capacity is allocated to the user who values it most highly. Operations will be less efficient if transmission is sold in non-transferable contracts, or via short-term tariffs.

Second, the allocation of the *short-run costs of constraints* (i.e. the costs of redispatching generation to cope with constraints) will decide who has an incentive to expand transmission capacity efficiently. Allocation of these costs will therefore determine whether system users or the transmission company should be responsible for investment.

If transmission contracts can be "curtailed", or are subject to "bottleneck charges" when constraints bite, the short-run costs of congestion are borne by system users. These types of contract put the incentive for network investment on system users, so the role of the transmission company should be rather limited. It should only build and run the network in accordance with the instructions of system users (or from a regulator acting on their behalf).

It is possible to give the transmission company a larger role, by allowing it to sell contracts for transmission service, in which the duration of interruptions to the service is strictly limited. To fulfil such contracts, transmission companies must incur whatever short-run costs are necessary to meet the contractual standard of service. The list of such costs includes the short-run costs of redispatch, voltage control, maintenance and so on. Since the transmission company bears the short-run costs, the transmission company can safely be given the responsibility to plan and carry out network investments.

It is by no means clear whether companies in the electricity system and their regulators will prefer to assign responsibility for investment decisions to transmission companies or to system users. The decision will depend upon considerations of efficiency, risk, regulatory policy and corporate governance. In the UK, we have recently observed a tendency for the National Grid Company to assume a wider range of responsibilities. Arguments in favour include:

● the transmission company is legally responsible for investment in transmission and requires a financial incentive to carry out the responsibility efficiently;
● neither system users nor the regulator are well placed to supervise such decisions on a day-to-day basis, without incurring major costs.

However, the arguments are not one-sided and it has already been suggested that:

- system users may be reluctant to award too much responsibility to one company; and
- the transmission company may be reluctant to carry the risks associated with the short-run costs.

The relative weights of these arguments change slowly over time, as the risks and behaviour of an independent transmission company become better understood. The position will become clearer as competition expands in the way described in Part 1 of this book, and more independent transmission companies are established. This debate is therefore likely to continue for some time and the design of transmission contracts will no doubt develop accordingly.

APPENDIX C:
THE CASE OF THE
YORKSHIRE PYLONS

"The Yorkshire Pylons" refer to a new transmission line across the Yorkshire Dales. The NGC was required to make the investment in 1993, to accommodate new plant connected to the National Grid in the North East of England and expansion of the interconnector from Scotland. The project was delayed for several years by opposition in the planning stages. This appendix describes the NGC's transmission prices and shows how they fail to meet the criteria for economic efficiency. The last section explains the consequences for Yorkshire.

The following discussion was prepared and delivered as a speech in 1993. The original flavour has been retained, since it was apparently found to be instructive.

NGC's CHARGES FOR TRANSMISSION

The UK transmission company, the National Grid Company (NGC), is the only independent high-voltage transmission company in the UK. It has sole responsibility for investment in transmission in England and Wales. It makes two charges for its services: the connection charge, which is a plant-specific life-of-plant annual charge paid for attaching to the central network; and the use of system charge, which is a tariff for the use of the network.

Technical standards

The NGC can insist on technical standards for generators attached to the system, and is itself governed by technical standards written into its licence which govern the degree of security it must provide. For example, one licence requirement is for double fault standards (triple lines) for groups of net generation in excess of 1320 MW. The old CEGB had worked out alternative economic standards, where the degree of fault protection depended on the costs of potential faults, but these were not implemented before the privatisation.

Connection charges

The connection charges are based on the cost of investments made to connect the generator to the central network. For old plant, these charges are based on sunk costs, and approved by the regulator. For new plant, the NGC must offer terms for connection, although the generator may get someone else to construct the line. These charges are not regulated, because of the competitive element. The connection charges are sometimes called entry and exit charges, and are customer specific. Customer-specific charges which apply only to the cost of getting power to and from the network are called "shallow entry charges".

Transmission use of system (TUOS) charges

The transmission use of system charges are very simple tariffs. Those applicable from April 1993 are shown in Table C.1.

The country is divided into 14 areas; each area has a per-MW price for a generator, and a per-MW price for a customer at a bulk supply point in that area. The prices vary with location. The higher the generator price in an area, the lower the distributor price in the same area. In general, the prices vary with the marginal costs of adding a producer or a customer to the system

Table C.1   NGC's transmission use of system charges, as of April 1993†

Zone	Generation £/kW	Demand £/kW
North	5.648798	7.612786
Yorkshire	3.450149	9.043849
N. Wales & W. Lancashire	3.453450	9.542485
E. Lancashire	2.510125	10.003966
Nottinghamshire	2.537283	9.195032
W. Midlands	1.808322	10.348089
Anglia	0.897744	12.101864
West & Wales	0.688797	12.077377
Estuary (Thames)	2.055715	10.289090
Outer London	0.056402	13.780465
Inner London	−1.881839	15.563223
South Coast	0.184509	13.199920
Wessex	−0.177883	13.656434
Peninsula	−0.949719	13.656434

† Transmission Licence Condition 10 Statement of Charges for Use of System and Connection to the System (for the year 1993/94), April 1993, NGC.

in that area. There are some negative charges, indicating that the addition of a generator in the south-west peninsula would *reduce* total system costs.

The per-kW charges are levied on each user's maximum demand, which is measured by the "triad"—1/3 of the three highest demands during the high demand period. When a new customer comes onto the system, the costs assigned to the area in which he or she is located will change, and the change will be reflected in the charges to all users in that area. This is also typical of "shallow entry" charging—"deep entry" charges would assign all the increase in network costs to the new customer.

Regulation of revenues

NGC's total revenues are regulated by OFFER,[1] the UK electricity Regulator, who sets them every three or four years, taking into account planned investments. Between reviews they rise at the annual rate of RPI − X, where RPI is the rate of inflation (the retail price index), and X is the real reduction in revenues required by the regulator. In 1993, X was set as 4%, so NGC's price formula is RPI − 4 for five years. This price decrease is partially offset by an allowance for forecast load growth of 1% per annum. There is no provision for increased revenues to cover unforeseen increases in investment in this period, nor is there any reduction for planned investments not made in the period.

NGC and the pool

NGC's relation to the pool is complex, and need not bother us here in its entirety. The pool is an unincorporated association of its members; its members are sellers to the pool and buyers from the pool. Sellers are generators and buyers are customers, mainly distribution companies and others who have a licence to buy out of the pool. The pool rules provide that when bids from generators are received each day, NGC constructs a schedule for generation, as if there were no transmission constraints. It then re-schedules with transmission constraints. The difference between these two schedules is the cost of transmission constraints, which is borne by the pool and shared out on a per-kWh basis between buyers.

---

[1] OFFER is the OFFice of Electricity Regulation. The regulator is officially called the Director General of Electricity Supply—the DGES.

CRITIQUE OF NGC CHARGES

There are four basic principles which need to be incorporated in transmission prices:

● locational differentials in prices should reflect the true cost differentials;
● the transmission company should be responsible for the costs of transmission constraints, or else users should be allowed to determine investment in the National Grid;
● tariffs should be replaced with tradable, long term contracts, which reflect all the system (deep entry) costs; and
● the standards embodied in the licences should be replaced with economic standards.

NGC's charging principles failed to meet any of these four points. The resulting distortion of incentives caused real problems, which NGC has tried to solve, step by step. The following sections explain what problems arose and why.

Transmission Costs Differ by Location

Consulting firms are located in London and not the Shetland Islands, even though office space is undoubtedly cheaper there, because there is very little demand in the Shetland Islands for sophisticated economic advice. A consultant located in Shetland, would spend the whole day on the phone to clients, and one of the telephone companies would charge a fortune for it. If such a consultant wanted to visit clients he or she would have to absorb the air fare if he or she wanted their prices to be competitive. Would you say that, if he or she had an office in the Shetland Islands, they should pay only local rates for the telephone when calling London, or be entitled to reduced air fares simply because clients are in the South of England? Of course not.

Governments and central planners like "non-discriminatory pricing", by which they usually mean sharing out the costs equally. Some even want the same price for everyone, like a postage stamp. But when a market is introduced it becomes important to make sure that prices are aligned with cost causation.

The cost of providing transmission to a new generating plant or customer is *first*, increased losses, *second*, the cost of constraints on the system, and *third*, the cost of building new lines to reduce the losses and constraints. If most of the generation is located in the north, and most of the load is located in the south, transmission prices should be higher for northern generators and southern customers. Conversely, if a new generator or a new customer is located so as to oppose the dominant flow, *the losses would be reduced, the constraints relieved, and the need for new lines reduced, so the cost is negative.*

NGC's new transmission tariffs do indeed have locational differentials— they even have negative charges; this is a big step in the right direction. Unfortunately, the regulator has bowed to pressures from southern customers to whittle the differentials away even further. This all goes to show that these things really should have been done before privatisation, since they are so hard to change afterwards.

Constrained-Plant Costs should be borne by NGC

For those who are not familiar with the UK system, the pool price is determined by "dispatching" the system without transmission constraints to determine the price of energy; then re-dispatching it with actual constraints to determine which plants should run. The plants that *would have* run if transmission had been available but *did not* run because it wasn't, are called "constrained off". These plants are reimbursed for the profits lost because access to the transmission was denied. The plants that are "constrained on" in their place are paid their costs. These extra costs of the transmission constraints, namely, that more expensive plants have to generate, are borne by the pool members jointly in the uplift.[2]

Why is this done? Let us turn to what happened in 1991 in Corsica. Mandarin orange producers brought their output to the ferry docks. Then, they were told that the ferry was not running and their oranges were left to rot on the quays. Mandarin producers did what you would all have done: they asked the ferry company for compensation.

In the present electricity system in England and Wales, the analogy is exact: there is compensation for the lost profits due to not transporting the output. The ferry company effectively offered a *firm contract*, because they had to pay compensation if they did not run; this gives them the right incentives when they decide whether to invest in extra capacity so as not to lose the load. They will pay compensation up to the point where it pays to invest in another ferry.

Unfortunately, in the UK system, the pool members share out evenly the compensation and the extra running cost. The regulator has sensibly suggested that the cost of the transmission constraints should be borne not by the pool members but by the NGC. This would place the right incentives on the NGC. *The costs and benefits of expanding the transmission should both reside in the same*

---

[2] The Report on Constrained On Plant (OFFER, 1992) was concerned with the prices the generators had been charging for the constrained-on plant. These charges appear as part of the so-called "uplift" payments, which are added to the pool price. The uplift payments have been a cause of contention, since due to a design error in the original pool, the generators have been able to charge whatever they wanted, subject only to their concerns about regulatory action. The solution to this is to make contracts for the plant which is to be "constrained on", rather than relying on a spot price, as at present.

place so that the cost of denying access is borne by the same body as the cost of providing access.

There is nothing wrong with not providing access: it may be cheaper to reimburse for lost profits than to put in a new line. The airlines overbook and pay compensation if they cannot seat you. One of my colleagues was paid £100 for staying an extra night in Paris. It may be cheaper to do that than to roll out another plane, and similarly, it may be cheaper to pay for access denied than to pay overtime to get a transmission line back into service quickly. *There are other alternatives.* Even in the context of a monopoly transmission company, the NGC should be able to choose between calling generators to provide constrained-on plant, or to contract with customers to cut load, or to put in more capacity, whichever is the cheaper.

As it is, the NGC has no incentive at all to reduce constraints; if it does so it incurs costs with no equivalent revenues.[3]

Contracts for Transmission

Transmission in most cases is a natural monopoly. This implies, therefore, that prices should be regulated, and we are used to thinking of regulated prices as being governed by a tariff—an offer price, as it were, for immediate delivery of full requirements. Also, the nature of the network is that everyone uses the same wires, and it is physically impossible to tell whose electricity is flowing where. The easiest and fairest thing to do seems to be for the regulator to share out the costs of the network in a sort of club fee: everyone pays a fee to join the club and then shares the costs, perhaps in proportion to their maximum use.

In fact, we can resort to several interesting market solutions before having to ask the regulator or any other administrative body to step in. The first thing is to understand that even if everyone used the same network, it is possible to cost individual transactions. They do not have to share out the costs: some cost more and some cost less, even negative amounts. Whoever wants to use a transmission network to transport power should be able to purchase a *firm right to transmission, i.e. the right to have electricity transported at all times or to receive compensation.* These contracts should be priced to cover the (different) costs of each user.

Tariffs are a single-year contract and this reinforces the bargaining power of the transmission company. Once you have built a power station, or located your factory, it is easy for the transmission company to raise its tariff, as there is little you can do about it. *Long-term contracts*, for the life of the plant, are therefore preferable. This would make the use of monopoly power less likely

---

[3] This problem is now being addressed, at the request of the regulator; see Appendix B. The issue remains whether NGC should undertake the costs of transmission constraints, or whether the pool should rent the wires from NGC.

and reduce the need for regulatory scrutiny of transmission tariffs. *Long-term contracts make regulation much easier*, since most of the transmission company's revenues would be contracted for, and regulation need only oversee the contracting process. There are a variety of ways to make contracts; long-term contracts do not have to be one-dimensional fixed-price contracts.

Having signed a contract to provide access to the pool, and determined the price and the consequences of failing to deliver, the grid operator could meet the contract any way it chose. If the plant potentially creates a transmission constraint, *the generator would pay in the contract for the expected constraint costs, which it would then claim back when and if the constraints occurred*. If it is more cost effective to upgrade the system and build new lines, the grid operator would make the investment and save the constraint costs. By a parallel argument, the grid operator should also bear the cost of losses, buying the energy to meet the losses and charging the expected value in the contract price.

The monopoly power of the transmission operator would be further reduced by the possibility offered to users of the transmission system to *sell or buy existing transmission rights—tradable rights*. As far as the network is concerned, it docs not matter whether a load of 100 MW is created by an old coal plant or by a new Combined Cycle Gas Turbine (CCGT) built next to a retired coal plant. So the transaction should be neutral for NGC: the owner of the coal plant would simply sell its transmission rights to the owner of the CCGT.

The main feature of the contracts is that they should be priced to cover all the costs imposed by the user. *A new user of the system should pay the full cost of expanding the system to meet the new load, all the way through the system*. In the jargon, these have been called *deep entry costs or deep exit costs*, as opposed to shallow entry/exit costs, which make a new user pay only for the costs of getting into the main network.

Under the present tariffs, new loads are only charged for the cost of connecting them to the nearest point, while everyone else in the area shares the costs of upgrading the central system. This makes no sense. The new user should pay *all* the costs imposed by adding a load to the system, or generation and loads will be added in the wrong place. This includes all the costs of reinforcing the main system, if that is necessary, as well as the specific connection to the system.

Contracts would also match costs to payments: under the present tariff structure, NGC has an incentive not to build, since the cost of building has already been incorporated in the tariffs, and NGC gets paid no extra when the line goes into operation.

Economic Standards

Once upon a time in New York, there used to be flats which had bathtubs in the kitchen. Along came some well-meaning bureaucrats who said no-one should have to live with a bath in the kitchen. And they imposed standards of construction which made flats so expensive that now there are people with no flats at all—they live on the streets without a bath or a kitchen.

The UK planning standards for transmission are designed for high security—but why? For instance, under planning standard PLM SP1, stations over 1320 MW must be able to transmit output with any two circuits failing, so three are always installed. So, belt, braces and a piece of string around the waist in case two systems fail! The chances of any two circuits failing are small; the right question is, how much more spinning reserve and replacement energy would be required if the third circuit were not there? But PLM SP1, and several other planning standards, developed by the CEGB, are written into NGC's licence.

Therefore we have to build new lines across the Vale of York, one of the great beauty spots of England, to take the output of new plants located on the coast. *The irony is that, under a special derogation from two of the planning standards, the new plant will be able to operate until 1995 without the upgrading the standards require,* but with an intertrip mechanism to protect reliability. Apparently the sky has not fallen in, so one has to wonder whether the planning standard means anything, and whether the line is really necessary.

But even under this derogation, the addition of the new plant is not costless, notwithstanding the intertrip scheme. Constraints and losses on the system are increased, but the new generator does not have to pay for them. The cost is spread over all the pool purchasers and eventually the customers. Or, if the line is eventually built, everyone will share the costs. Furthermore, expansion of the Scottish interconnector, which will also use the new line, might never have gone ahead if the full costs were borne by the users.

Sharing costs is for communes, not competitive markets. Eventually, someone whose costs have been raised by taking the burden of other people's decisions will want out. Economic plant will be closed to avoid the charges. Private generating and distribution facilities will be built and not connected to the grid. Building the Yorkshire pylons, and charging others for the cost, only adds to the potential for bypassing the grid altogether, and rendering the pylons in the end unnecessary.

This returns us to a point made earlier about tradable contracts. The tightly constrained north east ring includes a 1000 MW plant at Blyth, and a similar one at Hartlepool, which use the same facilities to send power south. One of these might well close down early *if they could sell their transmission rights* to the new plant, thus freeing up enough transmission capacity to obviate the need for the pylons.

This brief summary shows that economics is not just about equations and curves and theories: it can end up being about pylons across the moors. By violating the basic rules of economics, we may have ended up violating the landscape unnecessarily.

Suppose that a new generator (N) signs a contract to supply an existing customer of the incumbent utility (I). The new generator's output will displace the output of a generator owned by the incumbent. The resulting cost savings are referred to as the incumbent's "avoidable cost" of generation. The purpose of top-down pricing is to ensure that new generators only enter the market to supply a utility's customers, when the *full costs* of the new source (G_N) lie below the *avoidable costs* of the existing source (G_I). This condition is used to define efficient entry by new generators:

$$\text{Efficiency gain} = e = G_I - G_N \geq 0$$

However, a new generator will only enter the industry if it is possible to make a profit in the face of competition from the existing utility. If P_N is the price earned by the new entrant, and T_N is the price paid for transmission by the new entrant, then a generator will only enter the market when the following condition applies:

$$\text{Profit of entrant} = \pi_N = P_N - G_N - T_N \geq 0$$

It is possible to fulfil these conditions in a number of ways, but some additional assumptions reduce the number of solutions to one. First, it may be assumed that competition will force the new entrant to charge the same price as the incumbent, so that $P_N = P_I$. Second, as a matter of policy, it may be decided that the new entrant is allowed to earn profits equal to the full amount of the efficiency gain, i.e. $\pi_N = e$.

Combining these equations gives the following:

$$\text{Profit of entrant} = \pi_N = e = P_N - G_N - T_N$$
$$\Rightarrow G_I - G_N = P_I - G_N - T_N$$
$$\Rightarrow T_N = P_I - G_I$$

In other words, the price for transmission (T_N) which fulfils the conditions of efficient entry under competition is equal to the current retail price (P_I)

minus the incumbent's own incremental cost of generation (G_I). This pricing rule has been described as "efficient component pricing", but may be thought of as "top-down pricing" in the following sense; prices for new network users are derived by *subtracting incremental cost savings* from the current bundled consumer tariff.

Of course, if this rule is adopted, incumbent utilities will have an incentive to understate the value of G_I, in order to maximise the charge for transmission and minimise the scope for competition. Regulatory bodies will therefore have to check the estimate of G_I to ensure that it accurately represents the future avoidable cost of the incumbent utility's generation.

INDEX